GULLAH
SPIRITUALS

GULLAH SPIRITUALS

The Sound of Freedom and Protest in the South Carolina Sea Islands

ERIC SEAN CRAWFORD with
BESSIE FOSTER CRAWFORD

THE UNIVERSITY OF
SOUTH CAROLINA PRESS

Published by the University of South Carolina Press
Columbia, South Carolina 29208

www.uscpress.com

Manufactured in the United States of America

30 29 28 27 26 25 24 23 22 21
10 9 8 7 6 5 4 3 2

Library of Congress Cataloging-in-Publication Data
can be found at http://catalog.loc.gov/.

ISBN: 978-1-64336-189-5 (hardcover)
ISBN: 978-1-64336-190-1 (paperback)
ISBN: 978-1-64336-191-8 (ebook)

The following material was reprinted with permission:

Thirty-Six South Carolina Spirituals by Carl Diton. Copyright 1928 (renewed) by
G. Schirmer, Inc. International Copyright Secured. All Rights Reserved.
Reprinted by Permission.

Walk in Jerusalem, Just Like John
I'm Going to Eat at the Welcome Table
May Be the List Time, I Don't Know
I've Got a Home in the Rock, Don't You See
Ring the Bells

Guy Carawan, Sing for Freedom: The Story of the Civil Rights Movements Through
Its Songs. Music examples reprinted by permission of New South Books, Inc.

Support for publication was provided by the AMS 75 PAYS Fund of the
American Musicological Society, supported in part by the National Endowment
for the Humanities and the Andrew W. Mellon Foundation.

CONTENTS

ACKNOWLEDGMENTS

First, I give thanks to my Lord and Savior Jesus Christ for giving me patience in this long process. I must also recognize my mentors, Ernest James Brown, DMA, Carl Gordon Harris, DMA, and Marjorie Scott Johnson, PhD. They have made this journey possible, and I am eternally grateful.

I am indebted to my dear friend Alli Crandell, director of the Athenaeum Press at Coastal Carolina University, and the staffs at Penn Center, the American Folklife Center at the Library of Congress, and the Southern Folklife Collection at the University of North Carolina at Chapel Hill for granting me access to historical collections and permissions to use the reproductions in this document. I also thank ethnomusicologist Sandra Graham, who offered feedback and a tender shoulder in the early stages of this book.

I cannot fail to recognize my parents, Pastor Timothy and Dr. Bessie Crawford, who are the benchmarks for my life. They are truly the "Wind Beneath My Wings." To my son Sean Timothy Crawford, I am a proud father, and I know you will accomplish great things. I am also thankful for the support of my brother, Dwayne Andre Crawford and his wife Kathy, Angie, and their children Andre, Taylor, and Kayla Marie.

Last, I recognize that this book would not have been possible without the help and inspiration of Deacon James Garfield Smalls, Minnie (Gracie) Gadson, and Deacon Joseph and Rosa Murray. Their commitment to keeping the Saint Helena Island song tradition alive makes them true ambassadors of the Gullah Geechee culture. I am truly fortunate to have them in my life.

Introduction

De ole sheep done kno' de road
De ole sheep done kno' de road
De ole sheep done kno' de road
De young lam' mus fin' de way.

—*Saint Helena Negro spiritual*

Each time I hear this popular refrain from Saint Helena Island, South Carolina, I think of those elderly singers on the island who continue a Gullah song tradition with unbroken ties to America's slavery past. Indeed, they still remember traveling to church services by mule and watching their mothers and grandmothers singing and moving in the emotionally charged ring shout. Some can even recall singing more dignified spirituals during chapel services at Penn Normal, Industrial, and Agricultural School, one of the earliest educational institutions for newly freed slaves in the South. Yet readers will discover that these spirituals traveled well beyond Saint Helena Island's shores. Remarkably, these songs persevered despite the immense emotional and physical atrocities of the transatlantic slave trade and southern plantation life to influence many of the major events in American history.

My initial interest in Saint Helena Island's spirituals stemmed from a thesis entitled "Music Education Through Gullah: The Legacy of a Forgotten Genre" by former student Marianne Rice. She grew up near Saint Helena Island, and her mother Marlena Smalls is a well-known singer, actress, and educator. Marianne wrote about Gullah's ties to West Africa and the many well-known Gullah spirituals from the island, revealing a culture whose contributions to American history had been largely unacknowledged. Her writing caused me to reflect upon my undergraduate years at a Historically Black College and University (HBCU), where there was surprisingly little if any mention of Gullah culture in my classes, including the university's choir, where spirituals were a staple of our musical repertoire. This awakening moment was the driving force in my decision to visit Saint Helena Island in the summer of 2009.

When I arrived on Saint Helena Island in Beaufort County, South Carolina, I was struck by its scenic marshlands, unspoiled beaches, and tree-lined roads defined by the hanging Spanish moss. Undoubtedly, such elements contributed to a much slower pace of life, and residents drove their cars below the speed limit so they could wave to the many walkers on the side of the road. It is obvious that they still remembered when walking was the norm and not the exception.

I attended a Sunday morning worship service at Historic Brick Baptist Church on Saint Helena Island, where I anticipated hearing some of the old spirituals. Before the Civil War, plantation owners brought their enslaved laborers to Brick Baptist to Christianize them and remove their perceived "heathenish" practices. These enslaved Africans had to sit unseen in the upstairs balcony, but they still took an active role in the congregational singing, especially the Europeanized hymns that would later serve as free musical material for their Negro spirituals. To my dismay, I heard none of the Gullah spirituals during Brick Baptist's worship service, only hymns and popular gospel songs. However, a kind church member informed me of an evening pray's (praise) house service not far away where I might hear the old songs.

I vividly remember hearing Deacon James Garfield Smalls fervently raise several of his songs at the Jenkins Praise House, one of two pray's houses still holding Sunday evening services. His voice swept through this tiny wooden structure with a force that seemed to bring us all back to the bygone era of slavery when Negro spirituals were first forged. Indeed, such singing seemed to honor all those who had come before, and I felt an instant connection to my own childhood as a kid growing up in Millington, Tennessee, where I attended Saint James Christian Methodist Episcopal Church. After forty years, I can still recall the foot-tapping of my pastor's wife to the cadence of her husband's sermons and the ever-present congregational responses of "Amen" and "Preach Pastor." My own cultural past found a kinship and common ground within this pray's house.

A few months later, I returned to the island and attended another service at Jenkins Praise House featuring a guest singer named Minnie "Gracie" Gadson, who sang many of her favorite spirituals. The power and emotion in her voice rivaled Deacon Smalls, and as the old saints in church used to say, "The spirit was high!" Many of Gracie's spirituals contained Gullah-infused texts that were unfamiliar to me, and she accompanied each song with a handclapping pattern she undoubtedly learned as a child. Gracie's performance confirmed the survival of the West and Central African rhythms and linguistic elements on the island. But the absence of younger members made me keenly aware of the uncertain future of this art form.

The amount of study and preservation of its artwork, language, folktales, and music situate Saint Helena Island as the center of Gullah Geechee culture. The island's geographic isolation, the continued presence of Penn School, now known as Penn Center, weekly pray's house services, and immense scholarly interest have all contributed to a high retention of its Gullah cultural elements. But the shouting and rowing songs, containing the strongest West African retentions, are mostly lost and forgotten. This book illuminates the remarkable history, survival,

Jenkins Praise House, Saint Helena Island, South Carolina; reproduced courtesy of the Athenaeum Press, Coastal Carolina University.

and influence of this island's music from early recordings in the 1860s. However, I focus on more than just song retentions and analyses in this book.

Though it is difficult to remain completely impartial, I attempt an honest assessment of the policies of Penn School's principals Laura Towne and Rossa Cooley. These educational pioneers struggled to appreciate an enslaved people's culture very different from their own, and they were at times clearly biased, especially toward the Gullah language and music. However, most visitors (Black and White) struggled to understand and appreciate the islanders' unique creole-based Gullah language, which began as pidgin spoken by slaves during passage from Africa and gradually developed distinctive grammatical, phonological, and syntactical rules.[1] The islanders' speech and singing seemed unintelligible, and few could translate its strange patois. It took the laudable efforts of the White missionaries William Francis Allen, Charles Pickard Ware, and Lucy McKim, in their 1867 publication *Slave Songs of the United States*, to finally present a serious study of the Gullah language and music.

There were, however, shining moments when Towne and Cooley openly embraced the islanders' culture and integrated their spirituals into Penn School's curriculum. Such apparent inconsistency was partly due to the difficult instructional choices these two women made in the wake of the great debates between Booker T. Washington and W. E. B. Du Bois over the education of the Negro. Towne and her assistant Ellen Murray supported a strictly academic curriculum for their students, garnering praise from W. E. B. Du Bois, while Cooley firmly believed in the vocational model used at Hampton Institute and Booker T. Washington's Tuskegee Institute. Historian Orville Burton notes that Towne and Cooley faced opposition from many who were against any education for African Americans.[2] To their credit, each woman's educational approach proved effective in giving the island's children an opportunity for a better life.

In this book, I present evidence linking Saint Helena Island's music to the spirituals performed by the famed Hampton Singers, the main rival of the legendary Fisk Jubilee Singers. Hampton's first choir director, Thomas Fenner, took several of the island's songs from *Slave Songs* and made choral arrangements for his fundraising concert tours in the 1870s. Later, Hollis Frissell, principal of Hampton Institute and chairman of the Board of Trustees at Penn School, sent the school's folklorist, Natalie Curtis, to Saint Helena Island before the start of World War I, where she made her own arrangements of these spirituals. From these efforts, island favorites such as "Nobody Knows de Trouble I've Had," "In Bright Mansions Above," and "Ride on, Jesus," were published in Hampton Institute's *Religious Folksongs of the Negro*.[3] This collection's several editions attest to its great popularity, especially under Hampton choral director and composer R. Nathaniel Dett, who, according to Lawrence Schenbeck, was the most well-known of all serious African American composers during the 1920s.[4] As a result, Saint Helena Island's spirituals were extremely popular among Historically Black Colleges and Universities and now enjoy growing popularity among institutions regardless of racial makeup.

Further use of the island's songs occurred at the turn of the century when they helped rally support for America's involvement in World War I and calm racial tensions between Black and White soldiers in army camps at home and abroad. Curtis added patriotic texts to several of these spirituals and gave special performances of her arrangements to garner support for the war effort. Her anthem "Hymn of Freedom" contains the melody of the Saint Helena spiritual "Ride On, Jesus" and became such a popular wartime song that church groups and school choirs requested special choral arrangements for their own use. Soon, the US Army enlisted Saint Helena's own song leader, Joshua Blanton, to teach this anthem and other island favorites to soldiers throughout the country.

Blanton, who was the charismatic lead singer of Penn School's quartet, sang many of the island's songs at several war camps, at home and abroad, in his role as Negro song leader for the US Army. The army wanted Blanton to diffuse the frustration of many Black soldiers toward their mistreatment in the service and help promote racial tolerance between Black and White troops. Yet Blanton proved to be more than a mere "Yes Man" or the proverbial Uncle Tom. In 1919, the *New York Age,* a leading Black periodical, recognized his success in building up the morale of the Negro troops and inspiring the White community to sing

Negro spirituals.[5] Blanton was so effective with both Black and White troops that the Army soon hired more Negro song leaders and included two spirituals in the 1918 official *Army Songbook*. After the war, Blanton left Saint Helena Island to become principal at Voorhees School, now Voorhees College, in Denmark, South Carolina. During his twenty-five-year tenure, Blanton continued to sing the island's songs around the country to raise money for the construction of many of the buildings that stand today on the Voorhees campus.

In the 1960s, civil rights leaders recognized the suitability of Saint Helena Island's songs as tools of nonviolent protest and reintroduced these spirituals into the nation's consciousness. Through the work of Guy and Candie Carawan, Bernice Johnson Reagon, Bessie Jones, and Pete Seeger, these songs were disseminated throughout the country as freedom or protest songs. In this role, the old spirituals assumed contrafactum texts that personalized the struggle for equality and strengthened the resolve of members of the movement who took part in sit-ins, boycotts, mass meetings, and the freedom rides. Reagon remembers that "the singing was essential to those of us involved in the action, it was galvanizing, it pulled us together, it helped us to handle fear and anger . . . it was powerful music, the freedom songs."[6]

In recent years, a growing list of scholars give increased attention to the role Black popular music played during the civil rights movement. Michael Castellini's "Sit in, Stand Up, and Sing Out: Black Gospel Music and the Civil Rights Movement," Robert Darden's *Nothing but Love in God's Water: Black Sacred Music from the Civil War to the Civil Rights Movement,* and Reiland Rabaka's *Civil Rights Music: The Soundtracks of the Civil Rights Movement* are notable contributions. An explanation for this trend may lie in Darden's assertion that the use of spirituals in the movement is already well documented.[7] Castellini and Rabaka, however, strongly argue that Black popular music best communicated Black cultural values and reinforced Black identity during the 1960s, thus becoming in essence a mouthpiece for the civil rights movement.[8] Within this climate of Black pride and Black power, could the Negro spiritual speak to the immediate concerns of African Americans who tired of the passivity of this art form so aligned to slavery?

Without question Saint Helena Island's music constitutes the most studied body of Negro spirituals in America. From 1867 to 1939, scholars routinely visited the island to examine and record West African retentions in its spirituals; however, the building of Ladies Island Bridge in 1927 signaled for many the loss of this unique art form. This book confirms the continued survival of this music and builds upon the findings of six major studies: *Slave Songs of the United States* (Allen, Ware, McKim), *Thirty-Six South Carolina Spirituals* (Carl Diton), *Saint Helena Island Spirituals* (Nicholas Ballanta-Taylor), *The Carolina Low Country* (Society for the Preservation of Spirituals), *Folk Culture on St. Helena Island*

(Guy Johnson), and "The Religious Life of South Carolina Coastal and Sea Island Negroes" (Samuel Lawton).[9] Even before these efforts, Lucy McKim released early accounts of the islanders' singing that first awakened public interest in this music and eventually led to the groundbreaking efforts in *Slave Songs*.

Lucy McKim made one of the first recordings of Negro spirituals in an open letter to *Dwight's Journal of Music* on November 1, 1862, entitled "Songs of the Port Royal Contrabands." Earlier that year, McKim accompanied her father James Miller McKim on his inspection of the Sea Islands region, and she described the songs they encountered as possessing a "curious rhythmic effect produced by single voices chiming in at different irregular intervals."[10] Eventually, McKim published vocal and piano arrangements of the Saint Helena spirituals "Poor Rosy, Poor Gal" and "Roll, Jordan Roll."

Nine months after McKim's letter, Henry George Spaulding, a Unitarian minister, published spirituals in an article entitled "Under the Palmetto" in the August 1863 edition of the *Continental Monthly*.[11] During the Civil War, Spaulding traveled to Saint Helena Island as a member of the US Sanitary Commission, and he transcribed several of the islanders' songs. His article received much attention as he fascinated readers with accounts of "peculiar hymns and chants" like "Times Hab Badly Change' Old Massa Now" and "Lord, Remember Me," which were in his view crude in nature.

Four years later, Colonel Thomas Wentworth Higginson, Unitarian minister and Commander of the First South Carolina Volunteers, compiled an even larger collection of spirituals that were popular among his all-Black regiment. From November 5, 1862, to October 27, 1864, Higginson heard and transcribed the lyrics of thirty-seven spirituals sung by men who had often been former slaves on Saint Helena Island. After the Civil War, he published his "Negro Spirituals" collection in the June 1867 edition of the *Atlantic Monthly*.[12]

Lucy McKim and her husband Wendell Phillips Garrison, literary editor for *The Nation*, recognized the public's growing interest in Negro spirituals and the need for a more serious examination. They also became aware of an even larger repository of Saint Helena spirituals collected independently by William Allen and Charles Ware, who agreed to join the Garrisons in forming a study of unprecedented breadth. In their work with the Port Royal Experiment, Ware was a superintendent of plantations while Allen and his wife served as schoolteachers on the island. In these job capacities, both men worked closely with the newly freed slaves, gained an intimate knowledge of the islanders' songs, and with surprising attention to detail, notated unique melodic and textual elements in the singing.

To gather as many Negro spirituals as possible, the *Slave Songs* editors (Allen, Ware, and McKim) added Higginson's earlier collection and spirituals from other southern states. Initially, they wanted to publish a heterogeneous collection representative of the musical output of slaves throughout the South, but Allen admitted that most of the spirituals came from a few plantations on the northern end of Saint Helena Island. Specifically, fifty-five songs were part of Ware's collection from the Coffin Point Plantation, headquarters of the Port Royal Experiment, and twenty-two came from other areas of the island. In the end, 77 out of 136 spirituals in the *Slave Songs* come from one singular source—Saint Helena Island.

Transcriptions made by the *Slave Songs* editors, Diton, Ballanta-Taylor, and the Society for the Preservation of Spirituals are central to many of the musical analyses in this book. The nearly four hundred musical examples in these collections reflect the immense musical creativity that sprung forth from the Sea Islands region, and there were many more undocumented Negro spirituals. After his departure from Saint Helena Island, Allen regretted leaving a "wealth of material still awaiting the collector."[13] The island's major song collections encompass the years from 1867 to 1939 and give evidence of musical alterations and retentions occurring during dramatic educational and social reforms taking place on the island. These transcriptions further reflect the seven editors' various backgrounds, which influenced their decision-making process in regard to this music.

Born into musical families, cousins William Allen and Charles Ware took piano lessons as children, spent their formative years learning harmonic principles, and were proficient singers.[14] However, their collaborator Lucy McKim was an accomplished pianist, piano teacher, violinist, and the only full-time musician among the *Slave Songs* editors.[15] Josephine and Caroline Pinckney, who transcribed songs for the Society for the Preservation of Spirituals, came from an influential Charlestonian family who stressed fine singing and proficiency on the parlor piano in their grand music room.[16] Finally, Carl Diton and Nicholas Ballanta-Taylor were the only professional musicians among these song collectors, having received degrees in music from the University of Pennsylvania and Institute of Musical Arts (The Juilliard School), respectively. Diton was the first African American concert pianist to tour America and composed popular organ works based on Negro spirituals.[17] The Sierra Leonean Ballanta-Taylor composed organ works and two operas, *Afiwa* and *Efua*.

Despite their musical training, these early folklorists often faced, in the words of musicologist Ronald Radano, "living vestiges of primordial sound impossible to notate."[18] But their greatest hurdle lay in their preconceived judgments of the islanders' music. For example, the Unitarian teacher Allen referred to the island's songs as either "barbaric" or "civilized" based upon the perceived degree of White influence. Diton, a member of the Black elite of the New Negro Movement or Harlem Renaissance, insisted on standard English spellings instead of the Gullah texts he assuredly heard during his summer on the island.

Ballanta-Taylor's singular preoccupation with proving West African elements resulted is his oversight of clear White hymnal influences. Last, the Pinckney sisters' ardent commitment to achieving accurate Gullah texts, melodies, and even clapping patterns is laudable, but they were the only editors without substantial input from a native islander.

I must also address those folklorists and ethnomusicologists who argue for less reliance on musical transcriptions and more on the study of the music makers themselves. Christopher Waterman famously stated, "adequate analysis of the music itself—a classic example of scholarly animism—must be informed by an equally detailed understanding of the historically situated human subjects . . . Musics do not have selves people do."[19] While these editors' personal biases governed to some extent their analytical constructions and musical decisions, there is unquestioned importance in their musical contributions and an equally valuable historical record of the island's songs.

Similarly, to some extent my own biases governed my transcriptions in this book. Like Allen, Ware, and McKim, I concentrate on mainly single-melody notations. Ethnomusicologist Bruno Nettl criticizes this tendency on the part of many folk scholars to concentrate on monophonic music in lieu of the more courageous task of representing two or more voices.[20] Although I made several transcriptions of four-part group singing from audio recordings of the Penn School film *To Live As Free Men,* which were courageous indeed, the vast majority of my transcriptions derive from personal interviews of the island's song leaders Gracie Gadson, Deacon Joseph and Rosa Murray, and Deacon James Smalls. My intent was to focus on these soloists to give the broad term Gullah or Geechee an identity, a story, through the singing and personal accounts offered by these special people.

Numerous weekends and summers I stayed in a small trailer in the backyard of Gracie's home and eagerly waited for an invitation to come inside her home to eat wonderful Frogmore stew and fried shrimp. It was during these moments I realized that her singing was even more powerful and emotional when she sang inside her home, where the only audience seemed to be the Lord. During my visits with Deacon Smalls at his farm, I spent time with him as he fed his cows and sang on his sofa for many hours. During our times together at his home, I learned more about the old songs than I ever did from my recordings of him at the pray's house or church. Smalls gave insightful information concerning the scriptural basis for each song, told stories about how the "old people" used to sing, and reflected on his many years as a choral director.

Last, my visits with Rosa and Joseph Murray in their home provided great insight into their rich backgrounds as church singers and their memories of experiencing the ring shout. Their love for each other was most evident when

Rosa Murray and Gracie Gadson performing at the Heritage Days Festival, November 9, 2014; reproduced courtesy of the Athenaeum Press, Coastal Carolina University.

they sang, laughed, and created beautiful harmonies together. All four singers are featured in the compact disk *Gullah: The Voice of an Island.*

This book's singular focus on Saint Helena Island overlooks to some degree influences from the more than 100 islands of the Sea Islands region. Natural interactions between families, friends, and churches located on different islands occurred, often blurring the exclusivity of any island's culture. When needed I relied upon studies conducted on Johns Island (Guy and Candie Carawan, 1966), McIntosh County (Art Rosenbaum, 1998), and Saint Simons Island (Lydia Parrish, 1942).[21] Parrish's *Slave Songs of the Georgia Islands* was the first and most extensive study done on a sea island outside of Saint Helena, and she provided one of the earliest discussions of the West African influences within the ring shout tradition.

My discussion of the Saint Helena Island Negro spirituals traces the development of these songs from their beginnings in West Africa and later oppression by White missionaries to their height as songs for social change and Black identity in the twentieth century. I concentrate primarily on the shouting songs, rowing songs, the Penn School musical curriculum, song usage during the World Wars and Prohibition, and the adaptation of these spirituals into freedom songs. In providing vital historical overview, I contextualize song usage and performance tradition and identify those factors most responsible for song retentions or song loss.

Chapter 1 details the rowing songs which contained important West African cultural retentions. White owners prized those slaves from the Gold Coast of

Deacon Joseph and Rosa
Murray performing at the
Heritage Days Festival, No-
vember 9, 2014; reproduced
courtesy of the Athenaeum
Press, Coastal Carolina
University.

Angola and Congo because of their skillful rowing, which was often accompanied by a unique repertoire of songs. These rowing songs served as a form of
musical entertainment as White visitors traveled throughout the Sea Islands
region. Although slave rowers worked incredibly long hours and carried heavy
loads, numerous accounts describe the cheerful nature by which these men went
about their jobs. However, there were moments when these oarsmen inserted
song texts that complained openly about their difficult working conditions and
mistreatment by passengers. My discussions offer a rare insight into the hidden
meanings in these rowing songs.

The latter part of the chapter analyzes the West African-derived counterclockwise movement in the ring shout and the 3+3+2 handclapping rhythm
employed during shouting. To many White people the ring shout crossed the line
between sacred and secular, and Towne and Cooley worked hard to eradicate this
highly emotional and frenzied art form. These White missionaries and even a
few educated Blacks deemed the shout as barbaric, causing islanders to establish
clear performance rules to validate its sacredness and appropriate use. I discuss
West African ties to the ring shout and the accompanying handclapping pattern
still popular today.

Chapter 2 provides an overview of Penn School's early musical and educational curriculum. Towne's use of northern educational methods and patriotic
songs resulted in her students' mastery of standard English, but in this process,
students stopped speaking and singing in their Gullah language. Under Cooley,
Penn School implemented a comprehensive community curriculum involving

adult classes, Bible classes, and chapel services that modeled a more restrained religious experience. Cooley endeavored to affect change in her students and even in their parents in order to achieve, in the words of her favorite scripture (John 10:10), "the abundant life."

The Penn School administrators consistently favored the use of slower, less emotional songs in marked contrast to the ever-present emotionalism in shouting songs. Many of the school's few surviving graduates call these spirituals "Penn Favorites," and they continue to sing songs such as "Nobody Knows De Trouble I've Had" and "Roll, Jordan Roll" while shouting songs are all but forgotten. The dominance of the Penn Favorites on the island and the negative views of Towne and Cooley toward the ring shout were major reasons that the shout came to an end.

Cooley's many community outreach efforts are the focus of chapter 3. For example, her house blessings celebrated the building of a new home with a formal church service featuring spirituals, hymns, and even a lecture. She used these occasions to display a restrained religious service devoid of the emotional shouting songs and even the characteristic call and response of Black preaching. Cooley's Community Sings outreach program was her most enduring legacy because it allowed the islanders to worship in their own manner—with emotion. I argue that this monthly service survives today because of this freedom.

Later, I examine the influences of Hampton Institute on the island's songs. I focus mainly on Penn School's Saint Helena Quartet, who brought many of the Negro spiritual arrangements they learned as members of Hampton Institute's choirs to the island. Over time, the quartet's immense popularity made these imported spirituals nearly indistinguishable from the islanders' own music, and the group's conservative repertoire of nonshouting songs came to embody the Penn School-approved spiritual. Yet there was also the migration of the island's songs to Hampton Institute where many Penn School graduates attended. These students played a pivotal role in teaching their unique song texts, rhythms, and melodies to students in Hampton's famed choirs and quartets.

The use of the island's songs during the World Wars and Prohibition is delineated in chapter 4. I begin by examining efforts by folklorist Natalie Curtis and Penn School teacher Joshua Blanton to inspire American troops fighting on the battlefields of Europe. Blanton was extremely effective in using his race's music to lift the morale of African American troops. Although the country's interest in Negro spirituals diminished greatly during World War II, these songs continued to give strength to the island community and hope to African American soldiers in the European theatre. Later, a battle was fought on the island itself over alcoholism during the Prohibition era. In response to the problem of public intoxication, religious leaders on the Saint Helena Island added new texts to the island's songs that threatened the loss of salvation for excessive drinking.

The adaptation of the island's songs during the civil rights movement is highlighted in chapter 5. The early part of this chapter concentrates on efforts by Zilphia Horton and later Guy Carawan, music directors at Highlander Folk School, to collect and disseminate Saint Helena Island's songs to union workers and later civil rights organizations such as the Student Nonviolent Coordinating Committee, Southern Christian Leadership Conference, and Congress of Racial Equality. The latter part of the chapter focuses on the pivotal Highlander-sponsored workshops of the 1960s, where internal battles among civil rights leaders occurred over the use of Negro spirituals in the movement.

Chapter 6 focuses on Minnie (Gracie) Gadson and Deacon James Garfield Smalls, song leaders whose performances have been instrumental to the survival of the Saint Helena Island spirituals. I examine their personal histories, pertinent community structures, and familial influences in order to identify the social factors most responsible for their continued retention of the Gullah music traditions while so many others have discarded these songs. It is my desire to share Gadson's and Smalls' unique history with readers so that they can perhaps recognize, in their own families, a similar person who is the genealogist, historian, the cultural bearer.

I close with a Gullah songbook of spirituals taken from cited collections or transcribed from my field interviews. I organize these spirituals according to their liturgical use in response to those scholars who overlook the sacred functions of Negro spirituals and the organized manner by which slaves conducted their church services. While many of these Saint Helena Island spirituals are no longer performed, it is hoped that this wealth of sacred music will be of interest to church leaders, musicians, and the general public.

Finally, it is my intent to make my discussions clear to the scholar, general reader, and those islanders who have given me such invaluable help. I am guided by the impressive listing of scholars who understood that the Saint Helena Island spirituals represented not only a legacy from the West African past but also the creation of a new art form—the Negro spiritual.

ONE

The West African Song Tradition

ROWING SONGS

Michael row de boat asho, Hallelujah!
Michael row de boat asho, Hallelujah!

The Sea Islands region provides the greatest number of accounts and transcriptions of rowing songs during the antebellum period. These boat songs, performed by physically imposing enslaved men, served as entertainment, secret codes, and much-needed accompaniment during long and arduous trips. Yet there is some uncertainty regarding their exclusive use for boating. A rower named Paris informed William Allen that boat songs were "sometimes the same as the shouting songs but sometimes used only for rowing."[1] While there was an obvious crossover of song usage, countless observations confirm a unique body of songs utilized by enslaved rowers as they carried White passengers between Charleston and the Georgia islands.

Historian Peter Wood traces the first appearance of Black oarsmen in the Sea Islands region to the 1600s, when slaves acquired valuable knowledge of trade routes and navigation from interactions with Native American tribes at trading posts along the Savannah River.[2] As the number of Native Americans declined and the cotton and rice industries boomed, plantation owners placed an even higher value on those slaves possessing navigational expertise to transport these products. This growing market resulted in numerous entries in local newspapers advertising for enslaved Blacks with boating experience. The following notice appeared in the *South Carolina Gazette* on October 8, 1772:

> To be Sold by private Contract
> Eight as valuable boat Negroes
> As any in the Province,
> Two of whom are Patroons [boat captains], who are well acquainted with
> most of the Rivers and Creeks on the Northward and Southward, being

used to them for upwards of Twelve Years. Their Honesty and Care with Respect to the Rice that they may be Entrusted with, can be answered for. They would answer Extremely well for a Country Gentleman who has Boats of His own.[3]

In Lynn Harris's view, plantation owners particularly valued slaves from the Gold Coast of Angola and Congo because of their boating and fishing expertise. Within these ancestral communities, oarsmen navigated up and down the shores in brilliantly colored boats decorated with crescent moons, stars, and sea-life symbols from their mythological stories.[4] In the 1860s, English naturalist John George Wood traveled extensively throughout West and Central Africa and discovered excellent boatmen and swimmers in the tribes along the rivers. In his discussion of the Mpongwé tribe (currently Gabon), who were "admirable boatmen," Wood gives this detailed description of their canoe-making abilities:

> When a Mpongwé has settled upon a tree which he thinks will make a good canoe, he transplants to the spot and builds a new homestead for himself, his wife, his children, and his slaves. When the trees are felled and cut to the proper length—sixty feet being the ordinary measurement—they are inge- niously hollowed by means of fire, which is carefully watched and guided until the interior is burnt away. . . . A clever man with a large family will make several such boats in a single dry season.[5]

Slave boatmen, descendants of these "clever men," built similar long, slender dugout boats as they transported passengers and cargo along Lowcountry waters.

Another cultural tradition retained by enslaved boatmen was the singing of songs to ease the strenuous physicality of rowing. In the 1964 film entitled *Sing- ing Fishermen of Ghana*, Pete Seeger captures a Ghanaian boat crew of thirteen men singing in waters forty miles northeast of Accra. This film vividly depicts the struggle of these oarsmen to overcome high waves and the importance of music in synchronizing rowing movements. Visible is the patroon song leader, positioned in the back of the boat, who leads high-energy songs.[6]

On December 19, 1864, James P. Blake of New Haven, Connecticut, gives this account of his boat trip from Saint Helena Island to Hilton Head.

> Coming over from St. Helena yesterday, in a row boat with about twenty of them, they were singing all the way strange responsive chants or melodies, of which the women would sing the burden, and the stout oarsmen every once in a while burst out with the refrain "An' I heard from Heaven To-day." These songs, much to my surprise, were all cheerful in their tendency, and all in the major key.[7] (Example 1.1.)

EXAMPLE 1.1. From Allen, Ware, and Garrison, 1867,
Slave Songs of the United States, 2.

Blake cites a rare instance in which passengers, the enslaved women, take the lead in singing verses while the oarsmen respond with the refrain. Usually published reports refer to a lead oarsman or patroon who sings the verses and the remaining rowers sing the chorus. As a young boy, South Carolina State Senator William Grayson, who was born in Beaufort, South Carolina, remembers oarsmen singing during trips to Charleston. "One served as chief performer, the rest as chorus."[8]

From Blake's account, it is apparent he expected slaves on board to sing sorrow songs more reflective of their everyday struggles than upbeat, happy tunes. He naively failed to understand the constraints placed on oarsmen. These men not only transported passengers but also were the main source of entertainment during trips lasting many hours and even days. In this capacity, they had to sing songs designed to keep their passengers in high spirits.

In the 1830s, actress and abolitionist Fanny Kemble, wife of Georgian slaveowner Pierce Butler, recorded words to a typical rowing song ditty:

Jenny shake her toe at me,
Jenny gone away;
Jenny shake her toe at me,
Jenny gone away.
Hurrah! Miss Susy, oh!
Jenny gone away;
Hurrah! Miss Susy, oh!
Jenny gone away.[9]

Kemble keenly observed that many of the masters and overseers on plantations prohibited melancholy tunes or words but encouraged cheerful music and sense-less words, deprecating the effects of sadder strains upon the slaves.[10] Another example is the upbeat rowing song "Sandfly Bite Me" discovered by folklorist Robert Gordon:

Sandfly bite me, sen' for de doctor
Farewell, Lord, I gwine!
Sandfly bite me, sen' for de doctor
Farewell, Lord, I gwine!

O-o-h carry me over!
Farewell, Lord, I gwine!
O-o-h carry me over!
Farewell, Lord, I gwine!

When I git over yonder I kick back Satan!
Farewell, Lord, I gwine!
Git over yonder I kick back Satan!
Farewell, Lord, I gwine!

The enslaved oarsmen, like most slaves, wore jovial masks to placate ever-watchful White owners and overseers. Political scientist James Scott insists that a subordinate group is incapable of open resistance but expresses their opposition through what he terms a "hidden transcript," which is a critique of power spoken behind the back of the dominant group.[11] Within the context of slavery, Michael Castellini sees the hidden transcript as a veiled realm free from the direct aggression of White people, thus allowing a degree of freedom for the enslaved Africans.[12] In the last verse of "Sandfly Bite Me," the rowers' hidden transcript expresses their confidence in a day of recompense in heaven (yonder), when they can finally express their anger and "kick back" their white oppressor (Satan)." Often, the rowing process provided enslaved boatmen with a rare opportunity to express their anger on earth. While most Negro spirituals detour from address-ing the White master directly, many rowing songs offer fascinating moments in which subordinate slaves take off their masks and reveal their true feelings.

Slave oarsmen took advantage of the distractive sounds emanating from the oars, wind, and waves to insert personal texts in response to unpleasant passen-gers, unbearably heavy loads, and extremely long hours of rowing. For example, Bartholomew Carroll, a Charlestonian editor, describes a boat ride to Edisto Island in 1842 involving a rather drunk passenger, his uncle Ralph. In his inebri-ated condition, Ralph is rather quarrelsome and curses at length at the oarsmen before taking his seat at the helm of the boat. Then each oarsman takes his place, releases himself of his jacket, and seems to wonder in his mind, if uncle Ralph goes on drinking, whether his cheeks will not surpass in color said oarsmen's red flannel shirt . . . "Big-Mouth Joe," the leading oarsman, announces his departure from the city with a song in whose chorus everyone joins.

> Now we gwine leab Charlestown city,
> Pull boys, pull!
> The gals we leab it is a pity,
> Pull boys, pull!
> Mass Ralph 'e take a big strong toddy,
> Pull boys, pull!
> Mass Ralph 'e aint gwine let us noddy,
> Pull boys, pull![13]

As the boat takes off, Joe's improvised verses begin with the expected upbeat farewell, but once the rowing is at full speed, he cleverly addresses Ralph's excessive drinking and even hints at this gentleman's antagonism toward the oarsmen. This adaptation of the hidden transcript allows "Big Mouth Joe" to sing words that express his true feelings toward Uncle Ralph without evoking anger from the White passengers and perhaps eventual punishment.

In another example, Irish war correspondent William Russell describes his fishing trip from Pocotaligo to Barnwell Island, South Carolina, in 1861. On the evening of April 26, Russell's party interrupts the dinner of four stout oarsmen, who must stop and carry these passengers and their heavy loads on a nighttime voyage through unpredictable Lowcountry waters. Although this trip lasts for only an hour, the patroon's song contains a hidden transcript revealing his dismay at being forced to work and his desire for rest:

> Oh, your soul! Oh, my soul!
> I'm going to the churchyard to lay this body down.
> Oh, my soul! Oh, my soul!
> We're going to the churchyard to lay this nigger down.[14]

This patroon also begins with a benign, nonthreatening statement "Oh, your soul, Oh my soul, I'm going to the churchyard to lay this body down down" before dramatically using the derogatory term "nigger" to describe his dehumanized condition. The editors of *Slave Songs* confirm the use of "Lay this Body Down" when the load was particularly heavy and the tide was against the rowers, thus producing a slower tempo.[15]

Toward the end of the Civil War, six newly freed oarsmen of the First Regiment of South Carolina Volunteers sang a rowing song that expressed the emotion closest to their hearts—freedom:

> No more driver call for me,
> No more driver call;
> No more driver call for me,
> Many a thousand time.
> No more fifty lashes for me,
> No more fifty lash;
> No more fifty lashes for me,
> Many a thousand time.

With increasing intensity and focus on their deliverance from whippings, these men defiantly remove their mask of obedience and without pretense of a hidden transcript proclaim in solidarity, "No more!" Indeed, these words are in marked contrast to the conciliatory tone in the regiment's more typical boat songs, such as "I Want to Go to Canaan," "Praise Member," and "My Army Cross Over" recorded by the soldiers' commander, Colonel Thomas Higginson (Examples 1.2 and 1.3). Unfortunately, the *Slave Songs* editors could provide only a text for "I Want to Go to Canaan."

> I want to go to Canaan
> I want to go to Canaan
> I want to go to Canaan
> To meet 'em at de comin' day
>
> My brudder, you—oh!—remember (Thrice)
> To meet 'em at de comin' day.[16]

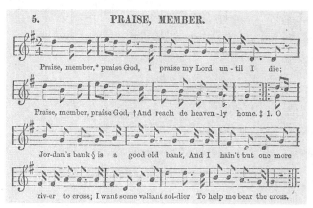

EXAMPLE 1.2. From Allen, Ware, and Garrison, 1867,
Slave Songs of the United States, 4.

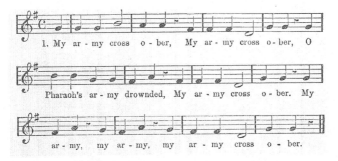

EXAMPLE 1.3. From Allen, Ware, and Garrison, 1867, *Slave Songs of the United States*, 38. In regard to the unusual word "Myo," an old man in Higginson's regiment informed him that it meant the river of death. Higginson reasoned that it was African in origin.

Northern visitors traveling to Saint Helena Island in the 1860s cite an extraordinary singing crew operating the ferry boat between Beaufort and Whitehall Landing at Lady's Island. Although another crew rowed a connecting ferry boat from Lady's Island to Saint Helena Island, it was the Beaufort boatmen who received praise for their outstanding singing. Allen states, "I have only heard good boat singing once—in crossing the ferry to Beaufort. That crew sings finely."[17] Penn School teacher Charlotte Forten agreed with Allen's assessment and wrote this account on October 28, 1862:

> The row was delightful. It was just at sunset—a grand Southern sunset;
> and gorgeous clouds of crimson and gold were reflected in the waters below,
> which were smooth and calm as a mirror. Then, as we glided along, the rich
> sonorous tones of the boatmen broke up the evening stillness. Their singing
> impressed me much. It was so sweet, strange, and solemn. "Roll, Jordan
> Roll" was grand and another

> Jesus make de blind to see
> Jesus make de deaf to hear
> Jesus make de cripple walk
> Walk in, kind Jesus
> No man can hinder me.[18]

While "Roll, Jordan Roll" was popular in diverse settings such as Penn School, pray's houses, and on boats, the few reports of "No Man Can Hinder Me" allude to its primary use as a rowing song. The editors of *Slave Songs*, specifically Charles Ware, provide the following transcription of "No Man Can Hinder Me" (Example 1.4).

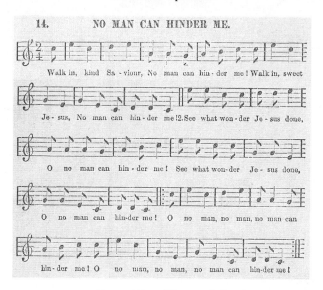

EXAMPLE 1.4. From Allen, Ware, and Garrison, 1867,
Slave Songs of the United States, 10.

Finally, Wendell Garrison, literary editor for the weekly newspaper *The Nation*, published this account on November 21, 1867, which describes his trip to Saint Helena Island with his wife, the aforementioned Lucy McKim:

> Then there is the quaint "O Deat' He is a Little Man," which we remember ourselves to have heard sung by a crew rowing across the ferry between St. Helena and Beaufort. The fugleman [leader] on that occasion—a fellow of inky blackness, with the sweat of a summer's day streaming from every pore, and his eyes squinted under the sun's glare—can never be forgotten as he poured forth energetically, "O Lord, remember me; do Lord, remember me."[19]

The names of these oarsmen are largely unknown except for Charles Ware's singular reference in the preface of *Slave Songs*. In his description of the oarsmen's slower song tempo, Ware cites a crewman named Jerry who often hung onto his oar on the word "holy" in the spiritual "Believer Cry Holy." Assuredly, Jerry and the rest of the crew's commitment to entertaining visitors through the beauty of Negro spirituals should not be forgotten!

Of the *Slave Songs* editors, Ware seemed most interested in the boat songs of the islanders. For example, he observed that rowing strokes accented the first measure of a rowing song while the rattle of oars in the row locks served to accentuate the second measure. He even counted the rowing strokes of the Beaufort crew, finding an average of twenty-four strokes per minute. Ware's curiosity with rowing songs continued even after he left the islands. Among his personal papers were three unpublished rowing melodies and two boat refrains "Halle, Hallelu" and "O Zion." These were handwritten in his personal copy of *Slave Songs.*

Ware's greatest contribution may have been his listing of the most common rowing songs: "Praise Member," "Heaven Bell A-Ring," "Jine 'em," "Rain Fall and Wet Becca Lawton," "No Man Can Hinder Me," "Religion So Sweet," "Bell da Ring," "Can't Stay Behind," "Rock o' Jubilee," "Lay this Body Down," "Bound to Go," "Sail O Believer," "Satan's Camp A-Fire," and "Michael Row the Boat Ashore." Even though some of these rowing songs were used as shouting songs, Ware's research confirms a specific repertoire of boat songs performed by the enslaved boatmen he heard. Due to the immense popularity of "Michael Row the Boat Ashore," I reserve a later discussion for this rowing song, which was born in camp meetings and brought to life during the civil rights movement.

According to Allen, "Michael Row the Boat Ashore" was the only exclusive rowing song. He states, "I know only one pure boat song, the fine lyric, 'Michael Row the Boat Ashore'; and this I have no doubt is a real spiritual—it being the archangel Michael that is addressed" (Example 1.5).[20]

EXAMPLE 1.5. Allen. 1867. *Slave Songs of the United States,* 23.

A closer examination of "Michael Row the Boat Ashore" reveals striking similarities to Samuel Hauser's camp meeting hymn "Old Ship of Zion."[21] Although many spirituals originated from slave plantation life, some grew out of camp meetings during the Second Great Awakening in the 1830s.[22] From these highly charged evangelical services, important musical exchanges occurred between Black and White people, blurring lines of ownership. After the camp meetings dismissed, many slaves continued to sing all night. At a camp meeting in Charleston, South Carolina, in 1850, Swedish writer Fredrika Bremer describes the behavior she witnessed after midnight:

> We went the round of the camp, especially the black side. And here all the tents were still full of religious exaltation, each separate tent some new phasis. We saw in one a zealous convert, male or female, as it might be, who with violent gesticulations gave vent to his or her newly awakened feelings, surrounded by devout auditors; in another we saw a whole crowd

of black people on their knees, all dressed in white, striking themselves on the breast, and crying out and talking with the greatest pathos; in a third women were dancing "the holy dance" for one of the newly converted. . . . In a fourth, a song of the spiritual Canaan was being sung excellently.[23]

The slaves in attendance continued to sing and rework hymns such as "Old Ship of Zion" because this music offered solace and even hope. Such a refashioning process may account for the popularity of this hymn's text and its many different versions. For example, the editors of *Slave Songs* presented two versions in their collection, and Higginson presented three more. In fact, Allen states, "We have received two versions of the 'Old Ship of Zion,' quite different from each other and from those given by Colonel Higginson."[24] To facilitate a better comparison, I transpose Higginson's Georgia version of "Old Ship of Zion" a whole step lower to the E♭ key of "Michael Row the Boat Ashore." The text is "Think she'll be able to take us all home. O glory hallelujah" (see Example 1.6).

Think she'll be   a-ble-to   take us all   home.   O - glo ry ha le lu   jah.

EXAMPLE 1.6. Hauser, "Old Ship of Zion," mm. 1–8.

1.   Michael   row   de boat   a - shore,   Hal - le - lu - jah!

"Michael Row the Boat Ashore." From Allen, Ware,
and Garrison, 1867, *Slave Songs of the United States.*

The shared melodic material and reoccurring hallelujah refrains suggest "Old Ship of Zion" as the probable melodic stem of this valued rowing song. Notably, the added texts and subtle melodic variations highlight the ability of slaves to create new, more personal songs from the camp meeting hymns they encountered. Evidence shows that even more alterations occurred to this melody on Johns Island, South Carolina, where Guy and Candie Carawan recorded "Row, Michael, Row" during a New Year's Eve service in the Moving Star Hall. In this rendition, verses include a reference to Michael, Sister Mary (presumably the Virgin Mary), and the personal plea "Just gimme a living chance."[25] In fact, over time the people of Johns Island created an entirely new melody for "Michael" that bears little resemblance to Saint Helena Island's version.

During the 1950s and 1960s, "Michael Row the Boat Ashore" enjoyed commercial success as a folk song and a civil rights anthem. Folklorist Pete Seeger explains its genesis into the American cultural mainstream:

In 1867, an ex-officer of the army published in the North a book entitled *Slave Songs*. In 1954, Tony Saletan found a copy in a library in Boston and went through it page by page. He selected this song and these verses to teach me. I taught it to the Weavers, who sang it at their '55 reunion concert. In '59 some pop singers made it a hit record. Then (not before) it spread through the South again and got many new verses.[26]

The new verses added during the civil rights movement are as follows:

> Michael's boat is a freedom boat, Alleluja
> If you stop singing then it can't float, Alleluja
>
> Jordan's river is deep and wide, Alleluja
> Get my freedom on the other side, Alleluja
>
> Jordan's river is chilly and cold, Alleluja
> Chills the body but not the soul, Alleluja
> Christian brothers, don't you know, Alleluja
> Mississippi is the next to go, Alleluja

Seeger made few alterations to the original transcription. He lowered the key a half-step to D major, a more accommodating key for a guitar or banjo, and made subtle changes to the melodic line. In chapter 5, I will discuss the use of several other Saint Helena Island songs as the soundtrack for the civil rights movement.

Aside from the *Slave Songs* transcription, I found no reference to "Michael Row the Boat Ashore" in the five other major collections of the island's music. In fact, only one islander, Deacon James Garfield Smalls, remembers hearing this spiritual sung on the island. Presumably, the building of the bridge linking Saint Helena to the mainland ended the community's reliance on boats for transportation and diminished the need for rowing songs. The later recording of "Row, Michael, Row" on Johns Island suggests this community's continued reliance on rowboats over a longer time period.

In numerous historical accounts, rowing songs gave White visitors their first introduction to the music of the Sea Islands region. Often, these visitors described lively spirituals that provided entertainment and a much-needed distraction from the monotony of a long boat ride. Within the constraints of slavery, boatmen had little choice but to appear happy and cheerful for passengers and overseers. Indeed, as one slave sang:

> Got one mind for white folks to see
> 'Nother for what I know is me
> He don't know, he don't know my mind
> When he see me laughing
> Laughing just to keep from crying.[27]

Deacon James Garfield Smalls at home, 2017. Photograph by Haley Yarborough, Courtesy of The Athenaeum Press at Coastal Carolina.

Eventually as freedom became a reality, oarsmen expressed through songs their innermost feelings without fear of retribution as they proclaimed an end to the physical and mental atrocities of slavery. The singular survival of the popular "Michael Row the Boat Ashore" represents an important legacy for those African American boatmen who entertained so many despite unmentionable hardships. By the 1920s, there was no longer a need for boats and rowing songs on Saint Helena Island, bringing to an end one of the most important genres of Negro spirituals. The encroaching outside world and Penn School had equally devastating effects on the other great legacy—shouting songs.

SHOUTING SONGS

O Eve, Where's Adam
O Eve, Adam in da gaadin pickin' up leaf

Due to high profitability of rice, South Carolina plantation owners placed a higher value on enslaved Africans from the rice-growing areas of Africa: Senegambia, Sierra Leone, and the Windward Coast, which extends from Cape Mount to Assini (modern Liberia and the Ivory Coast).[28] On Saint Helena Island, the enslaved workers proved equally effective in growing the highly prized long-staple cotton. According to Charles Kovacik and Robert Mason, the silky-fine quality of long-staple cotton brought the highest prices and was the most valued cotton in the world, resulting in a powerful aristocratic plantation society with more slaves per owner than in any other part of South Carolina.[29] These slaves differed in their languages and customs, but they shared the centrality of the circle dance in their religious life. Historian Sterling Stuckey notes that use of the circle for religious purposes in slavery was so consistent and profound that it gave form and meaning to Black religion and art.[30] Moreover, the circle dance, known as the ring shout, required little conversation, needing only a communal desire to escape from the difficulties of slave life and connect to what had been lost during the transatlantic slave trade, sometimes referred to as the Maafa (Great Disaster).[31]

In the 1950s, Argentine historian Vicente Rossi made this observation of a circle dance in the Rio de la Plata region:

> There is something there, in the middle of the circle of black men, some-
> thing that they alone see, feel, and comprehend . . . the voice of native
> soil, a flag unfurled in harmonic syllables. There is something there, in the
> middle of the dancing ring of black men and it is the motherland! Fleeting
> seconds of liberty have evoked it, and, once brought into being it fortifies
> their broken spirits . . . they have, forgetting themselves, relived the Kongo
> nation in one of its typical expressions . . . in sudden homage, with an ex-
> panded power of observation they dance around the vision.[32]

The small white structure known as the pray's house on Saint Helena Island offered enslaved Africans a safe haven where they could experience these "fleeting seconds of freedom" in the performance of the energetic and frenzied ring shout. Joseph Murray, deacon at Ebenezer Baptist Church on Saint Helena Island, often shares his memories of watching his mother, who was a large woman, gyrate her hips in performance of the shout. He is fond of saying, "she was a big woman who could really shout." *Slave Songs* editor William Allen offers one of the earliest and most detailed descriptions of the shout after the scripture reading, prayer, and hymn lining of the hymn took place:

> The benches are pushed back to the wall when the formal meeting is over,
> and old and young, men and women, sprucely dressed young men, gro-
> tesquely half-clad field-hands—the women generally with gay handkerchiefs
> twisted about their heads and with short skirts—boys with tattered shirts
> and men's trousers, young girls barefooted, all stand up in the middle of the
> floor, and when the 'sperichil' is struck up, begin first walking and by-and-
> by shuffling round, one after the other, in a ring. The foot is hardly taken
> from the floor, and the progression is mainly due to a jerking, hitching
> motion, which agitates the entire shouter, and soon brings out streams of
> perspiration.[33]

Allen elaborates on the role of the ring shout participants:

> Sometimes as they shuffle they sing the chorus of the spiritual, and some-
> times the song itself is also sung by the dancers. But more frequently a

band, composed of some of the best singers and of tired shouters, stand at the side of the room to 'base' the others, singing the body of the song and clapping their hands together or on the knees.[34]

Sociologist T. J. Woofter Jr. traces the pray's house and shouting tradition back to the period when "slave laws were implemented to discourage the gathering of slaves away from their own plantations." Yet many slaves continued to hold secret evening pray's services in the woods or ravines called hush harbors even at the risk of severe punishment. Presbyterian minister Charles Colcock Jones recalls that slaves were "willing to risk threats of floggings at the hands of their earthly masters in order to worship their 'Divine Master' as they saw fit."[35] To lessen the danger, the enslaved would wet quilts and rags or place an iron pot or kettle upside down to absorb the sounds from the praying, singing, and dancing. Slaveowners, realizing the futility of trying to prevent these gatherings, built pray's houses on their plantations to keep slaves from stealing away and gave slaves complete authority over all pray's house matters.

In his book *Four Moments of the Sun,* Robert Thompson's examination of the Bakongo burial ceremony gives important insight into the West African traditions of the circle dance. During this ritual, the body of the deceased is laid out in state in an open yard "on a textile-decorated bier," as bare-chested mourners dance to the rhythms of drums "in a broken counter-clockwise circle," their feet imprinting a circle on the earth, as cloth attached to and trailing on the ground from their waists deepen[s] the circle. If the deceased lived a good life, death, a mere crossing of a threshold into another world, was a precondition for being "carried back into the mainstream of the living, in the name and body of grandchildren of succeeding generations."[36]

Thompson relates this counterclockwise movement to the Kongo cosmogram, which involves four moments of the sun: dawn (birth), noon (life at its fullest), sunset (the end of life's journey) and, finally, for those who lead exemplary lives, a second dawn (rebirth). He elaborates:

> Coded as a cross, a quartered circle or diamond, a seashell's spiral, or special cross with solar emblems at each ending—the sign of the four moments is the Kongo emblem of spiritual continuity and renaissance. . . . In certain rites it is written on the earth, and a person stands upon it to take an oath, or to signify that he or she understands the meaning of life as a process shared with the dead below the river or the sea—the real sources of earthly power and prestige.[37]

Sierra Leonean Earl Conteh-Morgan confirms a similar counterclockwise movement around the deceased during Bandu burial services in his country, where sacred dance holds a prominent place in traditional societies. This strong connection between the circle of life processes such as marriage, the birth of children, and death permeates much of Sierra Leone society and predates the transatlantic slave trade. In his study of the Kongo cosmogram, Corey Stayton concludes that it

> provides a unique model of religious and social values which have paved the way for the creation of this theory and the very foundation of many African-American traditions. The reification of the cosmogram upon the earth's surface [is] through African funeral.

The horizontal and vertical lines, which are also found in slavery pottery, are also addressed by Stayton:

The horizontal line, which stretches from the farthest right point of the circle to the farthest left point, symbolizes a wide river or deep forest. This horizontal line divides the circle into two hemispheres: the world of the living and the world of the dead. More specifically, the top half of the circle represents the world of the living and the bottom half represents the world of the dead. The vertical line, which stretches from the circle's highest point to its lowest point, traces the path across the two worlds of the living and the dead.

A celebrated example of enslaved Africans observing this dance-funeral ritual was the Mende song recorded in the summer of 1931 by linguist Lorenzo Turner. In his book *Africanisms in the Gullah Dialect,* Turner provides the longest preserved West African text in a song by Amelia Dawley, who lived in Harris Neck, Georgia. Dawley learned the tune from her mother Tawba Shaw and her grandmother Catherine, both born in slavery. The song and language had no meaning to them, but they sang it to entertain the children and make them dance.[38]

In 1990, scholar Joseph Opala found Dawley's daughter, Mary Moran, still performing this song more than fifty years since Turner's interview, and he traced this song's origin to Sierra Leone. Inspired by this discovery, Opala and ethnomusicologist Cynthia Schmidt took a recording of Dawley's song to Sierra Leone and eventually found the remote Mende village of Senehum Ngola in Sierra Leone, where a woman named Baindu Jabati recognized the melody and lyrics. Jabati recalled her grandmother singing this song during a graveside ceremony called Tenjami or "crossing the river." This Mende funeral song had been a dirge that featured body movements in honor of the village's ancestors.[39] With the help of linguist Tazieff Koroma, Opala and Schmidt translated Amelia's Song:

Mende Language

> Ah wakuh muh monuh kambay yah lee luh lay tambay
> Ah wakuh muh monuh kambay yah lee luh lay kah.
> Ha suh wileego seehai yuh gbangah lilly

Ha suh wileego dwelin duh kwen
Ha suh wileego seehi uh kwendaiyah.

English Translation

Everyone come together, let us work hard;
the grave is not yet finished; let his heart be perfectly at peace.
Everyone come together, let us work hard:
the grave is not yet finished; let his heart be at peace at once.

Sudden death commands everyone's attention
like a firing gun.

Sudden death commands everyone's attention,
oh elders, oh heads of family
Sudden death commands everyone's attention
like a distant drum beat.[40]

Lorenzo Turner traced the word "shout" to the Arabic term "saut" or "sha'wt," which referred to a single circumambulation (the act of moving around a sacred object). As part of their pilgrimage to Mecca, Saudi Arabia, Muslims process around the Ka'bah, a cube-shaped building at center of Islam's most sacred mosque Al-Masjid al-Haram, seven times in a counterclockwise direction. Turner's suggestion of a Muslim presence among slaves in the Sea Islands region is supported by Allan Austin in his book *African Muslims in Antebellum America: A Sourcebook*. Austin identifies a large number of Muslims who still practiced their religion among the West Africans enslaved in the Georgia Sea Islands.[41] More recently, Michael Gomez uncovered evidence, through an examination of slave names, of several Muslims living on the John Stapleton Plantation on Saint Helena Island. He writes:

In May 1816, a list of the 135 slaves on the Frogmore estate [Stapleton Plantation] was drawn up, on which the following individuals appear: Sambo, eighty-five years old and African-born; Dido, a fifty-six year old "Moroccan"; Mamoodie and his wife Eleanor, both African born and age twenty-eight and twenty-nine, respectively; and the family of Nelson, Venus, and child Harriett. Sambo and Dido were probably Muslim. Mamoodie and Eleanor had a child named Fatima [an Arabic name] in 1814 (who died in infancy), so they were very likely Muslim. The more interesting individuals are Nelson and Venus, who were twenty-nine and twenty-seven, respectively, and both African-born. In a subsequent slave list drawn up in 1818, their child Hammett appears. Hammett (Hamid or Ahmad) is a Muslim name, which would strongly suggest that one or both parents were Muslim.[42]

The ring shout reconnected the enslaved (Muslim or Christian) to the major phases of life: birth, adolescence, adulthood, and afterlife in the ancestral worlds. Stayton states, "it was an African way of restoring an African community to its natural circular form."[43]

Penn School principals Laura Towne and Rossa Cooley, however, expressed a very different view toward the ring shout. They considered the shout on the island to be heathenish and barbaric because its overt emotionalism went against their Christian beliefs. In particular, Towne and Cooley objected to the extreme body movements, especially the dancing. Towne writes the following entry in her journal on Sunday, April 27, 1862:

> To-night I have been to a "shout," which seems to me certainly the re-
> mains of some old idol worship. The Negroes sing a kind of chorus—three
> standing apart to lead and clap, and then all the others go shuffling round
> in a circle following one another with not much regularity, turning round
> occasionally and bending the knees, and stamping so that the whole floor
> swings. I never saw anything so savage. They call it a religious ceremony,
> but it seems more like a regular frolic to me, and instead of attending the
> shout, the better persons go to the "Praise House." This is always the cabin
> of the oldest person in the little village of Negro houses.[44]

The "better persons" Towne references were those islanders who also viewed the ring shout as being outside of the Christian faith and inappropriate for true believers. These men and women preferred to attend the more formal prayer service preceding the ring shout, where they could read scriptures and pray together. African American writer James Weldon Johnson remembers the negative connotations associated with the shout at his church in Florida. As a boy, he would hear whispered invitations going around at the end of service to certain members asking them to "Stay after church; there's going to be a ring shout." The educated ministers and members eventually overcame the primitive elements in the church and placed a ban on the ring shout.[45]

Those islanders participating in the ring shout responded to this criticism by proclaiming their movements to be within the tenets of the Christian faith because their feet never crossed—they were not dancing! To this point, the elders watched carefully to ensure that shouters observed this important rule and disciplined anyone who broke it. Importantly, the shout occurred after a "vociferous exhortation or prayer of the presiding elder," lining of a hymn, and the formal church service were over.[46] The timing and freedom of the ring shout made it in essence a social dance according to Mary Twining; a time for joyful expression for people so restricted geographically from other social outlets.[47] William Allen gives this assessment:

Perhaps it [the shout] is of African origin, with Christianity engrafted upon it just as it was upon the ancient Roman ritual. At any rate, it arises from the same strange connection between dancing and religious worship which was so frequent among the ancients, and which we find in the dervishes, shakers, etc. These people are very strict about dancing but will keep up the shout all night. It has a religious significance, and apparently a very sincere one, but it is evidently their recreation.[48]

The ring shout seemed to be a perfect example of having fun in church—a concept very much ahead of its time.

The ring shout tradition has come to an end on Saint Helena, and there are only three surviving pray's houses: Coffin Point, Croft, and Jenkins. Once there was a pray's house on every plantation and, depending on the number of members, as many as three. Currently, there is only one pray's house service on Sunday evening at either Croft or Jenkins, where a few faithful members attend. As late as the early 1980s, pray's house services on the island occurred on Tuesday, Thursday, and Sunday evenings and were led by the pray's house's leader (usually a deacon) at the Thursday and Sunday services and by a female member at the Tuesday service.

In her book *Catching Sense: African American Communities on a South Carolina Sea* Island, Patricia Guthrie states that the pray's house leader was responsible for "collecting money from plantation members . . . , officiating at sessions of the religious court held at the praise house, and speaking at the funerals of deceased praise house members." Although pray's houses are often spelled with the more grammatically correct "praise" spelling, older residents on Saint Helena Island refer to these sacred clapboard buildings as prayer houses or pray's houses. From his 1939 study of the religious practices on Saint Helena Island, Samuel Lawton confirmed pray's house as the most consistent pronunciation of this structure.[49] Over time, the growing emphasis on standard English on the island resulted in an unfortunate substitution of "praise" for "pray's."

Despite the strong evidence of West African influences on circular body movement in the Sea Islands region, folklorist Art Rosenbaum cautions against relating all ring shouts to the cosmogram. Rosenbaum found that ring shouters in McIntosh, Georgia, were unaware of any symbolic meaning attached to the ring shout. These dancers simply regarded the shout "as a way of honoring God and of evoking at the very least thoughts of departed ancestors."[50] In my own study of the ring shout on Saint Helena Island, none of the islanders could explain the purpose of the counterclockwise movement beyond "having a good time in the Lord."

Musical Analyses of Shouting Songs

In *Slave Songs,* Allen lists eight favorite shouting songs on the island: "Pray All de Member," "Bell da Ring," "Shall I die?," "I Can't Stay Behind, My Lord," "Turn, Sinner," "My Body Rock 'long Fever," "Rock o' Jubilee," and "O Jerusalem, Early in de Morning." All of these spirituals contain short, repetitive refrains that were ideal for the monotony of the ring shout, for they served as a percussive counterpart to the hand clapping and foot stamping. The *Slave Songs* transcription of "Pray All de Member" shows the characteristic textual and melodic repetition common in shouting songs (Example 1.7).

EXAMPLE 1.7. From Allen, Ware, and Garrison, 1867,
Slave Songs of the United States, 35.

An even more repetitive example is the shouting song "Shall I Die?" In fact, Allen admitted that the song leader eventually just repeated the word "die." (Example 1.8)."[51]

EXAMPLE 1.8. From Allen, Ware, and Garrison, 1867,
Slave Songs of the United States, 35.

Stuckey states, "the repetition of stanzas as the dancers circled around, with even greater acceleration, reinforced and deepened the spirit of familial attachment, drawing within the ancestral orbit slaves who may not have known either a father or a mother, their involvement being an extension of that of others, the circle symbolizing the unbroken unity of the community."[52] To fully realize this unifying experience, there had to be cohesive interaction between the song leader, who stood apart and improvised verses, and the chorus of singers known as the basers, who provided the clapping, foot-stamping and sang the refrain, and the dancers.[53] If any of these elements was missing, the ring shout could not sustain itself.

In 1973, Penn Center (formerly known as Penn School) recorded the spiritual "Jubilee" during a dramatization of old plantation spirituals presented by a local ensemble known as the Saint Helena Group.[54] This group of islanders attempted to reenact the slave experience through song, dance, and short skits as part of a Spring Festival celebration. Despite their efforts to give an authentic rendition, their singing of this shouting song bears little resemblance to the *Slave Songs* version. Originally, "Jubilee," entitled "Rock O' Jubilee" in *Slave Songs,* had a minimum of nine short verses (Example 1.9).

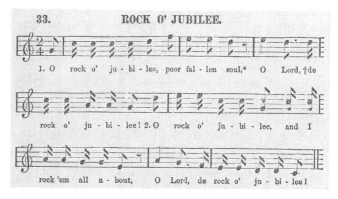

EXAMPLE 1.9. From Allen, Ware, and Garrison, 1867,
Slave Songs of the United States, 25.

Rock O' Jubilee

In the 1973 Spring Festival, the lead singer omits improvisatory textual interjections, such as "O Lord" in measures 3 and 7 in the earlier version, which help to inspire and push the basers. The soloist simply repeats "Got a home in Jubilee," leaving the "basers" with little to sustain the spiritual's momentum, and this song ends abruptly.[55]

On August 20, 1983, Rosenbaum recorded a similar version of "Jubilee" performed by the McIntosh County Shouters.[56] He relates this spiritual to Lydia Parrish's recording entitled "My Soul Rock on Jubilee," but more accurately it originated from "Rock O' Jubilee" in *Slave Songs.*[57] Due to Rosenbaum's ability to record "Jubilee" within an actual ring shout ceremony, the listener receives a more accurate representation than the earlier performance on Saint Helena. In his adaptation, the song leader provides more than ten song verses and inserts vocal interjections that drive the dancers and basers to stomp and perform the characteristic 3+3+2 handclap pattern.

The use of hand clapping in the ring shout was due in part to a ban on drums after the death of at least twenty Whites during the Stono Rebellion of 1739. South Carolinian slaveowners realized that drums had been an important communicative tool for the twenty Angolan slaves involved in the insurrection, and they moved quickly to eliminate this threat. Left with only foot stamping, hand clapping, and their voices, slaves managed to organize the ring shout around a complex layering of progressively faster beats, grunts, moans, and the final 3+3+2 handclapping pattern. The positioning of this pattern at the end provided a critical syncopation that further heightened the emotional levels of shouters.

According to ethnomusicologist Johann Buis, the 3+3+2 pattern is an African rhythmic signature that is consistently found in all ring shouts. Early efforts by the jazz historian Gunther Schuller in the 1960s traced this pattern to a West African Gankogui drum rhythm, and he argued that the bimetric approach of the African native had been forced into a 2/4 European musical framework.[58] This rhythmic pattern is normally reflected as a dotted-quarter note followed by an eighth note and quarter note tied together and an ending quarter note.

Musicologist Samuel Floyd identified the 3+3+2 pattern in the rhythm of the tresillo, a Caribbean-based dance, and in his view this pattern is ubiquitous to all Black music-making in the Americas.[59] Ethnomusicologist A. M. Jones offers this assessment of the importance of the clapping pattern in the performance of Negro spirituals:

> Claps never give way but preserve an inexorably steady beat, we see that it is the song which depends on the claps and not vice-versa. . . . A whole song will consist of a multiple of two or three claps or clap-patterns or of simple combinations of multiples of these numbers. . . . It is quite extraordinary that these apparently free songs should be found to rest on such a strict mathematical foundation.[60]

More important, the ring shout needed this clapping pattern's rhythmic thrust in order to reach its culminating point—the vamp. James Weldon Johnson gives this graphic description of the emotionalism and frenzied environment of the vamp:

> The music, starting, perhaps, as a spiritual, becomes a wild, monotonous chant. The same musical phrase is repeated over and over one, two, three, four, five hours. The words become a repetition of an incoherent cry. The very monotony of sound and motion produces an ecstatic state. Women, screaming, fall to the ground prone and quivering. Men exhausted, drop out of the shout. But the ring closes up and moves around and around.

The vamp began when the song leader reached an emotional apex and stopped singing the song verses.[61] With this signal, the basers and dancers repeated a single line or word of the refrain over the 3+3+2 clapping pattern and stamping as the leader verbally urged them on. After one of his trips to the pray's house, Allen transcribed the vamp section of the shouting song "Can't Stand the Fire" (Example 1.10).

EXAMPLE 1.10. From Allen, Ware, and Garrison, 1867,
Slave Songs of the United States, 42.

Allen admits that his rendering was only a fragment of the original spiritual. Since it appears to have been sung in different parts of Saint Helena Island, Allen's abbreviated version of "I Can't Stand the Fire" represents the community's decision to retain the popular vamp text and discard the less successful verses.

From its origins in the ring shout (an earlier form in West African music) to its use in such musical styles as blues, jazz, rock and roll, and gospel music, the vamp continues to function as the culminating emotional apex; in fact, a musician's improvisational skill within the vamping section often determines the overall effectiveness of a song. Due to its unbroken tradition in the African American religious experience, the vamp has stood as a rite of passage for gospel artists such as the Clara Ward Singers in the mid-1950s, the Hawkins Singers of the 1980s, and more recently Kirk Franklin. Indeed, gospel scholar Horace Boyer considers the repetitive vamp section to be the single most important element in gospel music.[62]

Clearly, the shout provided a rare opportunity for many African Americans to feel the fleeting seconds of liberty. Outside the purview of White society, Black people could openly complain, cry, laugh and, above all else, shout as they moved within the safety of the ring. Sterling Stuckey posits a tendency to treat spirituals as a musical form unrelated to dance and certainly unrelated to particular configurations of dance and dance rhythms.[63] Invariably, we overlook the inherent movement and syncopated nature of Negro spirituals that is driven by the 3+3+2 clapping rhythm and foot stamping. Deacon Garfield Smalls often remarks "any spiritual can be a shouting song if you set them right." The end of the ring shout on Saint Helena Island broke the islanders' ties to the West African cosmogram and its circle of life. Forever lost was the unique shuffling of feet, swaying of upper bodies, and the ever-increasing tempo of the circle that sustained the community for so long.

TWO

The Penn School

I know I would like to read
Like to read,
Like to read dat sweet story ob ole,
I would like to read
Like to read

—*Saint Helena Negro spiritual*

During its eighty-six years of existence, Penn Normal, Industrial and Agricultural School was the most influential organization on Saint Helena Island. Even before the federal and state governments offered aid to the islanders, this little school raised the necessary funds to support its northern-based educational and social programs.[1] Penn School administrators pursued a singular commitment to create a better, more "abundant life" for the island community through an effective teacher training program and equally successful vocational training program.[2] The school's first two principals, Laura Towne and Rossa Cooley, viewed the Gullah language as an impediment to their students' educational progress and instituted a standard English-only policy and substituted northern hymns for their students' own Gullah-infused songs. Despite my criticisms, Towne and Cooley faced nearly insurmountable obstacles in keeping the school open and at times battled a skeptical island community and Union Army. Furthermore, in the beginning, Towne encountered students who had no formal education and saw little need for the northerner's school.

PENN SCHOOL'S FOUNDERS

Laura Towne (1825–1901), a White missionary from Philadelphia, founded Penn School in September 1862. Initially, many of the island residents believed that Towne and her close friend Ellen Murray (1834–1908) had come to steal their children, so there were only nine students counted on their first day of classes in the Oaks Plantation House, the headquarters of the Union Army. However, within a month Towne and Murray had gained the islanders' trust, and the

Penn School founder Laura Towne with three of her students, Dick, Maria, and Amoretta Photo Courtesy New York Public Library.

school's enrollment swelled to 100 students, forcing a move to larger accommodations at Brick Baptist Church in the center of the island.[3] The immediate need for additional teachers brought Charlotte Forten (1837–1914), the first African American instructor, to the island in October 1862.[4]

Later, the Pennsylvania Freedmen's Association sent a three-room, ready-built schoolhouse by boat to the island, and Towne personally donated a brass bell for the new school with the inscription "Proclaim Liberty." As it rang, the school's students, a heterogeneous group of men, women, and children, marched across the road and took their seats in one of the first schools for Blacks in the South.[5] During this early period, Towne realized that her greatest educational hurdle was the students' peculiar Gullah language. Although Gullah borrows its lexicon from English, its grammatical structure actually lies in West African languages such as Igbo, Yoruba, Efik, Twi, and others.[6] As a result, Towne faced the difficult task of teaching her students an entirely different syntax. For example, "s" and "g" endings are absent in the Gullah language, and there is no differentiation between masculine, feminine, or neuter gender when using a singular pronoun. Instead, they use "she" or "he" to refer to all genders in the nominative case.[7] Towne describes her early students:

They had no idea of sitting still, of giving attention, of ceasing to talk aloud. They lay down and went asleep; they scuffled and struck each other. They got up by the dozen and made their curtsies, and walked off to the neighboring fields for blackberries, coming to their seats with a curtsy when they were ready. They evidently did not understand me, and I could not understand them, and after two hours and a half of effort I was thoroughly exhausted.[8]

In response to such daunting challenges, Towne and Murray implemented a regimented curriculum of reading, writing, arithmetic, Latin, history, physiology, geography, and Bible classes.

Towne and her assistant, Ellen Murray, based this educational approach, in part, on their own experiences in the North, where the standard curriculum was primarily the three R's, Latin, and Greek.[9] Edward L. Pierce, Special Agent for the Treasury Agency, approved of the school's emphasis on reading, writing, and arithmetic but insisted that Towne and Murray stress the "moral and intellectual culture of [their] wards."[10] It was Pierce who gave one of the earliest accounts of instruction at the school

One hundred and thirty-one children were present on my first visit, and one hundred and forty-five on my second, which was a few days later. Like most of the schools on the plantations, it opened at noon and closed at three o'clock, leaving the forenoon for the children to work in the field or perform other service in which they could be useful. One class, of twelve pupils, read page 70 in Willson's Reader, on "Going Away." They had not read the passage before, and they went through it with little spelling or hesitation.[11]

Soon, Towne and Murray instituted student dialogues and exercises in spelling and grammar that reinforced rudimentary grammatical skills, culminating in year-end school ceremonies demonstrating their students' remarkable progress.[12] As one observer noted, "To Miss Towne and her faithful companion was turned over not only the task of teaching the Negro the three R's but also instilling in him the rudiments of civilization. The Negro had to be torn down and rebuilt according to the white man's conception of civilization."[13] Upon Towne's death, long-time Penn School supporters George Peabody and Dr. Hollis Frissell, principal of Hampton Normal and Agricultural Institute, sent Rossa Cooley (1872–1949) to Penn School to implement a new industrial educational model.[14]

Cooley had taught at Hampton Institute, and she adopted the school's vocational curriculum for Penn School, where service to the community would become equally as important as the ability to read or write. Before her arrival, Penn School's main focus was its teacher training program, which prepared students to pass the county's certification examinations. As a result, the curriculum empha-sized test questions in the areas of pedagogy, arithmetic, grammar, and history. Cooley recognized the importance of teacher training, but she felt that too much time had been allocated to test questions, leaving great areas of life on the island untouched.[15]

Cooley understood Towne's initial need to prove to a skeptical Union Army that field hands were capable of learning through books rather than through force, but she questioned academic excesses such as pages of history recited with hardly a word changed; long lines of presidents and dynasties given, dates included; and blackboards covered with examples of cube root and algebra.[16] Cooley and her assistant Grace Bigelow House refuted the importance of identi-fying "the black lines on the map as water courses when these had nothing to do with the blue and shining tide rivers that some of the boys and girls had crossed coming to school."[17] In their view, the curriculum needed changing in order to address the immediate needs of the community.[18] However, Cooley maintained Towne's standard English requirement for students, and she shared the former principal's disdain for the emotional behavior of the islanders during their wor-ship services.

Cooley's administration implemented a year-round program at Penn School that eliminated the long summer vacation; instead, students and teachers had mini-breaks throughout the year.[19] She proudly boasted that the school's new cal-endar "brought the children farther along in their studies than they had been able to go" in the old schedule.[20] Cooley added high school classes to Penn School's curriculum, and upon graduation many students pursued a college education. But as students graduated and went on to college, fewer and fewer returned to the island.

Cooley also organized a more structured Bible class curriculum according to the following schedule:

> Every session is commenced by Bible memory verses, prayer in concert, and hymns. Their own "spirituals" are kept up as religious songs, not amusements. The lower grades learn selected verses, Psalms and Com-mandments. The higher read the Testament and Bible History. In the Eighth Grade, morals are especially insisted upon and in the Ninth there is a course of Bible Study.[21]

Her reference to spirituals as religious songs and amusements alludes to the shouting songs she felt did not belong in sacred settings. In her view, they were an unneeded form of entertainment.[22]

Cooley naively attempted Bible classes with the island's older women in hopes of changing their religious views; however, they were less than receptive to her form of religion. One woman defiantly stated, "I goes ter some churches, an'

I sees folks settin' quiet an' still, like dey dunno what the Holy Sperit am . . . dey tells us we mustn't make no noise ter praise de Lord. I don't want no sich 'ligion as dat ar."[23] Admitting failure, she placed her hopes instead with the students.

Towne and Cooley's insistence on proper literary and speaking skills greatly affected their students' perception of the value of their own language. In many cases, these children stopped speaking in the "old way." These women, however, are not solely responsible because many parents, hoping for a better life for their children, forbade the speaking of Gullah at home. Actor and singer Ron Daise recalls his childhood:

> Because my mother, a school teacher, and my father, a carpenter, both were 1933 graduates of the Penn School, one of the first schools in the South for freed slaves, speaking Gullah at home wasn't allowed. In fact, throughout my childhood, absolutely no aspect of Gullah heritage was considered positive. To identify oneself as a Gullah or Geechee meant that you were destined not to amount to much in life. My sojourn to shedding shame about my culture began piecemeal. I never identified myself as Gullah during childhood, and whenever I spoke the language it was to poke fun at someone else. I didn't speak that way. I knew better. To be Gullah or Geechee, after all, was a mark of shame.[24]

Former Penn School graduate Ralph Robert Middleton states, "Penn teachers did not recognize Gullah, and they tried to get us out of Gullah. Our training was not to speak the Gullah language, we were taught English."[25]

Under Towne and Cooley, the northern-based educational curriculum and the Bible classes succeeded in providing students with basic literacy skills and a strong moral foundation, but these accomplishments came at the expense of the students' Gullah language. Both women also discouraged the use of shouting songs and effectively turned many students away from these songs. In their place, Towne and Cooley introduced northern hymns and patriotic songs and promoted the islanders' slower, more restrained songs.

PENN SCHOOL'S PATRIOTIC SONGS

In the early years of the school, Towne, Murray, and Forten showcased their students in special New Year's Day, Fourth of July, and year-end exhibition programs.[26] Because military officers and government officials attended these ceremonies, students learned to sing popular northern hymns and songs such as "Pull for the Shore" and the "John Brown Song."[27]

Verse 1:
John Brown's body lies a-mouldering in the grave,
John Brown's body lies a-mouldering in the grave,

John Brown's body lies a-mouldering in the grave,
His soul's marching on!

Chorus:
Glory, glory, hallelujah,
Glory, glory, hallelujah,
Glory, glory, hallelujah
His soul's marching on!

Verse 2:
He's gone to be a soldier in the Army of the Lord,

Verse 3:
John Brown's knapsack is strapped upon his back,

Verse 4:
His pet lamps will meet him on the way

Verse 5:
They will hang Jeff Davis to a tree!

Verse 6:
Now three rousing cheers for the Union!
Now three rousing cheers for the Union!
Now three rousing cheers for the Union!
As we are marching on![28]

The African American instructor Charlotte Forten took great pride in teaching her students about the "glorious old man" who died to save them, and by all accounts the "John Brown Song" was a favorite among the newly freed slaves.[29]

Murray, who played the organ, was responsible for much of the musical instruction at the school in the early years. She taught such northern hymns as "Pull for the Shore," "What Shall the Harvest Be?," and "Sound the Loud Timbrel," which Forten felt was too difficult for the students (see Example 2.1).[30] Murray's choice of "What Shall the Harvest Be?" was undoubtedly due to its focus on the reward (harvest) for those who followed the tenets of the Christian faith (sowing in the seed). Such a text effectively aligned with Penn School's emphasis on character building and modeled for students those texts suitable for sacred use. As one observer stated, "Our teachers discourage the use of their old barbaric chants, and besides our beautiful, patriotic, and religious hymns teach the virtues of industry, truth, honesty, and purity in rhyme and measure."[31]

Like Forten, Towne expressed concern with the difficulty of Murray's music, especially when students struggled to learn the challenging chorus in "What Shall the Harvest Be?" After a successful performance of this work, however,

Towne collaborated with Murray on even more difficult hymns, thus exposing students to music in marked contrast to their own spirituals.[32] From these experiences, students questioned not only the educational and moral value of their own songs but also the musical quality, and it was only natural for them to prefer this newer, more advanced music. As one teacher remarked, "I have seen them, when requested to sing some of their grotesque hymns, which were great favorites in slave-times, hide their heads while singing and seem heartily ashamed of them.[33]

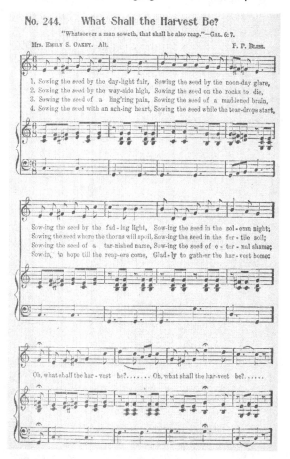

EXAMPLE 2.1. "What Shall the Harvest Be?" From Philip Bliss and Emily Oakey, "What Shall the Harvest Be?" in *The Songs of Zion: A Collection of Choice Songs* (Chicago: Church of Jesus Christ of Latter-day Saints, 1918), 264.

PENN SCHOOL'S CHRISTMAS SONGS

Under Cooley's administration, Towne's New Year's, Fourth of July, and year-end exhibition programs became less formal, and there was more focus on the agricultural accomplishments of the students. Students no longer needed to spend weeks learning challenging anthems because Cooley added a band class, chapel services, and an important Christmas play to the school's music curriculum. This latter addition, known as "The Great Mystery Play," became an event attended by the entire island community.

In 1916, Cooley brought this play to the island after her trip to Massachusetts, where she received a script, costumes, and old English carols from two former school principals.[34] These carols were "O Come, All Ye Faithful," "From Far Away," and "Draw Nigh, Draw Nigh, Emmanuel." To these carols, she added the spirituals "Go Tell It on the Mountain," and "Rise Up Shepherd and Follow." "Go Tell it on the Mountain" served as a processional song during the Mystery Play's last scene, when the entire cast came down the aisle (see Example 2.2). Later, everyone sang the spiritual "Rise Up Shepherd An' Foller" when the shepherds entered (see Example 2.3.) Cooley offers this account:

> The shepherds come in. They talk quietly about the strangeness of the night, as they stretch themselves out in the "field" in the early moonlight. (Yes, we have electric lights, red, blue, and white, so color effects on our stage are possible.) The night grows black. Something is wrong with their herds. Their fear as Gabriel appears to them, followed by the other angels, does not seem like acting at all. The voices of the unseen choir sing,

> Dere's a star in de east
> On Christmas morn,
> Rise up shepherds, an' follow
> It'll lead yo' to de place
> Where de Savior is born
> Rise up shepherds, an' follow.[35]

EXAMPLE 2.2. Ballanta-Taylor, "Go Tell It on de Mountain," (Philip Bliss and Emily Oakey, "What Shall the Harvest Be," in *Joy to the World: For the Church and Sunday School,* ed. E. O. Excell (Chicago: Hope Publishing, 1915, 90.)

The Mystery Play was an elaborate reenactment of Jesus's birth that routinely drew the entire island community to the Penn School grounds, and it is a testament to Cooley's foresight that, after nearly a century, this play still continues today. Although recent revivals feature an abbreviated form, the appearance of Deacon James Garfield Smalls in the play is always a special treat.

EXAMPLE 2.3. Ballanta-Taylor, "Rise Up, Shepherd an' Foller"
(Ballanta-Taylor, 91)

Cooley asserts that these two spirituals originated on the island, but there is little evidence supporting her claim. Ballanta-Taylor's transcription of these two spirituals during his time on the island references Fenner's Hampton Institute arrangements as the source of these songs. Since most of Cooley's teachers were graduates of Hampton Institute, it seems more plausible that they brought these Christmas spirituals to the island and taught them to the students. Supporting this premise is the lack of familiarity many of the islanders had with the Christmas story; in fact, they needed pictures to understand the story of Christ's birth before they performed the play.[36] But Cooley did incorporate the islanders' Marian spirituals as part of her successful midwifery community program.

PENN SCHOOL'S MIDWIFERY PROGRAM

Cooley and her staff wanted to eliminate the old home remedies and superstitions that many midwives on the island practiced, so they instituted an educational program to eradicate this problem. Surprisingly, midwives had better training during slavery because they were sent to Charleston for instruction and passed on their knowledge to other women.[37] After slavery, Cooley found that no records of births and deaths had been kept, and many babies were born with handicaps.[38] During their stays on the island in the late 1920s, Guy Johnson and T. J. Woofter cited these graphic examples of the superstitions practiced by some midwives during childbirth:

> Sometimes the midwives would put a hoe or a plow point or an ax under the bed to cut the after pains attending childbirth. Gizzard tea, or tea made from the nest of the mud dauber, were also thought to reduce the after pains. Even more extreme, one practice involved standing the woman in childbirth up in a corner and assisting the process by having several robust women beat, punch, and shake her.[39]

Cooley's midwifery program proved to be an effective tool in eliminating these unhealthy practices, and she reported the infant mortality rate to be 48 per 1,000 or 4.8 percent. This accomplishment was even more staggering when considering that the national average for Blacks was 100 infant deaths per 1,000 or 10 percent, and the national average for Whites was 60 infant deaths per 1,000 births or 6 percent.[40]

In support of her efforts, Cooley began an annual Christmas celebration that included the Marian spirituals "Mary Had a Baby, Aye Lawd," "Mary Had a Baby, Sing Hallelu," and "Mary Had a Baby." These texts reinforced the idyllic qualities of motherhood as exemplified by Mary, mother of Jesus. These three spirituals specifically addressed Mary's decisions for the name of her baby and choice of a suitable location to give birth (Examples 2.4, 2.5, 2.6).

This Christmas celebration continued long after Cooley retired and the school had closed its doors; in fact, in 1971, a recording of this event featured two of the three Marian spirituals, "Mary Had a Baby, Aye Lawd," and "Mary Had a Baby, Sing Hallelu."[41] Because of the popularity of these spirituals, there were few changes made to their texts and melodies in the intervening fifty-six years since Ballanta-Taylor's earlier transcription. "Mary Had a Baby, Aye Lawd" experienced popularity nationally when composer Ruth Crawford Seeger included this spiritual in her books *American Folksongs for Children* and *American Folksongs for Christmas*.[42] In both publications, Seeger cites Saint Helena Island as its origin. Although Minnie Gadson is familiar with these Marian songs, she says that they are rarely sung on the island today.[43]

EXAMPLE 2.4. Ballanta-Taylor, "Mary Had a Baby, Aye Lawd."
(Ballanta-Taylor, 40)

EXAMPLE 2.5. Ballanta-Taylor, "Mary Had a Baby, Sing Hallelu."
(Ballanta-Taylor, 41)

EXAMPLE 2.6. Ballanta-Taylor, "Mary Had a Baby." (Ballanta-Taylor, 41)

PENN SCHOOL'S FAVORITES

As discussed, early White missionaries were critical of the hand clapping, foot stamping, and body movements that characterized such shouting songs as "The Bell Done Ring" and "Bound to Go." Towne exclaimed that she never saw anything so savage as the ring shout, and even the African American teacher Charlotte Forten referred to the whole affair as barbarous. Through their personal letters it is clear that these women favored slower, less emotional songs like "Poor Rosy," described by Cooley as being a "croon in a minor key," "Roll, Jordan Roll," which Forten called "grand," the solemn "Lonesome Valley," and "Nobody Knows the Trouble I've Had."[44] Gradually, these slower-paced spirituals gained the overwhelming approval and support of Penn School's faculty and thrived at the expense of the once popular shouting songs. Lucy McKim Garrison provided the following transcription of "Poor Rosy" (Example 2.7).

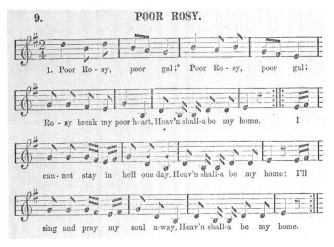

EXAMPLE 2.7. From Allen, Ware, and Garrison, 1867,
Slave Songs of the United States, 7.

While islanders no longer remember "Poor Rosy," older singers such as Deacon Smalls still sing "Roll, Jordan Roll," which holds the distinction as being the first Negro spiritual included in *Slave Songs of the United States.* Moreover, it was equally popular among Blacks and Whites (Example 2.8). Allen proclaimed it to be "one of the best and noblest of songs."[45] Charles Nordhoff, a White newspaper correspondent, noted the "glorious swing" in "Roll, Jordan Roll" and words that told of death and the happier life beyond.[46]

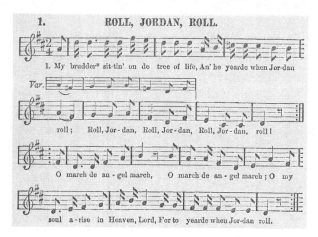

EXAMPLE 2.8. From Allen, Ware, and Garrison, 1867,
Slave Songs of the United States, 1.

Arthur Sumner, a White teacher who spent thirteen years on the island, gives the following details of the first Fourth-of-July celebration for the newly freed slaves on Saint Helena Island:

> The Negroes, marshalled by two young superintendents, came down the roads leading to the church in great processions bearing branches of greenery and singing one of their favorite songs, "Roll, Jordan Roll." The singing was intrinsically good, the songs strange and beautiful, and their swaying to and fro had a sort of oceanic grandeur in it.[47]

Later, historian W. E. B. Du Bois wrote of the mighty chorus and minor cadences in "Roll, Jordan Roll" that made it one of the ten master songs of sorrow.[48] Deacon Smalls currently sings a version of "Roll, Jordan Roll" more reminiscent of Theodore Seward's Fisk Jubilee Singers transcription than the *Slave Songs* version. He probably heard this version from Penn School's teachers, who sang many of the Fisk Jubilee Singers spiritual arrangements when they were members of Hampton Institute's choirs.

In 2013, singer-songwriter John Legend recorded a soulful rendition of "Roll, Jordan Roll" for the historical drama film *12 Years a Slave*. Clearly based on the Fisk Jubilee version, Legend slightly alters the melody, as Deacon Smalls often does, but he retains the original text and sings in virtually the same key (D major as opposed to E flat major). Later, Nicolas Britell, composer of the film, presents a new arrangement of "Roll, Jordan Roll" for a poignant scene in which the spiritual serves as an antithesis to the slave taunts of another *Slave Songs* spiritual, "Run, Nigger Run," and offers hope to the kidnapped free-slave Solomon Northup. Although altered, this spiritual remains as powerful as it was when first forged over a century ago.

Charlotte Forten considered "The Lonesome Valley" to be the most beautiful of the islanders' songs, and she referred to it as an "old favorite" at the school (Example 2.9).[49] The "valley" in this spiritual is a reference to the biblical story of Jesus being led by the Holy Spirit for his test in the wilderness. Similarly, a young person on Saint Helena Island had to undergo a test through a conversion experience known as "seekin'" before they could join a church or pray's house. When a teenager proclaimed to have been called by God, seekin' involved a vision quest supervised by a spiritual guide. During this process, the seeker wore a white bandana around the head and was physically isolated from the community until undergoing a test of Christian faith within the pray's house and the culminating religious ceremony—the water baptism.[50]

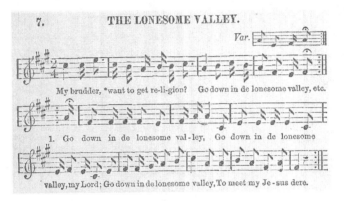

EXAMPLE 2.9. From Allen, Ware, and Garrison, 1867,
Slave Songs of the United States, 5.

This spiritual's importance in the pray's house and at Penn School resulted in few changes melodically or textually seventy-five years after its publication in *Slave Songs*. "The Lonesome Valley," along with the aforementioned "Roll, Jordan Roll," were two of ten favorite Saint Helena Island songs recorded during the filming of the 1942 Penn School documentary "To Live as Free Men."[51] Predictably, there was only one shouting song on this album, "I'm Goin' to Sing a New Song." Included also was the spiritual "Nobody Knows de Trouble I've Had," which Allen states was a favorite in the Charleston colored schools before spreading to Saint Helena Island. Later, I provide an extensive discussion of this Penn School favorite.

PENN SCHOOL'S CHAPEL SERVICES

Upon her arrival, Cooley immediately began chapel services in an attempt to become more involved in the religious life of the entire community. Ultimately, she endeavored to redirect the islanders away from the emotionalism found in their church services.[52] Like Towne, Cooley excluded the emotional shouting songs, preferring instead slower-paced spirituals. More important, these chapel services modeled disciplined and restrained worship that was fundamental to Cooley's own religious beliefs. The few living Penn School graduates still remember their teachers' emphasis on good behavior during weekly chapel services and the very organized processional for each service.

A long line of eager students marched in single file to a piano accompaniment, entered a building made of oyster shells and sand, stopped on cue from the piano, saluted the flag, then sat in their assigned seats. Such was the manner in which students entered Penn School's chapel service. Services were held every day at noon, and on Wednesday the school invited the community for a special Big Chapel service.[53] Cooley based most of the structure of these chapel services on the Hampton Institute model she observed during her time there. She describes Hampton's chapel service:

> All the School gathers for the afternoon service in the Memorial Chapel, where a service is held in which the Lord's Prayer, the Apostle's Creed, and the Ten Commandments hold a prominent part with chants, responsive readings, and the silent prayer of the Friends. Much prominence is given to music in all the religious services. Both races are not fond of it but are raised and helped by it.[54]

In Cooley's view, slower, less emotional songs, such as "Lead Me to the Rock," "We Are Traveling," and "We Are Climbing Jacob's Ladder," were better able to uplift the moral character of her students than shouting songs.

There were a few faster-paced spirituals in Cooley's chapel services, but she carefully chose nonshouting songs such as "One Morning Soon," "Little Wheel A-Turning in my Heart," and "Everybody Talking about Heaven Ain't Goin' There." These were sung during an undated Big Chapel service along with the ending lullaby "Go to Sleep"

Cooley's chapel services played a direct role in the retention of less emotional songs and the eventual loss of shouting songs. Cooley firmly believed that these emotional songs were a relic of barbarism the influence of which worked against the Christian teachings central to the school's mission.[55] Thus, when faced with the impending end of the shouting songs in the 1920s, Cooley refused to intervene and simply responded by saying, "The shouts were born and live in the praise house."[56]

She had championed the building of new homes on the island, the emphasis on agricultural improvement, midwifery, even the retention of spirituals (in certain contexts), but was unwilling to protect the ring shout.[57] Cooley was equally critical of the Gullah language and, like Towne before her, failed to realize its cultural significance until it was too late.

Proof of the effectiveness of Cooley's efforts can be seen in the 140th anniversary of Penn School's founding in 2002. Former students of Penn School compiled a commemorative booklet entitled "Memories of Penn School," which contained valuable photographs, historical information, and a listing of "Favorite Penn School Spirituals".[58] Virtually all of these spiritual favorites are either nonshouting songs or slower-paced spirituals such as "Lead Me to the Rock" and "We Are Climbing Jacob's Ladder." Remarkably, among the list are three *Slave Songs* spirituals, "There's a Meeting Here Tonight," "In the Mansions Above," and the previously discussed "Nobody Knows De Trouble I See." Unfortunately, none of the shouting songs copied by Allen, Ware, and Garrison survive in the memories of Penn school students.

The *Slave Songs* transcription of "There's a Meeting Here Tonight" is below (Example 2.10).

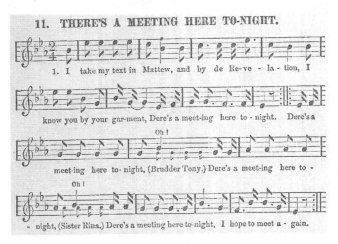

EXAMPLE 2.10. Allen. 1867. *Slave Songs of the United States.*
(Allen, Ware, and Garrison, 9)

I recorded "In the Mansions Above" during a pray's house service on May 10, 2009, and it showed surprising retentions of Allen's refrain. This spiritual is now known as "In Bright Mansions Above" and song leaders omit Allen's texts "Good Lord" and "My Lord" and their accompanying melodies (Example 2.11).

EXAMPLE 2.11. "In Bright Mansions Above, mm.1–9," Transcription by author.
(*In Bright Mansions Above,* led by Garfield Smalls, Mary Jenkins Praise House Service, Saint Helena Island, SC, May 10, 2009.)

Originally, Allen erroneously integrated the musical notes of these improvisatory texts into this spiritual's overall melody. Although he correctly heard these interjections during the song's performance, soloists used these words during momentary pauses in the melodic line to further the song's momentum, but they were never part of the spiritual's fundamental tune (Example 2.12).[59]

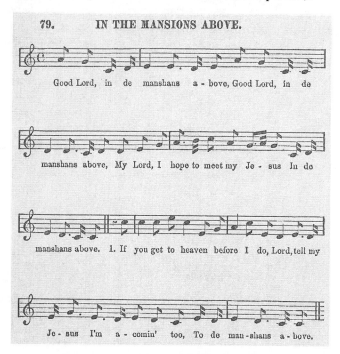

EXAMPLE 2.12. Allen, Ware, Garrison. 1867. Slave Songs of the United States.

Following "In Bright Mansions Above," someone began the spiritual "I Couldn't Hear Nobody Pray" with the exhortation "oh Lord." Other interjections such as "praise Lord," "oh," and "in the valley" infused this song with the needed forward thrust.[60]

> Oh Lord, I couldn't hear nobody pray
> Oh, I couldn't hear nobody pray,
> Oh, way down yonder by myself
>
> I couldn't hear nobody pray, Praise Lord
> I couldn't hear nobody pray, In the valley[61]

Usually the "Favorite Penn School Spirituals" are sung by an elderly group known as the "Echoes of Penn" ensemble during the monthly Community Sings event on the grounds of the old Penn School.[62] A surprising omission in the list of favorites is the well-known spiritual, "Roll, Jordan Roll," which Deacon Smalls, former leader of the Echoes of Penn, still sings today. He may be the only islander who keeps this spiritual alive.

Cooley's more aggressive attempts to change the islanders' music through a series of community-based initiatives would bring more of the community to Penn School, giving Cooley even more influence on the islanders' form of worship.

THREE

The Penn School Community Outreach Efforts

Dere's a meeting here tonight
Dere's a meeting here tonight
Dere's a meeting here tonight
I hope to meet again.

—*Community Class spiritual*

Shortly after her arrival in 1901, Cooley traveled by horseback to all parts of Saint Helena Island so she could witness firsthand the islanders' impoverished conditions. Cooley realized immediately that the school's success depended on its ability to improve the overall quality of living on the island. Cooley integrated Hampton Institute's industrial educational model into Penn School's curriculum and created special community educational programs to meet the islanders' immediate needs.[1] Through the "We Class," house blessings, Community Sings, and Saint Helena Quartet outreach efforts, the school disseminated information and offered much-needed aid to the islanders. These programs proved equally effective in giving Cooley even more influence on the religious practices of the island community.

THE "WE CLASS"

Cooley began Penn School's Community Class because she wanted to offer an enrichment opportunity for women ranging in age from forty to ninety. More specifically, she used these classes to encourage and enrich the lives of women who had endured unjust treatment during slavery. Cooley explains:

> We forget the sex relationships of slavery days. No Negro mother had any rights, and now when I hear white women speak of Negro women as if they all have a moral twist, my mind goes back to those days of the "Street," when the bodies and souls of the people were not their own. It is well to

know that there has been a spiritual fight for sixty years. And it has been the fight of the mothers.[2]

During each week, the women participated in quilt-making, basketry, and knitting, often accompanying these activities with the singing of spirituals. For example, Aunt Lily, a class leader, sang this spiritual from her youth:

> Jedus keep-a-listenin' all de day long
> Keep a-listenin' all de night
> Jedus keep a-listenin' all de day long
> For to hear some sinner pray.
>
> Oh, de Jews trow Dan'el in de lion's den,
> And how could Dan'el pray?
> But all God's chillum hoverin' about
> For to hear how Dan'el pray.[3]

Within the supportive environment of the Community Class, these women felt free not only to sing the old songs but also to move in the old manner. Cooley gives this account:

> A tapping on the floor, sometimes a soft clapping of the hands, makes the rhythm all the more distinct. Heads nod, and sometimes the bodies sway. There are old grandmothers with white head coverings, and very occasionally a bright colored bandanna. All are neatly dressed. And they so delight in "We Class."[4]

To promote this relaxed atmosphere, Cooley structured these classes according to the islanders' own church services and allowed hand clapping and body movements. She describes her "We Class" meetings:

> The class meets in the library, as do all our smaller groups of adults, and so they sit surrounded by books which will be open to their children but are closed to many of the older generation. . . . I listen to as many of the women as would like to talk, after we have opened with devotions. They do not come just to get for themselves, either, for as they sing the island spirituals after their "lessons," they sew busily on the quilt which will find its way to some home where there is a great need: Some one wussuh off dan we!—and many a time do they "throw up the collection" for the sick member or some community call.[5]

The "We Classes" included an opening devotional period (prayer, scripture), spirituals, and an offering for the needy.

The Community Class quickly gained popularity, and women even walked from the Fripp and Indian Hill Plantations, five miles away, to attend. From these more remote areas, they brought songs often unfamiliar to the Penn School faculty. During his interview of "We Class" members in the late 1920s, sociologist Guy Johnson discovered four forgotten spirituals from the *Slave Songs* collection: "There's a Meeting Here Tonight," "Tell My Jesus Morning," "The Graveyard," and "Satan's Camp on Fire."[6] Many elderly women in the Community Class were alive and lived near the Coffin Point Plantation, where Charles Ware recorded and transcribed his spirituals in the 1860s. Two of these women were Aunt Rina Miller, Community Class president, a "mother of 25, grandmother of 52, and great-grand of nine head of children and ninety-year-old Aunt Riah, who was the oldest woman Cooley had ever seen."[7]

HOUSE BLESSINGS

The poor living conditions for many of the residents on Saint Helena Island concerned both Towne and Cooley. When Towne first arrived in 1862, she provided an unsettling description of the homes on the island:

> The tiny clapboarded frame houses had small shuttered windows, mud-and stick chimneys, dirt floors beaten hard and worn in hollows. At one side was the open hearth before which the children slept on heaps of filthy rags. The household utensils consisted of one pot and occasionally a frying pan. The elders first helped themselves from the hominy pot, then it was given to the children, who finished all that could be easily scraped out. Then the dogs worked at it for hours and left it clean for the next meal.[8]

After Towne's retirement, Cooley noted the accomplishments of her predecessor in upgrading the appearance and construction of the islanders' homes:

> White-washed houses had become the rule, and they were gaily trimmed with splashes of blue, green, and purple. The one-room home had given way to three or four rooms—usually a living room, one bedroom, and a small lean-to kitchen. The father and mother slept in a double bed, rather than the old-time bunks, but the children still bundled themselves up and slept on the floor in front of the fireplace.[9]

These structures, called "jump up" homes, raised the standard of living for the community, but children still endured crowded living quarters, and many of the older siblings in families left for the city to find jobs to escape their impoverished existence.[10] In addition, returning World War I veterans brought new, more progressive ideas from the outside world, causing many islanders to question their isolated existence.[11] To slow the tide of migration and further help the island community, Cooley participated in the National Better Homes of America campaign of 1922.

The Better Homes of America was founded by Marie Meloney, editor of *The Delineator,* a Butterick publication that had a membership of one million female readers. The purpose of their national campaign was to increase home owner-ship through an educational program designed to teach self-reliance and thrift combined with household technology.[12] From the very beginning, Penn School teachers spearheaded a vigorous island-wide home-building campaign, resulting in a third prize award in its first year of participation, a second prize in its second year, and a special first prize in the campaign's third year.[13]

The Better Homes of America campaign brought a heightened awareness throughout the entire island of the importance of home construction, and new construction of a home brought the entire community together to celebrate the new dwelling. Since Christian doctrines permeated virtually every aspect of life on Saint Helena Island, the construction of a new home required the of-ficial blessing of church leaders and church members in a ceremony known as a "house blessing."[14] The house blessing services under Cooley's leadership played an important role in the retention of a select group of spirituals.

Cooley's house blessings contained many elements of a typical church service. There was an opening scripture, prayer, song, remarks, closing prayer, and bene-diction, but she included a discussion or talk in lieu of an emotionally charged sermon. Another feature of these services was a specific repertoire of Negro spiri-tuals containing texts such as "build," "building," "house," or "home." Examples are "I'm Working on a Building," "I'm Gonna Build," "I Know I Got Another Building," "Come and Go with Me to My Father's House," and "This Little House Gonna Fall."[15]

At a house blessing ceremony held on Monday, April 25, 1932, in the Land's End community, the spiritual "I'm Working on a Building" was sung as part of the devotional section of the service. Its use in the beginning of the house bless-ing was a natural choice because of its implication of an unfinished process.

The text for the spiritual "I'm Working on a Building" is as follows:

> I'm workin' on a building
> I'm workin' on a building
> I'm workin' on a building
> I'm workin' fo' my Lord
> Soon as I get finished up
> Working on this building
> Going home to Jesus
> Get my reward.[16]

Along with "I'm Working on a Building," the Land's End house blessing service featured the island favorites "Fisherman, Peter" and "Lawd hab mercy on Me," commonly known as "Let Us Break Bread Together." The guest speakers were Dr. Alice Headwards, president of India's Young Women's Christian Association, and Mrs. Linnie Blanton, former Penn School teacher and wife of Joshua Blanton.

At a house blessing for the Bailey family on April 6, 1941, "I'm Working on a Building" was sung prior to the dedication of the home and a reading of the Sam Walter Foss poem entitled "House by the Side of the Road." Other spirituals were "I'm Gonna Build" and "I Know I've Got Another Building." Sixteen years earlier, Penn School students and staff sang "I'm Gonna Build" in a house blessing service for their Frissell Community House when it was built on Penn School's campus. Cooley recalls its text:

> I'm a-goin' to build
> Right on dis shore
> Yes, I'm a-goin' to build
> Right on dis shore
> Right on dis shore
> I'm a-goin' to build fo' muh Mastuh
> Fo' muh Mastuh till I die.[17]

She describes another house blessing service held in the home of Joshua Blanton, lead singer and organizer of the Saint Helena Quartet:

> When the new house for our superintendent's family was furnished, a group of school boys, girls, teachers, men who had worked on the house, and some plantation neighbors gathered together. This is always a religious service and that afternoon, as the sun was setting across the little march river, lighting the great pines that surround the new cottage . . . spiritual after spiritual was raised by Joshua B. Blanton. The scripture reading from the Songs of David followed, and then one of the Island men who had a large share in the work of the house . . . offered a prayer of dedication and consecration. [This] was followed by more spirituals which filled the rooms with their melody. "Except the Lord build the house, they labor in vain that built it," is a vivid message on Saint Helena.[18]

From Cooley's description, Blanton's house blessing contained more spirituals in comparison to the Land's End and Bailey services. In fact, beyond the scripture reading and prayer, the entire house blessing involved singing by Blanton, an accomplished tenor.[19]

In the 1950s, house blessings broadened in scope to closely resemble the traditional Sunday morning church service. An audio recording of a house blessing at Penn Center in 1955 had a sermon entitled "Make Your Request" and a hymn "O How I Love Jesus" in a service lasting well over two hours.[20] Such a

Joshua Enoch Blanton directing Voorhees Choir.
Photo Courtesy Avery Research Center College of Charleston

duration was due in part to the singing of shouting songs such as "This Little House Gonna Fall," which were now a part of the house blessing service. Pastor Kenneth Doe of Bethesda Christian Fellowship Church on Saint Helena Island recalls that the lack of furniture in the new home produced an advantageous environment for shouting songs because of available space and the need for the people to stand.[21]

The appearance of shouting songs in house blessing ceremonies also reflects the decreasing influence of Cooley and Penn School in the 1940s and 1950s. Cooley retired in 1944, and Penn School faced mounting debts and diminishing financial support. Although house blessings still contained the formal structural elements Cooley introduced thirty years earlier, the informal shouting songs she wanted to relegate to the pray's house were now a part of this service.

The 1950s represent the height of the house blessing ceremony before the immense resort development in the 1960s and 1970s turned cheap farm plots into million-dollar properties that attracted a massive influx of White outsiders.[22] With the rise in real estate taxes, more islanders left in search of employment and important aspects of the Gullah culture were lost.[23] Currently, house blessings, or house christenings as they are now called, are more intimate affairs involving close friends and occasionally a deacon from the family's church.[24] A sermon is no longer included, and shouting songs are a distant memory. However, spirituals remain a major part of the service along with the popular gospel songs that have become an integral part of every sacred service on the island.

Cooley's house blessing ceremonies contributed to the survival of a special repertoire of spirituals. Although these songs appeared in other religious services, their unique textual link to house blessings maintained their continued use. Cooley's retirement allowed the islanders to have more freedom and emotionalism in house blessings and return for a fleeting moment to the shout songs.

THE COMMUNITY SINGS

Without question the most successful of Cooley's outreach efforts was the monthly program known as Community Sings.[25] Currently held every third Sunday evening, this service begins with a reenactment of the old Penn School chapel service procession as elderly men and women march together in single file and sing the old favorite spirituals. Over time, the continued observance of this service for nearly a century made the greatest impact on the survival of the island's songs. This event proved equally important for the survival of the island community during the World Wars, natural disasters, and social unrest.

Cooley began the Community Sings services as a demonstration of patriotism during World War I when many of the island's men were drafted into military service.[26] She hoped to offer solace to families whose husbands and fathers went off to war by summoning the entire island together on the school's grounds to celebrate, sing, and pray. Community Sings included spirituals, an opening march by Penn School students, a prayer, quizzes, a guest speaker, important community announcements, and a closing benediction. There was the inclusion of Penn School-approved spirituals such as "We Are Climbing Jacob's Ladder" and "Walk Together Children," but Cooley permitted the singing of the islanders' shouting songs, expressive hand clapping, and even foot stomping.[27]

On November 18, 1973, the islanders clapped and stomped their feet to the ever-increasing tempo of the spiritual "Come By Here" during a Pre-Thanksgiving Community Sings program.[28] Such emotional behavior was usually forbidden on Penn School's grounds, but over time Cooley and later administrators made an exception with the Community Sings. Early on, Cooley knew that her best chance at bringing the entire community to the school's campus was to include the popular and fun shouting songs. Included in the 1973 event is the popular spiritual "Glory, Glory, Hallelujah," which closely resembles Ballanta-Taylor's transcription nearly fifty years earlier (Example 3.1 and 3.2). To facilitate an easier analysis, I transpose Ballanta-Taylor's version to the D-flat key of the 1973 recording.

EXAMPLE 3.1. Community Sings, "Glory, Glory, Hallelujah," Southern Historical Collection, University of North Carolina at Chapel Hill, T-3615, Transcription by author.

EXAMPLE 3.2. Ballanta-Taylor, "Glory, Glory Hallelujah," (Ballanta-Taylor, 53)

Currently, the Community Sings service has lost much of its popularity, and although publicized in the area churches each month, few come to the event.[29] At the Community Sings program I attended on April 19, 2009, there were approximately eighteen former Penn School graduates present and an audience of around fifty, but younger islanders were noticeably absent. Mrs. Willie Mae Alston was in charge of the Penn School Founder's quiz; Mrs. Gardenia Simmons-White, a Penn School graduate, gave the history of Penn School; special guest Terry Seabrook of the US Census Bureau discussed the importance of the census in obtaining federal funding for the island; and the audience sang a favorite Penn School hymn, "Now the Day is Over."[30]

This program, however, has lost the fervent singing, hand clapping, and foot stomping that were once an integral part of the Community Sings of the past. In a Community Sings service in the 1930s, visitor Samuel Lawton counted twenty-two spirituals being performed, and he observed that "as soon as one person finished leading a spiritual, another in the group would begin another."[31] During the April 19th Community Sings service, I observed none of the uninterrupted spiritual singing mentioned by Lawton. In fact, participants sang just six spirituals the entire evening.

In my estimation the Community Sings had the greatest impact on the survival of the island's songs. Its uninterrupted monthly services saved countless spirituals by exposing generations of islanders to the emotion-filled shouting songs as well as to Penn School's slower-paced spirituals. In the end, Cooley was willing to compromise her views toward the islanders' emotional music making to help unify the entire community.

THE SAINT HELENA QUARTET

The Saint Helena Quartet was the most popular organization at Penn School. Formed by members of the school's faculty in the early 1920s, this group served as a vital marketing arm for the school through their memorable performances of spirituals locally and nationally.[32] These men were graduates of Hampton Institute, where they sang in the school's choirs and quartets, and they brought Hampton's spiritual arrangements and singing style to the island. Through their many performances, the quartet's members became local celebrities, and listeners marveled at their strict four-part harmonies, tone quality, correct breathing, and restrained singing. In keeping with Cooley's policies, this group refrained from the emotionally charged shouting songs and favored a refined singing approach honed during their years at Hampton Institute. Below is a brief biography of each of the original members of the quartet and their musical training.

Joshua E. Blanton (1880–1970), organizer and song leader of the quartet, received academic and agricultural degrees from Hampton Institute in 1902 and 1905, respectively. During his tenure at Hampton Institute, he was a member of the school's military battalion, where he served as Fifth Sergeant, and he sang in the choir under the direction of Bessie Cleaveland, a White musician from Essex County, Massachusetts.[33] Cleaveland designed the music curriculum for the school, which emphasized the use of the Holt system of sight reading for all students.[34] While at Penn School, Blanton taught agricultural education and eventually was promoted to superintendent of industrial education. Blanton's music training served him well during his singing tours for the War Department during World War I, his musical collaboration with Carl Diton, and his subsequent work as leader of the Saint Helena Quartet. Indeed, it was this musical foundation that was also responsible for his choice of similarly trained Hampton Institute men like Anthony Watson, James King, and Melvin Wildy.

Anthony D. Watson (1880–1956) received a degree in carpentry in 1904. As a student, he sang in Hampton's quartets, played in the band, and rang the school's chimes during chapel services.[35] While in school, Watson also took part in Hampton Institute's northern campaign tours that resulted in much-needed money for new construction on campus.[36] Watson's musical versatility would prove beneficial when he later formed Penn School's first band. Upon his death, he was remembered as having "given a great deal of pleasure and done much good."[37]

James P. King (1886–1967) received academic and business degrees in 1910 and 1912, respectively, and was a member of Hampton's quartet.[38] With Cleaveland's departure in 1904, Bessie Drew, a White musician from Atlantic, Massachusetts, became director of choirs. Yet the emphasis on sight-reading and tonal quality continued. King later taught at Penn School and eventually replaced Joshua Blanton as superintendent of Industrial Education at Penn School and leader of the quartet. King was an important collaborator with Ballanta-Taylor on his *Saint Helena Island Spirituals* collection and was an influential leader at Brick Baptist Church.

Last, Melvin T. Wildy (1888–1959) received trade school and academic degrees in 1912 and 1915, respectively, and served for three years in Hampton's choir under the direction of famed choral director R. Nathaniel Dett. In 1913, Dett replaced Drew as director of the Hampton choirs, and he brought a decided preference for European music.[39] Soon after his arrival, Dett introduced Russian anthems to the choirs, especially the music of Tchaikovsky, because of the "unusual number of parts in most cases and the fact that choruses were designed for unaccompanied singing."[40] As a member of Penn School's faculty, Wildy taught blacksmithing shop and was director of church choirs at Brick Baptist Church for many years.

The quartet members' strong musical foundations resulted in a disciplined approach to the island's spirituals. Their performances featured strict four-part harmony (tenor I, II, and bass I, II), which differed greatly from the islanders who, according to Allen, tended to "follow their own whims, beginning when they please and leaving off when they please, striking an octave above or below . . . or hitting some other note that chords."[41] The islanders' undisciplined singing may have been a major reason the editors of *Slave Songs* were able to present only single-line melodies for their spirituals.[42] On the other hand, the precise part-singing of the Saint Helena Quartet, under the leadership of James P. King, enabled Ballanta-Taylor to transcribe their songs in his *Saint Helena Spirituals* compilation into four parts.[43]

Members of the quartet also emphasized clarity of pitch and beauty of tone as opposed to the islanders whose Gullah-influenced tones and sliding notes were more dissonant in nature.[44] Former Penn School student Thomas Barnwell provides this account of the quartet's level of singing:

As a youngster living on Hilton Head Island, I heard uncles who attended Penn School and my father, Thomas S. Barnwell, Sr., a Penn School graduate, describing the "sweet music" of the St. Helena Quartet. When I became a student at Penn and got to hear the quartet for myself, I understood why they were so impressed. The students, school staff and community always looked forward to hearing the quartet sing the old spirituals of our forefathers. Their performances helped develop our appreciation for this beautiful music.[45]

With Penn School trustee George Peabody's help, the Saint Helena Quartet performed on October 3, 1928, at Carnegie Hall. This concert was the ensemble's crowning achievement, and it fulfilled Cooley's desire to show the artistic genius of the Negro race to White society. Over time, the island community learned many of the quartet's Hampton Institute spiritual arrangements and adopted them as their own, often forgetting their Virginia roots. The community also grew to value the quartet's emphasis on four-part singing and beauty of tone, which left indelible imprints on their own singing.

THE SAINT HELENA QUARTET SPIRITUALS

Most of the spirituals performed by the Saint Helena Quartet were the arrangements of Thomas Fenner, director of Music at Hampton Institute from 1872 through 1875. The five editions of these songs attest to the importance of this collection and reflect its continued use by the Hampton Institute choirs for well over fifty years. General Samuel Armstrong, founder of Hampton Institute, brought Fenner to the school to establish a Department of Music and assemble a money-making vehicle for the school. Within a year of Fenner's arrival, Hampton's choir embarked on a tour of the northern states, giving concerts and raising funds for the school.[46]

Through the efforts of the 1873–75 tours, the Hampton Student Singers raised most of the $75,000 needed for the construction of Virginia Hall, a main building for dormitories, classrooms, a dining room, and a chapel. The tours, although successful, were extremely grueling for the students who gave 500 concerts in eighteen states and Canada.[47] To meet this concert demand, Fenner arranged fifty Negro spirituals, and in 1874, he published these songs in a collection entitled *Cabin and Plantation Songs As Sung by the Hampton Students*.

Like Allen and McKim, Fenner questioned his ability to properly notate the Negro singer. In his view, they sang tones that were difficult to represent using traditional musical characters, so he enlisted the aid of his student singers, such as Alice Davis, J. M. Waddy, J. H. Bailey, and J. B. Towe, with some of the spiritual arrangements. For example, Towe provided much of the notation for "A Great Camp-meetin' in de Promised Land," including the "bent" tones in measures 10 and 11 of this Negro spiritual (see Example 3.3).[48] According to Fenner, Towe brought this spiritual to Hampton's campus; thus, he obviously knew the unique altered pitches in the spiritual. The Saint Helena Quartet members taught this song to Penn School's students, but they added a fourth inspirational verse "Work together children," which is still sung today.

EXAMPLE 3.3. Armstrong, Ludlow, and Fenner, *Hampton and Its Students.*

Among Du Bois's master songs, "Nobody Knows the Trouble I've Seen" is well known for its reoccurring descending sixth interval. Yet the transcription in *Slave Songs,* originally titled "Nobody Knows the Trouble I've Had," shows that the islanders initially sang an opening ascending perfect fourth ("Here Comes the Bride") interval (Example 3.4).

EXAMPLE 3.4. Allen, Ware, Garrison. 1867.
Slave Songs of the United States.

By the 1920s, Ballanta-Taylor transcription shows a dramatic change to an opening descending sixth interval by the islanders, and he cites Fenner's *Religious Folksong of the Negro* as the source of the "altered" melody. The Saint Helena Quartet members could have informed Ballanta-Taylor of Fenner's role in this alteration (Example 3.5).

EXAMPLE 3.5. Ballanta-Taylor, "Nobody Knows de
Trouble I've Seen." (Ballanta-Taylor, 89)

Evidence shows that Fenner possessed a personal copy of *Slave Songs* and taught this spiritual to his Hampton students. For example, Fenner's description of a performance of "Nobody Knows De Trouble I've Seen" on nearby Edisto

Island was taken verbatim from a citation written seven years earlier by the editors of *Slave Songs* (Example 3.6).[49]

> This song was a favorite in the Sea Islands. Once when there had been a good deal of ill feeling excited and trouble was apprehended, owing to the uncertain action of the Government in regard to the confiscated lands on the Sea Islands, Gen. Howard was called upon to address the colored people earnestly. To prepare them to listen, he asked them to sing. Immediately an old woman on the outskirts of the meeting began "Nobody Knows the trouble I've seen," and the whole audience joined in. The General was so affected by the plaintive melody, that he found it difficult to maintain his official dignity.

EXAMPLE 3.6. Armstrong, Ludlow, Fenner,
Hampton and Its Students. (Fenner, 181)

Obviously, Fenner was aware of the alterations in his version, especially the opening descending major sixth interval. But did this interval originate with one of his singers, or was this alteration Fenner's alone? While the answer is unknown at this time, there is little doubt of Fenner's influence on the singing of "Nobody Knows de Trouble I've Seen." Artists as diverse and influential as Paul

Robeson, Marian Anderson, Lena Horne, and Louis Armstrong have given their interpretations of this song and its defining moment—the opening descending sixth interval.

The Saint Helena Quartet introduced other Fenner's arrangements such as "De Ole Ark A-Moverin'," "De Ole Sheep Done Know de Road," "Dust an' Ashes," "Hail, Hail, Hail," "Hear de Angels Singin'," "I Hope My Mother Will Be There," "I've Been A-List'nin' All de Night Long," and "Swing Low, Sweet Chariot."[50] While Hampton's version of "Nobody Knows de Trouble I've Seen" altered a preexisting song on the island, other Hampton imports such as "Dust an Ashes" and "De Ole Sheep Done Know de Road" introduced entirely new spirituals to the islands. Over time, these songs became so popular that the islanders forgot their true origins.[51]

Saint Helena Island native Ron Daise includes the words to "De Ole Sheep Done Know de Road" in his book *Reminiscences of Sea Island Heritage: Legacy of Freedmen on St. Helena Island*:

> Refrain
> De ol' sheep done kno' de road
> De ol' sheep done kno' de road
> De ol' sheep done kno' de road
> De young lam' mus fin' de way.
>
> Verse 1
> Shout, my brotha, you are free!
> De young lam' mus fin' de way.
> Christ has bought your liberty!
> De young lam' mus fin' de way.
>
> Verse 2
> Fight, my brotha, don't you run!
> De young lam' mus fin' de way.
> Don't go away 'til de battle is won!
> De young lam' mus fin' de way.
>
> Refrain
> De ol' sheep done kno' de road
> De ol' sheep done kno' de road
> De ol' sheep done kno' de road
> De young lam' mus fin' de way.[52]

Daise, son of Penn School graduate Kathleen Daise, fondly remembers this song as an old Saint Helena favorite, but it is actually a Hampton import (Example 3.7). On April 19, 2009, I recorded a performance of "De Ole Sheep Done Know de Road" led by James Garfield Smalls along with Penn School graduates of the 1930s and 1940s on the old Penn School grounds. Deacon Smalls's singing, especially, followed much of Fenner's original texts, melodic lines, and harmonizations because he heard the quartet sing and was taught by many of them.

EXAMPLE 3.7. Armstrong, Ludlow, Fenner. 1874.
Hampton and Its Students. (Fenner, 198)

As the leader of the Saint Helena Quartet, Blanton's departure from the island in 1922 had a dramatic impact on the survival of the group's songs. Indeed, Blanton was by all accounts an exceptional soloist who gave memorable renditions of his spirituals throughout the country, and singers were hesitant to lead "his" songs. As a result of his departure, some of Blanton's songs were never again performed by the quartet; however, Blanton's association with the island's songs would continue when he went on to lead Voorhees School.

Joshua Enoch Blanton was selected as principal of Voorhees School, in Denmark, South Carolina, because of his success at raising money for Penn School as leader of the Saint Helena Quartet. When Blanton arrived at Voorhees in 1922, he found a school in near collapse. Financial contributions were at a standstill during this post–World War I period and the school's matriarch and primary donor, Elizabeth Voorhees, was in poor health and incapable of continuing her support. With the help of George Peabody, Blanton successfully lobbied the

Protestant Episcopal Diocese and the Protestant Episcopal Freedman's Commission organization the American Church Institute to assume responsibility for Voorhees in January 1925. Blanton's agreement with the Protestant Episcopal Diocese, however, came with the understanding that he would form a Church Institute Quartet, similar to the Saint Helena Quartet, and tour nationally to raise money for Voorhees and the three other African American schools under the diocese's purview. These schools were Saint Augustine's College in Raleigh, North Carolina, Bishop Paine Divinity School in Petersburg, Virginia, and Saint Paul's School and Junior College in Lawrenceville, Virginia. Blanton formed the Church Institute Singers in 1925 and immediately began touring throughout the country. Through the group's singing of the spirituals he perfected on Saint Helena Island, he raised in excess of $200,000 for all four schools.[53] Such an achievement is on par with the groundbreaking work of the Fisk Jubilee Singers in the 1870s.

His efforts resulted in the construction of four buildings on Voorhees College: Massachusetts Hall, the Saint James Building, Wright Hall, and Saint Philip's Chapel. In the Church Institute's 1940 performance in Kansas City, Missouri, Blanton offered this insight into the performance of spirituals he encountered on Saint Helena Island:

> It is practically impossible to put down on paper the Spiritual as the Negro sings it. It is a matter of temperament and the ear—plus inspiration. The Negro sings today as the slaves before him sang—from the heart; and the rhythm and melody are echoes of life on the plantations, and beyond, that, from far off days in the African wilds.[54]

Shortly before Blanton's retirement, the school's Junior College Program received an "A" accreditation rating from the Southern Association and enrollment at Voorhees reached an all-time high of 919 students.[55] In 1947, Blanton retired after twenty-five years of meritorious service at Voorhees College. In 1968, three buildings on campus, the Science Building, Women's Residence Hall, and the Administration Building, were named in his honor.

FOUR

Saint Helena's Spirituals during the World Wars and Prohibition

To struggling Russia Freedom!
To the starving Pole Freedom!
The trumpet sounds within my soul,
Liberty is calling

—*Hymn of Freedom*

Natalie Curtis rallied support for World War I through her anthem "Hymn of Freedom" set to the melody of the popular Saint Helena Island's spiritual "Ride on Jesus." In fact, many of the island's songs helped to raise monies for the Great War and to encourage African American troops facing the horrors of war and racism. Later, the islanders sang a special repertoire of spirituals that offered comfort to families with loved ones fighting in World War II. And when economic depression and Prohibition brought increased crime to the island, new song texts gave Christian guidance for those struggling with alcoholism. I will begin with a discussion of Curtis's textual alterations to the spirituals "Ride on Jesus" and "God's a-gwineter Move All de Troubles Away." Although she replaced the original texts, her retention of these melodies helped these spirituals to ultimately survive.

THE WORLD WAR I SONGS

Curtis's first performance of "Hymn of Freedom" occurred in an evening program held on Penn School's grounds in July 1918. She hoped that the song's new words would encourage the eighteen islanders drafted into the war and bring comfort to those with a limited understanding of the war effort.[1] Penn School administrator Grace Bigelow House, in attendance at this service, gives the following description:

I wish [you] could picture that meeting in the dimly lighted hall, gay with flags and those rows of anxious, troubled faces listening so patiently to get an understanding of what their call meant—and then the easing of their burdens through song. We feel alright about going now! was the expression of the men after the meeting.[2]

Originally, Curtis went to Saint Helena Island to study primitive music untouched by outside influences, but with the outbreak of World War I, she witnessed prayer meetings even more intense and emotional than normal. From the fervor of these services, Curtis became aware of "the single-hearted submission of the islanders to what they felt to be the will of God."[3] She vowed to offer, through their spirituals, solace to these Black men trapped in the "white man's" war. She wanted to show the country the power of Negro song![4]

Curtis initially transcribed "Ride On Jesus" from the singing of Hampton Institute's Big Quartet, comprised of William Cooper, Timothy Carper, Ira Godwin, and Joseph Barnes—all from Virginia. Despite this group's Virginia ties, she insisted that this song was brought to Hampton from Saint Helena Island. Because there were at least four Penn School graduates who were classmates of the quartet's members, Fred Fripp, Benjamin Barnwell, Dovey Chaplin, and Emily Brown, one or more of these islanders probably taught the quartet "Ride On Jesus" and presumably other songs from the island. As discussed earlier, Hampton graduates, teaching at Penn School, introduced new spirituals and altered some of the preexisting spirituals on the island. However, evidence suggests a reciprocal influence in which Penn School graduates, attending Hampton Institute, brought their spirituals and unusual song making to the school, altering to some degree the singing there.

As an ethnomusicologist, Curtis attempted an authentic representation of "Ride On Jesus," so she incorporated Gullah spellings such as 'Jedus" and "hebben" and the islanders' harmonies, which she referred to as "simple and somewhat crude."[5] Her transcription captures to some degree the unique Gullah singing style. Curtis's version of "Ride on Jesus" is below (Example 4.1).

According to Curtis, this spiritual's opening triumphant ring of music with its clarion call was the inspiration for a battle song and a new text, the very embodiment of "a conquering power of righteousness riding through the world."[6]

Curtis intended her hymn to garner support for the war, and it quickly gained popularity in churches, service clubs, and in schools.[7] The success of the "Hymn of Freedom" prompted George Peabody to convince Secretary of War Newton Baker and the YMCA to send Joshua Blanton, leader of the Saint Helena Quartet, to southern and European service camps, so that many of the Black servicemen could hear and learn the "Hymn."[8] The "Hymn of Freedom" also renewed the island residents' interest in their old spiritual "Ride On, Jesus." For example, when

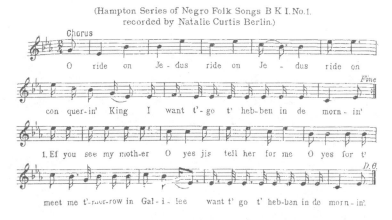

EXAMPLE 4.1. Nicholas George Ballanta-Taylor, "Ride on Jedus."
(Nicholas George Ballanta-Taylor, *Saint Helena Island Spirituals*
(New York: G. Schirmer, 1925), 92. Ballanta-Taylor's "Jedus" spelling
replicates the islanders' pronunciation of Jesus.)

hearing the "Hymn," one islander was so aroused emotionally that he began to
sing the melody using the original "Ride On, Jesus" text.[9]

Another Saint Helena Island spiritual altered by Curtis was "God's a-gwineter
Move All de Troubles Away." Unlike the collective emphasis of the "Hymn of
Freedom," this text specifically addresses the contribution of the Black soldier to
the war effort.

> God's going to move all the troubles away
> Sing the dawn of a better day!
> For years and years before the war
> Fate had been knocking at Europe's door;
>
> But men dreamed on, till the lightning's stroke
> Enveloped the world in a cloud of smoke.
> Nation by nation entered the fight
> To crush forever the despot's might.
>
> Soon when the war broke, came the call
> That summoned Africa's legions all;
> 'Twas the white man's fight, but the black man heard,
> And went without a questioning word.
>
> From Africa, east and north and west,
> The natives sailed on Europe's behest,
> Loyally spilled their blood in France,
> Checked with their bodies the German advance.

They did not know, but their lives were spent
That Freedom might live and the Kaiser repent, etc. . . . [10]

This spiritual's original chorus and first verse had the following text:

God's a-gwineter move all de troubles away
God's a-gwineter move all de troubles away
God's a-gwineter move all de troubles away
See 'm no more till de comin' day!

Genesis, you understan',
Methusaleh was de oldes' man
His age was nine hundred an' sixty-nine
He died and went to Heaven in due time.[11]

Curtis replaces the biblical story of Methuselah with a narrative of the Black soldier's entry into the White man's war.[12] This text reflects her admiration for those who went to war without a need to question why. In marked contrast to Curtis's patriotism that glorifies the battlefield, African American soldiers added texts to the island's spirituals that gave first-person accounts of the horrors of battle and the ultimate sacrifice of death.

Folklorist John J. Niles, traveling among Black troops during World War I, describes how these men forged new versions of songs containing war situations set to the familiar haunting melodies found in Negro spirituals.[13] In his book *Singing Soldiers,* Niles gives a transcription of the popular spiritual "Roll, Jordan Roll" sung by Elephant Iron, a Black soldier stationed in France. Elephant Iron transforms the old spiritual into a tribute to those comrades lost in battle.

The earlier *Slave Songs* version of "Roll, Jordan Roll" had the texts "My brudder sittin on de tree of life" and "My sister sat on de tree of life." Elephant Iron's version contains the words "there's a battle bein' fought in Argonne," which is a reference to the great battle at Meus-Argonne that claimed 26,000 American lives. More specifically, Elephant Iron honors the brave men of the 372nd Negro regiment who received the Croix de Guerre for their exceptional bravery and ultimate sacrifice at Meus-Argonne.[14]

In the second verse, Elephant Iron speaks of the many soldiers who died at the battle of Argonne, were given a eulogy by a military chaplain, and finally laid to rest to fight no more:

Roll, Jordan, roll—roll, Jordan, roll
Pastor, you'll be called on
To help some soldier pass on
'Cause he's never goin' to fight in de Argonne
Roll, Jordan, Roll.[15]

Such personal expressions are quite different from the song's original biblical text and even Burlin's patriotic strains, thus reflecting the adaptability of Negro spirituals.

Another island song transcribed by Niles is "Soldier in the Army of the Lord." In Niles's version, entitled "I'm a Warrior," a Black soldier named Prince sings this song (Example 4.2).

EXAMPLE 4.2. John J. Niles and Margaret Thorniley Williamson, "I'm a Warrior." (Niles and Williamson, 41–42)

The second chorus in this adaptation features a more familiar text:

> Oh, I'm a sojer in de army
> I'm a sojer for de Lord,
>
> I'm a sojer,
> I'm a sojer in de army of the Lord.[16]

In his version of "Soldier in the Army of the Lord," Prince uses the word "warrior" as the central theme in the first chorus before returning to the original "soldier" theme in the second chorus. Prince's use of this word order implies that he viewed himself first as a warrior and then a soldier. Andrew Huebner posits an important difference between a soldier and what he terms the "warrior image." He writes:

> The warrior image stresses the plight of the individual over the cohesion of the individual; the damaging rather than the edifying consequences of battle; isolation of the soldier instead of the enveloping presence of the military leadership, the government, and the home front.[17]

Ultimately, the stark realities of war, coupled with the many challenges facing African American troops at home and abroad, contributed to Prince's insertion of "warrior" into this spiritual.

In the 1920s, Guy Johnson cited a performance of "Soldier in the Army of the Lord" on Saint Helena Island, but he did not provide a transcription.[18] This spiritual currently features the following text:

> I'm a soldier in the army of the Lord
> I'm a soldier in the army
> I'm a soldier in the army of the Lord
> I'm a soldier in the army.[19]

Through the efforts of Joshua Blanton, Black and White troops sang many other Saint Helena Island songs. The War Department and YMCA hired Blanton to sing and teach spirituals that uplifted the morale of Black soldiers, and in doing so, these songs became an indispensable part of the war effort.

During the Great War, Blanton visited Camps Meade, Dix, Lee, and Jackson in the South and spent time in France to help those Black troops he felt had "a wrong view of the war."[20] He asked these men to have faith in the power of their spirituals to bring them through. Blanton states, "These are the songs that made it possible for your great-grandfathers and great-grandmothers to come through slavery, bearing heavy burdens, and at the same time keep close to their God."[21]

Blanton was called upon primarily to diffuse the anger of many Black soldiers who protested unfair treatment in the southern military camps. These soldiers experienced confrontations with local and governmental authorities and were denied the same provisions as White servicemen. In fact, before Blanton arrived at Camp Lee in Petersburg, Virginia, the African American soldiers stationed there submitted a list of their complaints to the War Department (see Figure 4.1).

To these disillusioned souls, Blanton sang Curtis's "Hymn of Freedom" and the Saint Helena spirituals "We Are Climbing Jacob's Ladder" and "Children, Hail, Hail, Hail." The first verse of "We Are Climbing Jacob's Ladder" appears below:

> We are climbing Jacob's Ladder
> We are climbing Jacob's Ladder
> We are climbing Jacob's Ladder
> Soldier of the Cross.[22]

The chorus and first verse of "Children, Hail, Hail, Hail" are below:

> Oh, children hail, hail, hail,
> I am going to join the saints above
> Hail, hail, hail,
> I am on my journey home

COMPLAINTS LODGED BY COLORED SOLDIERS IN CAMP

"Discrimination as to the issuance of passes to leave the camps—that white soldiers were allowed to go at will, while Negroes were refused permission to leave.

"Unfair treatment, oftimes brutality, on the part of Military Police.

"Inadequate provision for recreation.

"Unfair treatment, ofttimes brutality, on the part of Military Police. and denial of the enjoyment of privileges in the huts, where colored huts had not been provided.

"White non-commissioned officers over colored units, when the colored men were of a higher intellectual plane than the whites who commanded them.

"Lack of opportunity for educated Negroes to rise above non-commissioned officers in the Reserve Labor Battalions.

"Confinement to the guard house for long periods and compelled to pay heavy penalties for minor infractions of the rules of camp, or for disobedience of unreasonable commands.

"Frequently, lack of proper medical attention and treatment.

"Negro soldiers compelled to work at menial tasks, and denied sufficient drill work and not allowed training in manual of arms and denied an opportunity to fire a gun, in many instances.

FIGURE 4.1. Emmett Scott, Scott's Official History of the American Negro in the World War. (Scott, 107)

If you get there before I do
I am on my journey home

Tell all of my friends I am coming too
Tell all my friends.[23]

These song texts, which focused on soldiers of the cross climbing to a better future and the promise of a safe return home (earthly or heavenly), addressed the immediate concerns of these soldiers. More important, Blanton hoped to foster a better understanding between White officers and their Black troops.[24] After his tour of the camps, he came to this conclusion:

Those who felt at the beginning that Negroes should not be armed, and that, if they were armed, they should not be allowed to go into any of the Southern camps, have long since changed their minds, because Negroes have been drafted by hundreds of thousands: they have been put into nearly all of the camps, North and South; and as far as my observation goes in the ten camps visited, the Negro has turned out about as good a soldier in Camp Sheridan, Alabama or Camp Shelby, Mississippi, as he has in Camp Dix, New Jersey, or Camp Meade, Maryland.[25]

Blanton also reminded army officials of the overlooked role slaves played during the Civil War:

> Those who had the feeling that Negroes should be put into certain camps only, forget the tremendous loyalty of this race, especially that loyalty which made the Black slave stay at home four years to protect the wives and daughters of those who went away and fought from '61 to '65 to keep him in slavery. They also forget that thus far the Negro has held the Stars and Stripes to be sacred—a thing to be defended even at the cost of his life.[26]

Blanton's efforts raised the morale of Black troops, and military commanders quickly enlisted other Black song leaders such as William Elkins and Robert Hendrick.[27] The US Army assigned Elkins and Hendrick to camps in Newport News, Virginia, and Columbia, South Carolina, respectively, and with their help both Black and White troops embraced the singing of Negro spirituals. As a result, officials included the spirituals "Roll, Jordan Roll" and "Swing Low, Sweet Chariot" in the 1918 *U.S. Army Song Book*.[28]

Although Blanton, Elkins, and Hendrick helped popularize the island's songs during the war, many soldiers like Elephant Iron and Prince already knew many of these songs. Thus, the true legacy of Blanton and other Black song leaders may have been the credibility they gave to Negro spirituals. By singing these songs in the presence of White soldiers, they legitimized an art form so aligned to slavery and suppression, affirming to Black soldiers their rich legacy of song and the survivability of the human spirit. Blanton made this observation of Negro soldiers as they proudly sang during their daily drills:

> To see one thousand men with black faces stand in line, going through the different movements to the count of "one, two, three, four; one, two, three, four; one, two, three, four, r-e-s-t"—movements planned to develop every muscle in their bodies—makes one understand how it is that these men seem to grow stronger daily. To see the same thousand go through their rifle practice, then swing out on a hike to the tune of "Glory, Glory, Hallelujah . . ." makes one feel more than ever that Old Glory will always be protected as long as there is a drop of blood left on American soil.[29]

THE COMMUNITY SINGS DURING WORLD WAR II

By World War II, the Harlem Renaissance contributed to a perception of the old spirituals as outdated and irrelevant.[30] Jazz was in the forefront of the American consciousness and captured the imagination of a younger generation of Blacks who saw jazz performers as "less torn and damaged by the moral compromises and insincerities which had so sickened the life of the country."[31] As a result, the 1941 edition of the *U.S. Army Song Book* contained only one Negro Spiritual,

"Nobody Knows the Trouble I've Seen," and there was no longer a need for Black song leaders.[32] In their place, the War Department provided jazz bands for their African American troops and even added jazz-dominated radio broadcasts for all of their troops.[33]

Despite a diminished national role, there is evidence that a select group of Negro spirituals continued to be sung on Saint Helena Island. As it had in the past, the monthly Community Sings service was called upon to unify the community in prayer and in song. Specifically, the islanders chose those spirituals that offered hope and safety for the island's fathers and sons facing the horrors of the battlefield.

During a Community Sings held on January 17, 1943, the program was replete with patriotic hymns such as "Faith of our Fathers," "Battle Hymn of the Republic," "O Land of Lands, America," and "The Enlisted Soldiers."[34] The latter hymn, known as the Negro Battle Hymn, was first sung during the Civil War by the Ninth Regiment C. S. Colored Troops at Benedict, Maryland, in the winter of 1863.[35] Subsequently, R. Nathaniel Dett included this hymn in his song collection *Religious Folk-Songs of the Negro As Sung at Hampton Institute,* and Penn School faculty members brought it to the island. In Dett's transcription entitled "They Look Like Men of War," Dr. Herbert B. Turner, chaplain emeritus, provided the harmonization.

In addition to this hymn, the islanders sang three island songs, "Eagles Wings," "I'm Going to Build," "Stay in de fiel'" along with the popular spirituals "When the Saints Go Marching Home" and "Po' Little Jesus." Of particular interest are the spirituals "Eagles Wings" and "Stay in de fiel'," the refrains of which described the horrors facing soldiers on the battlefield.

Diton's transcription of "Eagles Wings" contains the following text:

Chorus:
Oh, I wish I have had an eagle wing, eagle wing,
Oh, I wish I have had an eagle wing, eagle wing,
Oh, Lord, I wish I, Oh, Lord, I wish I,
Oh, Lord, I wish I have had an eagle wing, eagle wing.

Verse:
I would fly all the way to Paradise,
I would fly all the way to Paradise,
Oh, Lord, fly all, Oh, Lord, fly all
Oh, Lord, fly all the way to Paradise.

Verse:
Oh, the lightning is flashing in my face,
Oh, the lightning is flashing in my face,

Oh, Lord the lightning, Oh, Lord the lightning,
Oh, Lord the lightning is flashing in my face.

Verse:
Oh, the thunder is rolling over my head,
Oh, the thunder is rolling over my head,
Oh, Lord, the thunder, Oh, Lord the thunder
Oh, Lord the thunder is rolling over my head.[36]

This song's second and third verses served as metaphors for the bombing and artillery fire facing Black soldiers during warfare; while the chorus and first verse expressed the family's faith that their loved ones could escape from such a dire situation and fly away to heaven.[37]

According to writer Cornelia Bailey, "flying" has a symbolic meaning in the Sea Islands region. She explains:

> Our ancestors could not move at all in those cramped boats they were in and when they got to the New World they wanted to go back to their home in Africa. They wanted to fly to Africa. You may not know this but the Africans who came to the Sea Islands believed in flying. They actually believed in it. There weren't any airplanes back then of course but they believed people could fly. We had song after song about flying, songs like "I'll Fly Away" and the one we sang at church that had the verse, "When I Get to Heaven, gonna put on my wings, gonna fly all over God's heaven."[38]

The imagery of flying took the islanders psychologically away from their enslaved condition, for "it made the row they had to hoe a little shorter, to think of freedom."[39] The uncertainty of World War II forced the community to call upon this cultural belief once again to give solace to the many families who were without their fathers, husbands, and sons. The singing of "Eagle Wings" gave them faith that their loved ones were safe from the dangers of battle.

The spiritual "Stay in de Fiel'" expresses the soldier's fundamental duty to stay on the battlefield until the end of the war. Originally, this song implored the believer to stay committed to the tenets of Christianity until the very end, but the chorus, "Stay in de fiel, Stay in de fiel, Stay in de fiel, 'til de war is ended" proved to be an effective war anthem. In fact, this spiritual survives today on the island, and many islanders remember its importance during the war years.

Although Dett transcribed "Stay in de Fiel'" in his *Religious Folk-Songs,* the popularity of this song among elderly singers throughout the Sea Islands region, including a ninety-five-year-old woman in Beaufort County, South Carolina, suggests a migration from the Sea Islands region to Hampton Institute.

Another popular Hampton Institute spiritual during World War II was "We'll End This Warfare," which was performed at a Community Sings program on

April 16, 1944. In keeping with the patriotic theme, the audience sang "The Star Spangled Banner" and the previously mentioned "The Enlisted Soldiers." R. Nathaniel Dett included a transcription of "We'll End This Warfare," also known as "Down by the River," in Hampton's *Religious Folk-songs* collection.

Originally, this spiritual's text was a narrative of the life of Jesus Christ with brief references to the Apostle Peter and the Rapture. Although the islanders valued this biblical message, the end of the war and the subsequent return of their loved ones were themes foremost in their minds and hearts. As their ancestors before them had done, the islanders adapted song texts that expressed their most immediate concerns.

Beyond the enormous impact of the World Wars, several natural disasters visited the island, causing heavy financial, environmental, and human losses. Prohibition further exacerbated economic concerns, forcing island residents to turn to illegal whiskey production to make a living. In response, the island's religious leaders added new song texts to spirituals in hopes of reducing the growing problem of alcoholism.

THE PROHIBITION SONG TEXTS

Beginning in the latter part of the nineteenth century and continuing to the early part of the twentieth century, Saint Helena Island experienced a series of devastating hurricanes. First, the Great Sea Island Hurricane of 1893 resulted in nearly 3,000 people being killed from winds up to 120 miles per hour and ten- to twelve-foot storm surges.[40] Then, eighteen years later, the Hurricane of 1911 exacted such a toll on the island that Rossa Cooley made this plea for help to the editor of the *New York Times:*

> The effects of the devastating storm of August 27 and 28 are more serious than first believed. Reports from the storm-swept Sea Islands off the South Carolina coast show conditions that demand immediate relief. On Saint Helena Island, where the hurricane struck with terrific force, the suffering is great. The storm raged for thirty-six hours; the wind blowing some of the time at the rate of 110 to 115 miles an hour. Houses were blown down, bridges carried away, boats were sunk or carried away . . . Over 100 families have lost everything—crops, horses, and animals. Winter is coming with no hope of making another crop before next year, and the people of the island are facing a year of famine, want, and suffering not experienced since the great '93 storm . . . Now they are looking to the school their oldest friend, for aid in this time of need, and the school sends out a most urgent appeal for relief for these suffering families.[41]

These catastrophic events affected all aspects of life on the island, requiring immediate housing, sanitation, clean water, and basic food. Guy Johnson argued that the devastation from the Great Storm of 1893 inspired the writing of the spiritual "Don't Let de Wind Blow Here No More."[42] This spiritual, in general, maintains a Christian message focused on the "day of judgment" when all of God's children will be marching home. The second verse's text, "when de sea gib up de dead," speaks directly to those who lost their lives in the two devastating storms. Ballanta-Taylor provided a transcription of "Don't Let de Wind Blow Here No More" along with additional verses (Example 4.3).

EXAMPLE 4.3. Ballanta-Taylor, "Don't Let de Wind Blow
Here No More." (Ballanta-Taylor, 39)

More calamity occurred after the 1893 and 1911 storms and with the arrival of the boll weevil, a small beetle—one-fourth inch long and one-third inch wide— that swept over the Atlantic Coast from 1892 through 1921. The boll weevil landed on Saint Helena Island in 1919, destroying 75 percent of the cotton crops.[43] The island's extra long-staple cotton crop never recovered and agricultural depression ensued.[44] The boll weevil had such an impact on the cotton industry that Blacks in southern states began to sing a song named for the beetle entitled "The Ballad of the Boll Weevil" containing a listing of all the states lying in its destructive path.[45]

> Oh, de boll weevil am a little black bug,
> Come from Mexico, dey say,
> Come all de way to Texas,
> Jus' a-lookin' foh a place to stay,
> Jus' a-lookin' foh a home,
> Jus' a-lookin' foh a home.
>
> De first time I seen de boll weevil,
> He was a-settin' on de square.
> De next time I seen de boll weevil,

He had all of his family dere.
Jus' a lookin' foh a home,
Jus' a-lookin' foh a home.

De farmer say to de weevil:
"What make yo' head so red?"
De weevil say to de farmer,
"It's a wondah I ain't dead,
A-lookin' foh a home,
Jus' a-lookin' foh a home."[46]

Many islanders (male and female) turned to illegal whiskey production to support their families during this devastation. With an estimated profit of $150 per batch of moonshine, Pierre McGowan, longtime resident on the island, estimated there were approximately fifty illegal whiskey stills active on the island between 1920 and 1965.[47] Ralph Robert Middleton, a Penn School graduate, remembers islanders transporting illegal whiskey in kerosene containers to avoid detection and even using their sailboats to elude authorities. McGowan tells the story of an islander woman who had been mailing moonshine to her son in Philadelphia before being caught by his father, the Gullah mailman. In fact, moonshining was so prevalent that the occupation of bootlegger was the third most common profession behind only fisherman and farmer during this time period.[48]

As a result of this illegal whiskey activity, the Beaufort County's Sheriff's Department was a constant presence on the island, and many of the older islanders remember with disdain the department's legendary leader Sheriff James McTeer. Despite the fondness White Beaufort County residents had for Sheriff McTeer, the islanders remember McTeer's unfair treatment and singular focus on Black moonshiners. For example, in 1931, of the twenty-seven Prohibition cases heard by the Beaufort County Court, all of the accused were of African American descent.[49] By 1944, this number had grown to thirty-two African Americans with approximately one-third of them being women.[50]

During the 1950s, illegal whiskey production was not only a problem for the sheriff's department but also the island's religious leaders, who were concerned about increasing numbers of alcohol-related arrests.[51] To combat this problem, church leaders added new verses to well-known spirituals such as "De Ole Ship Marie" and "Come and Go with Me to My Father's House" that criticized excessive drinking. Moreover, churches stopped singing the once popular spiritual "Drinkeen' Duh Wine" because of its suggestive lyrics.

Ballanta-Taylor's transcription of "De Ole Ship Marie" originally contained verses telling about a ship heavy loaded, filled with angels, and bound to see the Lamb of God (Example 4.4).

EXAMPLE 4.4. Ballanta-Taylor, "De Ole Ship Marie." (Ballanta-Taylor, 34)

However, in a 1956 wake service, new lyrics had been added to this spiritual, warning that the ship Marie "don't take no drunkards."[52]

In a recording taken from a house blessing in 1955, the fourth verse of the Negro spiritual "Come and Go with Me to My Father's House" includes a warning that there "ain't no drunkards" allowed in heaven.

> Come and go with me in my father's house
> Come and go with me in my father's house
> Come and go with me in my father's house
> There is joy, joy, joy.
>
> Milk and honey over there in my father's house
> Milk and honey over there in my father's house
> Milk and honey over there in my father's house
> There is joy, joy, joy.
>
> Ain't no lying over there in my father's house
> Ain't no lying over there in my father's house
> Ain't no lying over there in my father's house
> There is joy, joy, joy.
>
> Ain't no drunkards over there in my father's house
> Ain't no drunkards over there in my father's house
> Aint no drunkards over there in my father's house
> There is joy, joy, joy.[53]

One pastor on Saint Helena Island even forbade the singing of the popular communion spiritual "Drinkeen' Duh Wine." He wanted to reinforce his position against excessive alcohol consumption with this action and, to date, "Drinkeen' Duh Wine" is no longer sung in his church—or in many churches on the island.

Although this spiritual is no longer sung in many churches, the islanders fondly remember its repetitive text and catchy tune. I recorded song leader Minnie Gadson singing this rendition of the spiritual (Example 4.5).

EXAMPLE 4.5. "Drinkin' ob duh Wine," Transcribed by Eric Sean Crawford

CONCLUSION

During the World Wars, Saint Helena's spirituals inspired US soldiers and offered hope to those families with loved ones away in the war effort. In addition, Burlin's "Hymn of Freedom" and "God's a-gwineter Move All de Troubles Away" resulted in the use of the island's spirituals as rallying songs for democracy. At home and abroad, African American soldiers provided important textual alterations to spirituals as they interjected personal accounts of the horrors of battle and the many challenges facing Blacks in the Armed Services. As a result, many of the island's songs gained national and international exposure, contributing to their retention on and off the island.

Ravaged by the boll weevil's destruction of the long-staple cotton crop and an onslaught of natural disasters, the islanders were forced to find alternative sources of income. Understandably, many turned to illegal alcohol distribution that yielded great profits but resulted in a continual struggle with the sheriff's department and an increase in public drunkenness. In response to the latter issue, religious community leaders inserted new song texts that promised no place in heaven for those abusing alcohol. In this process, the Negro spiritual's original purpose changed from comforting despondent souls and offering communal expression of religious faith to serving as a vehicle for social change. In the 1960s, Saint Helena Island's songs gained broader use as tools of change when African Americans demanded equality during the civil rights movement.[54]

FIVE

Saint Helena's Spirituals during the Civil Rights Movement

We shall not be, We shall not be moved
We shall not be, We shall not be moved
Just like a tree planted by the water
We shall not be moved

Saint Helena Island's spirituals returned to the nation's consciousness during the 1960s civil rights movement, when they proved effective as tools of nonviolence. Songs originally created by slaves as expressions of their desire for freedom were now sung by folk singers, civil rights activists, and energized college students, who sought equal rights and freedoms under the law for African Americans in the South. In this more contemporary setting, song leaders added new words and altered melodies of the island's songs to personalize the emotions of the freedom rides, sit-ins, marches, and frightening confinements in local jails. Reverend C. T. Vivian, civil rights leader and close friend of Martin Luther King Jr., remembers how important it was "to take the music out of our past and apply it to the new situation, to change it so it really fit."[1] Although refashioned as freedom songs, this music still retained its inherent power, born in slavery, to convey openly the painful circumstances of the oppressed.

GUY CARAWAN AND HIGHLANDER

Guy Carawan is generally acknowledged as a guiding force in the integration of Negro spirituals, especially sea island songs, into the civil rights movement. Through Carawan's work as music director at Highlander Folk School in Monteagle, Tennessee, and as teacher on Johns Island, South Carolina, where he came in close contact with island music, he greatly influenced the three major civil rights organizations involved in mass demonstrations: Southern Christian Leadership Conference (SCLC), Student Nonviolent Coordinating Committee (SNCC), and Congress of Racial Equality (CORE). Musicologist Kristen Turner asserts that Carawan's activism with these groups increased after his frightening arrest on false charges of alcohol violation and his night in jail in the summer of 1959. During his confinement, the only comfort he felt came from hearing fellow activist Septima Clark sing "Michael Row the Boat Ashore."[2]

Shortly afterward, Carawan formulated the following seven-step plan of action in a letter to Highlander's supporters.

1. Put out a book of "songs for integration"
2. Hold workshops to train song leaders "who will go back and function in their own communities and organizations"
3. Put out records to go with the book to "help new song leaders (and the public in general) to learn these songs"
4. Organize a festival to bring together "different kinds of Negro and white music, song and dance, both old and new, that could and would be well attended and well integrated"
5. Plan "workshops for music educators and workers in schools and churches"
6. Hold workshops for folklorists
7. Organize a traveling performance group that would carry Highlander's message of brotherhood to southern communities through dramas, singing, dancing, and other kinds of performances.[3]

From this point forward, former SNCC song leader Julius Lester asserts that Carawan's influence on the music of the civil rights movement "can't be overestimated."[4]

Carawan's plan to publish "songs for integration" was in reaction to the music sung at early civil rights gatherings. He often heard stiff and overly formal songs from well-educated Black leaders who seemed to reject any traces of folk music. Ronald Cohen, historian, gives the example of the Montgomery bus boycott mass meeting held at Holt Street Baptist Church on December 5, 1955, the inaugural event of the civil rights movement. The only songs performed were the hymn "Onward Christian Soldiers" and the patriotic song "My Country Tis of Thee."[5] In 1959, Carawan also took exception to song sheets distributed by the National Association for the Advancement of Colored People (NAACP) to its local branches. These contained parodies of popular songs such as "Down by the Old Mill Stream," "Let Me Call You Sweetheart," and "The More We Get Together the Happier We'll Be." He exclaimed, "Not a single song out of Negro folk culture on it."[6]

Carawan's desire to publish a songbook was also an attempt to build on the work of his predecessor at Highlander, Zilphia Horton, who died in 1956 of accidental ingestion of typewriter cleaning solution.[7] Since its inception in 1932, the school had stressed integration and established a special training program for

Black and White union laborers. As music director, Zilphia, wife of cofounder Myles Horton, featured union workers in theatre productions, led singing at workshops and picket lines, and published union songbooks. One compilation was the Textile Workers Union of America (TWUA) songbook *Labor Songs* in 1939. This collection contained Native American songs, topical songs of organizations, and the Black sharecropper's song "Strange Things Are Happening."[8]

One year earlier, the Congress of Industrial Organizations (CIO) commissioned Horton to publish their own union songbook, and she sent petitions throughout the country for songs containing union-focused lyrics and Negro spirituals for the Black workers within the organization. The CIO publication never materialized, but she spent over a ten-year period amassing an impressive collection of songs and spirituals, which includes Saint Helena Island favorites "Hand Me Down My Silver Trumpet, Gabriel" and "We Shall Not Be Moved." These songs contain contrafacta texts clearly intended to inspire union sympathies. In Horton's version of "Hand Me Down My Silver Trumpet, Gabriel," entitled "My Silver Trumpet," the unknown author declares, "If life were a thing that money could buy, the rich would live and the poor would die" (Example 5.1).[9]

EXAMPLE 5.1. Unknown Author, "My Silver Trumpet."

In the 1920s, the Society for the Preservation of Spirituals recorded a similar version of this spiritual in the Sea Islands. However, their transcription contains the Gullah-infused couplets "Uh nebbuh bin tuh He(b)'m but uh has bin tol,' De street am silbuh en' duh gate am gol'," and "Talles' tree een Paradise, Duh Christian call'um duh tree ob life."

> Verse:
> Uh nebbuh bin tuh He(b)'m but uh has bin tol'
> Han' me down muh silbuh trumpit, Gay-brul,
> De street am silbuh en' duh gate am gol'
> Han' me down muh silbuh trumpit, Lawd.
>
> Talles' tree een Paradise
> Han' me down muh silbuh trumpit, Gay-brul,
> Duh Christian call'um duh tree ob life
> Han' me down muh silbuh trumpit, Lawd.
>
> Refrain:
> Han' me down, han' me down, han' me down, han' me down,
> Han' me down muh silbuh trumpit, Gay-brul,
> Han' 'um down, t'row 'um down, any way fuh git'um down
> Han' me down muh silbuh trumpit, Lawd.[10]

The second couplet in the Society's transcription can be traced back to the opening verse of the *Slave Songs of the United States* spiritual "Blow Your Trumpet, Gabriel," first recorded on Saint Helena Island in the 1860s:

> De talles' tree in Paradise,
> De Christian call de tree of life;
> And I hope dat trump might blow me home
> To de new Jerusalem.
> Blow your trumpet, Gabriel.[11]

In the union version, the author is no longer content to wait for heavenly rewards promised in the *Slave Songs* transcription but expresses an immediate need for earthly wealth that resonated with union laborers struggling after the Great Depression.

"We Shall Not be Moved" stands as one of the most popular union songs in the 1940s.[12] In fact, only Ralph Chapin's "Solidarity Forever," the anthem for the Industrial Workers of the World (IWW), was sung more.[13]

In this arrangement, the author immediately affirms the union's full support of its labor force in the event of a strike. Subsequently, the rhetoric in the next three verses, "we're fighting for our freedom," "we're fighting for our children," and "the government is behind us," serves to motivate workers and defends the purpose of a strong union. The fifth verse is more serious in tone as the author challenges workers to remain committed even when facing the fear of tear gas from local authorities ("we're not afraid of tear gas,"). Finally, the last verse is more personal in nature as workers are allowed to insert the name of their union leader or other important local and national figures ("-----(name) is our leader,").

In the late 1920s, sociologist Guy Johnson made an audio recording of "We Shall Not Be Moved" on Saint Helena Island. This version, however, had the slightly different title "I Will Not Be Removed." Song leaders who took part in union demonstrations and later the civil rights movement often dropped the "I" first-person singular because of the collective power of singing "We." The most famous example is the movement's anthem "We Shall Overcome," which is partially based on Charles Tindley's gospel song "I'll Overcome Someday." Lucille Simmons, an African American tobacco worker, changed the "I" to "We" during a strike in Charleston, South Carolina, in 1945. In addition, she dramatically slowed the tempo. Later, Simmons accepted an invitation to Highlander, where she taught her arrangement to Horton, who in turn sang it for Pete Seeger. It was Seeger who replaced "will" in the title with the more phonetically pleasing "shall."[14]

David Spener contends that union laborers chose spirituals such as "Hand Me Down My Silver Trumpet, Gabriel" and "We Shall Not Be Moved" because of the "intense religiosity of both Black and White workers in many industries, especially those laboring in coal mines, textile mills, and cotton and tobacco plantations.[15] Since workers sang many of these spirituals in church, there was a familiarity that negated any difficulty in adapting to the new texts. Folksinger Lee Hays also recalls the need for workers to occasionally break into the old hymn words when facing threatening situations "in backwoods or in dismal cotton country."[16]

When Carawan arrived at Highlander he inherited a tremendous musical library of union songs and Negro spirituals, but the school's focus was quickly shifting away from the labor struggle and to the most pressing social issue of the 1960s—civil rights. Carawan reflects:

> In 1959, a few years after Zilphia died, I went to live and work at High-
> lander, hoping to learn something about folk music and life in the South
> and to help carry on some of Highlander's musical work in Zilphia's spirit.
> I had no idea at the time that the historic student demonstrations would
> be starting in the next few years and that I would be in a position to be . . .
> involved in this new upsurge for freedom.[17]

THE CARAWANS' "SING FOR FREEDOM" WORKSHOPS

Carawan's seven-step plan articulated his vision for Highlander's outreach efforts during the civil rights struggle. In 1960, he initiated his second goal of "holding workshops to train song leaders" with a Highlander-sponsored event called "Sing for Freedom." From August 28 through September 3, this workshop brought together Black and White song leaders, primarily from Georgia, Alabama,

Tennessee, North and South Carolina, and Mississippi. Present also was Carawan's mentor Pete Seeger, who brought along his northern musician friends Gil
Turner, Waldemar Hille, Ernie Marrs, Ethel Raim, Julius Lester, and Hedy West.
The stated purpose of "Sing for Freedom" was for participants to learn new and
old songs, learn to be good song leaders, and to create new songs.[18]

Way Down in Egypt Land

Later, Carawan compiled the music from the 1960 workshop into a songbook ap-
propriately entitled *Sing for Freedom: In the Community, on the Campus.* One of
the songs in this collection is the Saint Helena Island shouting song "Way Down
in Egypt Land" by Waldemar Hille, musical editor of the folksong magazine
People's Songs Bulletin. In 1950, Hille visited the island and attended a prayer
meeting where he heard this shouting song. Hille's transcription is noteworthy
because it contains the only reference to Saint Helena Island in Highlander's
many songbooks.[19]

Carawan generally used the phrase "adaptation of traditional song" for spirituals such as "Walkin' for Freedom Just Like John" because of his uncertainty of
some of their origins.[20] Carawan includes this song's lyrics in the *Sing for Freedom* songbook (see Example 5.2). The Society for the Preservation of Spirituals
and Nicholas Ballanta-Taylor published versions of this song in the 1920s, but
Carl Diton's recording on Saint Helena Island is one of the earliest transcriptions.

EXAMPLE 5.2. Carawan, "Walkin' for Freedom Just Like John." (Carawan, 69)

During the 1960s, "Walk in Jerusalem, Just Like John" was commonly known as "I Want to be Ready" because of this threefold announcement in the song's chorus. Originally, Diton placed the threefold statement in the verses "Last Sunday morning," "Train am a-coming," and "She is loaded down with angels," which emphasize a Christian's preparation to ride on the gospel train to heaven. The text "I want to be ready" speaks directly to this process, and I believe it represents a later addition to Diton's verses. Moreover, it is sung to Diton's same melody. Gradually, the popularity of these words eliminated other verses and even shifted the song's emphasis away from the refrain "Walk in Jerusalem, just like John" (Example 5.3).[21]

EXAMPLE 5.3. Diton, "Walk in Jerusalem, just like John, mm 1–8."
(Carl Diton, *Thirty-Six South Carolina Spirituals: For Church, Concert and General Use* (New York: G. Schirmer, 1930), 50.)

The "Sing for Freedom" event on May 7–10, 1964, in Atlanta, Georgia, is of special importance because it added a song festival to the musical workshop. Organized by Guy Carawan, Ruby Doris Smith-Robinson of SNCC, Andrew Young and Dorothy Cotton from SCLC, and Freedom Singers pioneer Bernice Johnson, this "Sing for Freedom" brought together fifty southern singers and several northern singer-songwriters in often heated discussions about race and the appropriate music for the civil rights struggle. In the end, the spirituals from Saint Helena Island assumed an even larger place in the civil rights movement.

The most memorable event at the Atlanta "Sing for Freedom" was the Saturday morning workshop given by Bessie Jones and the Georgia Sea Island Singers, who demonstrated the ring shout and sang traditional children's game songs from Saint Simons Island. Most of the older singers in attendance enjoyed the music, but some younger ones whispered "Uncle Tom" under their breath, remembers journalist Josh Dunson who was in attendance. Dunson also recalls the tensions that arose when Charles Sherrod, organizer for SNCC, asked, "Why?

Why these songs here?" An older woman stated, "We can hear those songs any time back home. I came here to sing freedom." Bessie Jones responded, "Slave songs were the only place where we could say we did not like slavery, say it for ourselves to hear."[22] Yet the most poignant words came from Len Chandler, noted African American folk musician:

> I went through this scene, man. I was ashamed of grandmother's music. I went to school to get degrees, in Akron, and things were all put up in a nice little box, a package of the Western World's music. But there was nothing in that box about my music. Why, even the spirituals were fitted out for a white audience, made to sound nice and polite—you know the bit: Marian Anderson, Paul Robeson . . . It wasn't until this white professor took me to his house to listen to some tapes that I started to know what my music is about. It took a white man to teach me—about my own music: Why this music (Bessie Jones) is great, and the boys on the radios and the T-vees have stopped you from hearing it—but this is it, man, this is the stuff . . . [23]

At the evening concert organized by Reagon and folksinger Eleanor Walden, Bessie Jones and the Georgia Sea Island Singers were the only performers to receive a standing ovation from both old and young, and there was a general consensus that Negro spirituals, particularly the Sea Island songs, had gained a measure of respect from all.

Carawan remained outwardly neutral during the fiery debates in Atlanta, but he quietly distributed free copies of his published songbook *We Shall Overcome: Songs of the Southern Freedom Movement,* which contained twenty-three Negro spirituals.[24] Although there were popular songs, folk songs, and union songs included in *We Shall Overcome,* Carawan only taught the spirituals to the workshop participants. Later, he and his wife Candie published a second songbook entitled *Freedom Is a Constant Struggle: Songs of the Freedom Movement.* Songs in this collection came from the Mississippi Summer Project of 1964.[25]

The Carawans' songbooks feature ten Saint Helena Island favorites, including "I'm Gonna Sit at the Welcome Table," "This May Be the Last Time," and "How Did You Feel?" Guy was familiar with "I'm Gonna Sit at the Welcome Table" as he and his wife Candie had heard this spiritual during their time spent on Johns Island, seventy-five miles north of Saint Helena Island. The Carawans were an integral part of Johns Island's groundbreaking citizenship schools. Guy was Septima Clark's driver, and he assisted her and local leader Esau Jenkins in their efforts to help the residents pass the literacy requirements for voter registration. This song was equally popular on Saint Helena Island, where Diton transcribed it under the title "I'm Gonna Eat at the Welcome Table." The Diton and Carawan versions of this spiritual are remarkably in the same key of G major and have few melodic discrepancies (see Examples 5.4 and 5.5). Over the years, the natural interaction between both islands is probably responsible for such strong similarities.

EXAMPLE 5.4. Carawan, "I'm Gonna Sit at the Welcome Table." (Carawan, 12)

EXAMPLE 5.5. Diton, "I'm a-going to eat at the welcome table." (Diton, 22)

This spiritual's textual change from "eat" to "sit" seems subtle, but it contributed dramatically to this song's continued use in the 1960s. On February 1, 1960, the first civil rights sit-in occurred at the Woolworth's lunch counter in Greensboro, North Carolina. Within a week, there were sit-ins in Durham, Winston-Salem, Fayetteville, Charlotte, and High Point, North Carolina. Ten days later they spread to Virginia. During this time, Guy Carawan remembers being at a meeting and song swap at Highlander when Ernie Martin suggested that "I'm Gonna Sit at the Welcome Table" would make a great lunch-counter song.[26] Highlander quickly adopted this song and added new verses. One verse actually references the Woolworth sit-in:

> I'm gonna walk the streets of gold,
> I'm gonna tell God how you treat me,
> I'm gonna get my civil rights,   ·
> I'm gonna sit at Woolworth's lunch counter.[27]

The Carawans utilize the designation "traditional spiritual" again for their transcription of "This May Be the Last Time." However, they cite the citizenship schools as the primary source of the words (see Example 5.6). Because this freedom song was written between 1963 and 1965, this version probably originated during the Freedom Summer of 1964 when over 700 Black and White volunteers descended upon an unwelcoming Mississippi to establish freedom schools.[28] Based on the citizenship school concept pioneered on Johns Island, the Freedom Summer civil rights project focused on voter registration, but there was an additional emphasis on helping Blacks in Mississippi to become more socially and politically active. Dave Dennis, CORE delegate, took part in this project and remembers singing "This May Be the Last Time" each night before going to bed because of the uncertainty of tomorrow.[29] On August 7, 1964, Dennis gave the eulogy for fellow CORE member James Chaney, who was killed along with Andrew Goodman and Michael Schwerner near the town of Philadelphia, Mississippi.

Diton made one of the earliest recordings of this song, but Carawan's transcription features many more verses, such as "It may be the last time we sing together, . . . pray together, . . . walk together, and . . . dance together." By contrast, Diton's version, entitled "May Be the Last Time, I Don't Know," contains the singular verse "May be the last time you'll hear me pray" (Example 5.7).

Although Guy and Candie Carawan credited the freedom song "How Did You Feel?" to members of CORE, the *Slave Songs* editors William Allen, Charles Ware, and Lucy McKim Garrison made an earlier transcription of this spiritual entitled "Go in the Wilderness" in 1867. In "How Did You Feel?," the singers omit the original refrain's text "I'm leaning on the Lord, who died on Calvary" and any other direct biblical references. CORE's focus is primarily on the verse's ending line "come out the wilderness," which reverberates as they challenge the

Traditional spiritual; Words: Citizenship schools

EXAMPLE 5.6.
Carawan, "This
May Be the Last
Time." (Carawan,
Sing for Freedom,
211.)

EXAMPLE 5.7.
Diton, "May Be
the Last Time,
I Don't Know."
(Diton, 28)

willingness of civil rights workers to fight for freedom, walk a picket line, carry a sign, and even go to jail. In the last verse, there is even an attempt to recruit new members into CORE (see Example 5.8).

EXAMPLE 5.8. Carawan, "How Did You Feel." (Carawan, *Sing for Freedom,* 16.)

This spiritual appealed to Black Americans who saw similarities between their daily struggles and the "wilderness" experiences preached to them in church. The statement "come out the wilderness" thus represented to many Blacks an end to their hardships and ordeals as second-class citizens and a new day ahead. Martin Luther King Jr. referred to this exodus out of the wilderness as the "breaking aloose from an evil Egypt." In King's view, once Blacks achieved this goal, they could "move toward the promised land of cultural integration."[30] During the 1960s, the *Slave Songs* text "go in the wilderness" was of little value to Black Americans who had tired of settling and accepting continued bondage in the South.

Following the successful Atlanta event, the "Sing for Freedom" workshop organized by Willie Peacock and Willie McGee on May 6–9, 1965, in Edwards, Mississippi, was beset with continued infighting. The old issues were heightened even more in the aftermath of the Selma march just two months prior. A few months later, Guy Carawan, Bernice Johnson Reagon, Myles Horton, and SNCC held a smaller but more successful Conference for Southern Community Cultural Revival at Knoxville, Tennessee, on October 1–3, 1965. One of their main goals was to make plans for folk music revivals throughout the South that would focus the attention of the Black community on its cultural heritage and traditions. SNCC leadership recognized the success of folk festivals by Guy Carawan on Johns Island, Bernice Johnson Reagon in Atlanta, Jerome Smith in New Orleans, and the trio of Willie Peacock, Sam Block, and Willie McGee in Mississippi, and they asked them to help plan duplicate efforts in other southern areas.

Other attendees were singers Bessie Jones and Eleanor Walden, civil rights leaders Esau Jenkins and Charles Sherrod, and folklorists Alan Lomax and Willis James. As usual there were heated debates about the music of the movement; however, the presence of Lomax and James "were the most unifying aspect of the conference."[31] By the end of the conference, these two men successfully argued for the continued use of Negro spirituals in the civil rights fight.

During his lecture, Alan Lomax, ethnographer for the Library of Congress, focused on the importance of reinstating the singing of Negro spirituals into the Black church. He blamed the domination of choirs, musical instruments, hymn books, microphones, and written music for the elimination of the old unaccompanied style of singing spirituals. In his view, these more modern features ultimately excluded older church members and their form of worship. Lomax further asserted an attempt by Black church leadership to rid themselves of remnants of the slave past and assimilate more Europeanized values.

A year earlier, Lomax wrote an article in the Charleston *News and Courier* expressing these concerns, and he discussed his own efforts to preserve and archive the old spirituals and similar work done by Charleston's Society for the Preservation of Spirituals. However, in his opinion, "Neither of these efforts affected the Negro community itself, which turned its back on the old traditions on the grounds that they were the symbols of slavery and degradation."[32] At the conference, Lomax played recorded examples of African American, African, and West Indian music, showing musically shared traits. A few months earlier, Lomax lectured at the Mississippi "Sing for Freedom" but received some criticism for his patronizing tone. His efforts were more successful this time, and SNCC leaders believed that those in attendance at the conference "could hear and feel the purpose for which they had come together."[33]

Willis Laurence James, chairman of the Music Department at Spelman College, sang and clapped the rhythms of the old slave spirituals and ring shouts during his lecture. As one observer noted, "participants could see the beauty and feel the pride in a tradition that was theirs to preserve and enhance."[34] Twenty years earlier, James spent considerable time tracing the origins of African American music in his book *Stars in de Elements: A Study of Negro Folk Music.* In this study, he identified musical ties to African and Caribbean melodies and rhythms, and he posited an inherent complexity at work in African American music. James's lecture was so effective that SNCC leadership articulated a statement of intent to "show both young and old that the Negro folk artists and their songs show as much complexity, beauty, and cultivation as any other cultural tradition."[35]

In chapter 7 of *Stars in de Elements,* James argues that more spirituals were written in the Sea Islands region than in any other part of the country. To support this assertion, he cites Saint Helena Island's many song collections as proof of the "tremendous creative forces active in the so-called 'Gullah' country."[36] In his opinion, the thousands of slaves left abandoned on the island following the Battle of Port Royal were the composers of many of these folk songs. He notes, "With added responsibilities and privileges came new inspiration and ideas for song-making." James's understanding of Saint Helena Island's songs and their historical importance made him an invaluable resource for civil rights leaders who were trying to justify the use of this music in protest songs. SNCC leadership made plans to record and distribute James's lecture nationally and to combine with SCLC on a series of his lectures, but Willis James died in 1966, and the movement lost an irreplaceable supporter of the folk traditions.

Folksinger and social activist Eleanor Walden attended the Knoxville conference and experienced firsthand some of the contentious debates about music choice and performance style. In her view, there were basically three groups at odds: purists, who focused on the artistic and social value of folksongs; traditionalists, who favored the use of the historically significant Negro spirituals; and younger Black activists, who wanted to integrate popular Black music into the struggle. Often, their differences bordered simply on race.[37]

Many of the White northern folksingers, such as Phil Ochs, Tom Paxton, and Eleanor Walden, sang songs that appeared to have little in common with the southern spirituals performed by Bernice Johnson Reagon and Bessie Jones.[38] Paxton acknowledged "an enormous difference musically" because spirituals were oriented toward mass singing while folksongs were often more individual.[39] Some Blacks even took exception to the northerners' use of the guitar, a typically secular instrument. But their interactions had a tremendous impact on both groups, especially White folksingers. Paxton states, "Their [songs] are much more utilitarian than ours are. And there is no comparison as to their value to the civil rights movement. Our songs hopefully might line up a little support and a little bread, but their songs are right for the fight."[40]

SAINT HELENA ISLAND SONGS IN *SING OUT!* AND *BROADSIDE*

The northern musicians Tom Paxton, Gil Turner, and Pete Seeger, who attended the "Sing for Freedom" workshops and Knoxville conference, became strong supporters of the movement's music, and they immediately influenced editors of the widely popular *Sing Out!* and *Broadside* folk magazines to feature more Negro spirituals and protest songs. In 1964, there are five spirituals, featured in *Sing Out!* In particular, the April–May edition presents articles and songs that showcase Sea Island music just before the start of the Atlanta "Sing for Freedom." Included is also Carawan's transcription of the spiritual "That's All Right" and the words of the Johns Island and Saint Helena Island popular communion song "Drinkin' of the Wine."

> Drinkin' of the wine, wine, wine,
> Drinkin' of the Wine, oh yes my Lord,
> You oughta been to heaven ten thousand years,
> Drinkin' of the wine.
>
> Eatin' of the bread, bread,
> Eatin' of the bread, oh yes my Lord
> You oughta been to heaven ten thousand years,
> Eatin' of the bread.
>
> Callin' of the roll, roll, roll
> Callin' of the roll, oh yes my Lord
> You oughta been to heaven ten thousand years
> Callin' of the roll.
>
> If my mother should ask for me
> Tell her I've gone to Calvary
>
> You oughta been to heaven ten thousand years,
> Drinkin' of the wine.[41]

Five months after the Atlanta "Sing for Freedom," the more topical magazine *Broadside* featured five spirituals, including freedom versions of island favorites "Roll, Jordan Roll" and "Go Tell It on the Mountain" in its October 1964 edition. The freedom song "Roll, Freedom, Roll" is unusual because the unknown author alters both the melody and text of Theodore Seward's popular version. In most protest songs, the changes were made only to the text while the well-known melody was kept intact. This complete reworking of the spiritual interjects a complexity absent in most traditional freedom songs.

The text "Julius you should have been there," in the very beginning of "Roll, Freedom Roll," is an important alteration of Seward's opening statement, "brother you ought t'have been there." In this sentence, the author specifically addresses Julius Lester, the well-known SNCC song leader. Moreover, other verses reference "the singing group Peter, Paul, and Mary, and President Lyndon Johnson, who signed the Civil Rights Act of 1964 and Fair Housing Act of 1968. There are more interesting changes, however, in the melody accompanying the title text "Roll, Freedom Roll."

In Seward's version, the words "Roll, Jordan Roll" ascend in a melody that emphasizes a slave's ultimate desire "to go to Heaven when I die." By contrast, this unknown poet incorporates primarily a step-wise descending melody for "Roll, Freedom Roll." The lone exception is a rising melodic line on the second pronouncement of "Roll, Freedom Roll (measures 11–12), which is quickly followed by a similar melodic ascent (measures 15–16), accompanying the text "satisfy the very soul." With these four measures, the author asserts that freedom far exceeds a physical need but is equally a spiritual one.

Former United States Representative and SNCC Chairman John Lewis expressed these same sentiments in a well-known letter written to his mother in the spring of 1960. He responds to her request for him to leave the movement after being jailed four times. Lewis writes, "I have acted according to my convictions and according to my Christian conscience . . . My soul will not be satisfied until freedom, justice, and fair play become a reality for all people."[42] As a former minister, Lewis was more concerned with the potential harm to his soul than to his physical body if he did not fight for his freedom. I believe the poet of "Roll, Freedom Roll" knew of Lewis's letter and masterfully adapted his words to one of the oldest Saint Helena Island songs, "Roll, Jordan Roll."

Julius Lester describes the freedom song arrangement of "Go Tell It on the Mountain" as a curious mixture. He continues,

> It is sung in two versions in the South. One is the Peter, Paul, and Mary version which is sung most often by the Freedom Singers. The other version is . . . more traditional, with PP and M [Peter, Paul, and Mary] overtones. This song has most often been associated with Mrs. Fanny Lou Hamer of Ruleville, Mississippi, a great singer in addition to her other fine qualities and achievements. Television viewers during the Democratic Convention saw her leading the singing of this song at a rally outside Convention Hall.[43]

Lester contends that Peter, Paul, and Mary's version influenced Fanny Hamer, and the SNCC's Freedom Singers, who were the most popular civil rights singers of their time. The original Freedom Singers were Rutha Mae Harris, Cordell Reagon, Bernice Johnson Reagon, and Charles Neblett. This unique adaptation of "Go Tell It on the Mountain" combines the spiritual's popular chorus with slightly altered verses from "Go Down Moses":

Verse 1: Who's that yonder dressed in red? Let my people go!
It must be the children Bob Moses led, Let my people go.

Verse 2: Who's that yonder dressed in black?
It must be the Uncle Tom's turning back

Verse 3: There was a book given to me
Every page spelled victory.[44]

The unknown author omits the Christmas texts transcribed by Ballanta-Taylor on Saint Helena Island and interjects a more militant tone to the verses in "Go Down Moses." For example, the Moses in this version is not the biblical figure but Bob Moses, the revered director of SNCC's Mississippi Project of 1961. Moses was the first Black activist to file assault charges against his White attackers after he was viciously beaten in Amite County, Mississippi.[45] There is use also of the polarizing term "Uncle Tom" for those Black Americans who turned their backs on the civil rights fight. Based on the Black character in Harriet Beecher Stowe's book *Uncle Tom's Cabin,* an "Uncle Tom" came to represent a Black person who was working for White oppressors to keep the rebellion in reasonable bounds.[46] Finally, the author stands assured of the Bible's promise of victory for Blacks in the South.

Lester includes an important reference to Hamer's iconic performance of this song during the Democratic Convention of 1964. Hamer's haunting singing was in stark contrast to the more jubilant version performed by Peter, Paul, and Mary. In fact, it appeared that her performance conveyed to all who listened the tremendous obstacles she faced that day and her whole life. Undeterred by stark opposition, Hamer climbed the mountain at the Democratic Convention and loudly demanded, "Let my people go."

The Voting Rights Act of 1965 signaled for many the end of the civil rights movement and the freedom songs era. The highly effective sit-ins, marches, and boycotts, now known as the *heroic period* of the movement, were coming to an end.[47] Soon afterward, the tragic deaths of key civil rights leaders, rising Black unemployment, increased Black frustrations, and urban rioting brought to the forefront a new term—Black power. There was no longer a need for freedom versions of Saint Helena Island's spirituals. In their place, Lester contends was violence! He wrote these words in 1966:

> Now it is over. The days of singing freedom songs and the days of combating bullets and billy clubs with Love. We Shall Overcome (and we have overcome our blindness) sounds old, outdated and can enter the pantheon of the greats along with the IWW songs and the union songs. As one SNCC veteran put it after the Mississippi March, "Man, the people are too busy getting ready to fight to bother with singing anymore."[48]

From 1960 to 1966, Saint Helena Island's songs proved to be effective tools in motivating and encouraging Black and White activists, who voluntarily fought on battlefields throughout the South for social justice. The new textual additions to these antebellum songs contemporized their meanings and purposes in the new struggle for Black freedom, and for a brief period many of the island's songs experienced renewed use.

Although the freedom songs supported a nonviolent methodology, their ability to unify a group in a continual never-ending statement of defiance was perhaps the movement's greatest weapon. Bernice Johnson Reagon offers this example from a church meeting in Dawson, Georgia:

> I sat in a church and felt the chill that ran through a small gathering of blacks when the sheriff and his deputies walked in. They stood at the door, making sure everyone knew they were there. Then a song began. And the song made sure that the sheriff and his deputies knew we were there. We became visible, our image was enlarged, when the sound of the freedom songs filled all the space in that church.[49]

In their book Playing for Change: Music and Musicians in the Service of Social Movements, Rob Rosenthal and Richard Flacks assert music's ability to dissipate fear and raise collective courage.[50] Reagon's account demonstrates how freedom songs, when sung as one, could remove the crippling effects of fear and replace it with courage. Suddenly those who were invisible and powerless become visible and to be feared.

SIX

An Examination of Two Saint Helena Song Leaders

You told me to sing, and I done that, too
I done, done that you told me to do
I sang and sang till I come through
I done, done what you told me to do.

Historian Charles Joyner stated his belief in his book *Shared Traditions: Southern History and Folk Culture* that social, psychological, cultural, and environmental variables are strong determinants in folklore performance.[1] More specifically, Joyner proposes a folklore model to understand the complexities involved in the interplay of individual personality, society, and cultural experience.[2] To this end, he proposes four major classifications: a performer's individual characteristics, the structure of the community in which the performer lives, the relationship of the performer to family and significant others, and the performer's individual perceptions.[3]

Ethnomusicologist Regula Qureshi emphasizes a similar focus on the performer because the music is known best by the music maker "who alone knows the medium of performance."[4] While Qureshi concentrates on multiple performers, other ethnographers concentrate solely on one ideal representative of a musical culture. For example, David McAllester and Charlotte Frisbie examine the life and work of Navajo leader Frank Mitchell to understand his role in Blessingway rites, and Virginia Danielson analyzes the life of Egyptian singer Umm Kulthum to highlight her influence on twentieth-century Egyptian musical culture.[5]

Throughout I have presented societal, cultural, and environmental factors affecting the island's songs, but I have not offered a detailed analysis of the individual performer of these songs. From such a directed concentration, there is discovery of additional factors that contribute to song alterations and retentions. During the course of my research on Saint Helena Island, I interviewed song leaders Minnie (Gracie) Gadson and James Garfield Smalls, who are among a small group of islanders still singing the old songs. Through the lens of Joyner's folklore model, I identify those factors responsible for each singer's continued performance of the island's songs.

Minnie (Gracie) Gadson, age 74, was born in the Hopes Community on Saint Helena Island. As a child, she attended the Hopes Praise House on her family's property and the John Fripp Praise House, where she learned many of the old spirituals from family members and other singers.[6] Gracie, as she is commonly called, received an education from the local public schools, and as a young adult, she moved away from the island, like many islanders.[7] But within three years, she returned to raise her children, to be closer to her family, and to reestablish her membership at Ebenezer Baptist Church.

Gracie was baptized at Ebenezer Baptist Church, her family's church, and has served in the church choirs for several decades. Because Ebenezer Baptist Church has a traditional worship service, the church congregation continues to sing the old spirituals. In fact, during the annual Heritage Days event on the island, many visitors choose to attend Ebenezer's church service because of their traditional Gullah worship experience.[8] Ebenezer's strong connection to the past enables Gracie to retain many of the old songs, and she has an impressive catalog of spirituals. During an interview conducted on Tuesday, August 11, 2009, Gracie sang many of the island's spirituals and provided important information on service usages for these songs. The baptismal and communion songs performed by Gracie were as follows:

"Drinkin' of the Wine"
"Take Me to the Water"
"I'll Be Somewhere Listening for My Name"
"Leanin' on the Lord"
"Wade in de Water"
"Let Us Break Bread Together"
"We Are Climbin' Jacob's Ladder"[9]

Gracie classified these songs as general usage spirituals:

"I Couldn't Hear Nobody Pray"
"My Mind Done Changed"
"Remember Me, Lord"
"I'm Working on de Building"
"I'm Gonna Build Right on that Shore"
"We've Come a Long Way"[10]

Gracie's early indoctrination in the Hopes and Fripp Praise Houses and her continued participation in current pray's house services resulted in her large repertoire of shouting spirituals. Yet Gracie's involvement in these pray's houses is the result of her church's affiliation with these structures.

In the past, Saint Helena Island pray's houses belonged to specific churches and to those church members living on the plantation housing the pray's house.[11] Ebenezer Baptist Church was responsible for the Hopes and John Fripp Praise houses near Gracie's home, a proximity which explains her affiliation with these important community structures. In addition, Ebenezer Baptist Church oversaw the Eddings Point Praise house and the still active Mary Jenkins Praise house. In 1977, anthropologist Patricia Guthrie commented that Ebenezer Baptist Church had the largest number of functioning pray's houses.[12] Certainly, the continued presence of the pray's house in Gracie's life is responsible for her retention of many of the island's shouting songs. Later, as a member of the "Gullah Praise House Shouters," a local performing group, she learned additional shouting songs from the older singers in the group.[13] As a result, shouting spirituals constitute her largest category of songs. Gracie's repertoire of shouting spirituals include:

"Way Down in Egypt Land"
"Adam in the Garden Pickin' up Leaves"
"Give Up the World and Come On"
"Dese Bones Gonna Rise Again"
"Can't Hide Sinner"
"Satan Your Camp on Fire"
"I Done Done What You Told Me to Do"
"Holy Spirit You're Welcome"

Joyner defines the relationship of the performer to family and significant others as:

The individual experiences and memories of the family and significant others [that] are shared with one another; thus any individual is affected by a variety of historical experiences in which he has not directly participated, simply because they have affected the personalities and expectations of persons important to his life.[14]

Gracie recalls the important influence of her mother and grandmother, but she also gives credit to many of the older singers she encountered in church and in the pray's house. For example, Gracie fondly remembers hearing Jack Johnson, a deacon from Ebenezer Baptist Church, sing "I'm Workin' on a Building," and she recalls Mrs. Lula and Mrs. Rivers, who were members of the Gullah Praise House Shouters. She even remembers an "old lady deaconess," the mother of the church, who loved to sing the spiritual "I Know I've Been Changed."[15]

According to Joyner, the performer's individual perceptions involve the attitudes and cognitions of the folk performer.[16] Moreover, changes in perception will ultimately change the performance even when other variables have remained unchanged. When asked why she still sings the Negro spirituals, Gracie simply responds, "Someone has to sing the old songs."[17] As a member of Ebenezer Baptist Church, she carries on the tradition of the island's songs, and no church service is complete without her singing.[18] Gracie gladly accepts this responsibility, and she always includes a shouting spiritual such as "Adam in the Garden Pickin' up Leaves," which includes her clapping the 3+3+2 accompanying rhythm. Despite occasional health concerns, Gracie is dedicated to singing the spirituals as she learned them, and it is doubtful that her performance has changed much over time.

Deacon James Garfield Smalls, age 100, graduated from Penn School and worked in civil service for several years. As a young man, Garfield, as he is commonly called, received musical training from B. H. Washington, a member of the Saint Helena Quartet, and he fondly remembers Mr. Washington's first impression of his singing voice:

> I had a good voice to sing, but I sounded like a cow. Mr. Washington asked me to come so he could train me. So after I come from work, I would go to his house at 11:00 p.m. at night. He would get that book and he would start scaling the songs.[19]

Eventually, Garfield sang in Washington's community vocal group called the 100 Voices, and he assumed leadership of this ensemble when Washington became ill. Garfield received additional musical training from Mrs. Jackson, the musical director of his church choir, who was a local school teacher. Beyond his early musical indoctrination, Garfield faithfully served his country in the Seabees, the US Navy Construction Battalion, serving in the Pacific theater during World War II.[20] Upon his return to the island, he supported a wife and family, worked a civil service job, and managed a farm.

Garfield credits Saint Joseph Baptist Church, now known as Bethesda Christian Fellowship, the Penn School, and the pray's house as being his community influences. The late Reverend Joseph H. Heyward formed Saint Joseph Baptist Church with a "small prayer band" of followers who left Ebenezer Baptist Church in 1937.[21] Importantly, Mrs. Jackson, Ebenezer's musician, was among the band of followers Reverend Heyward brought to Saint Joseph Baptist Church. As a result of her musical training, Jackson taught the Saint Joseph choir members sight-reading and stressed hymn singing. Garfield continued this musical tradition, and as a long-time leader of the Senior Choir at Bethesda, he insisted upon strict adherence to the given musical notation.[22]

Bethesda's contemporary morning service provides few opportunities for Deacon Smalls to sing the old spirituals. The exceptions are the year-end Watch Night services, evening services, and midweek prayer meetings when Garfield raises the spirituals "Leaning on the Lord" and "I Couldn't Hear Nobody Pray," which are considered to be "his" songs. On Sunday July 11, 2010, I was privileged to hear Garfield sing one of his favorite spirituals at an evening service held at nearby Ebenezer Baptist Church.

As is customary with many African American evening programs, the visiting church (in this case Bethesda) provided the choir and speaker while deacons from both churches shared the opening devotional service responsibilities. During the devotional service, Garfield raised his song "I Couldn't Hear Nobody Pray," and immediately the entire congregation "took up" the old song in a fervent rendition. Because these churches are within walking distance of each other and often share familial bonds, there was an understandably high emotional level.[23] More significantly, Garfield's singing seemed to bring the congregants back to a bygone era when Negro spirituals were the norm instead of the exception.[24]

Penn School's insistence on standard English greatly influences Garfield's singing style. He recalls that the Penn School faculty ultimately wanted their students to speak as they spoke.[25] As a result, Garfield admits that Penn students had a more formal singing approach to spirituals.[26] During my interview of Garfield, I also noticed that he rarely incorporated the 3+3+2 clapping pattern. In fact, the only time he used the 3+3+2 rhythm was in a singular demonstration of ring shout clapping. Yet this is consistent with many Penn School graduates because the school's faculty frowned on this practice. On the other hand, Gracie, a non-Penn student, consistently maintained the 3+3+2 rhythm even for non-shouting songs.

The vast majority of the spirituals Garfield sang were the more formal Penn School song favorites and even a few songs from the Saint Helena Quartet repertoire. These spirituals are below:

"I Heard the Angel Singing"
"The Old Ship Marie"
"Fisherman Peter"
"Roll, Jordan Roll"
"I Wish I Had an Eagle's Wings"
"How Can I Pray"
"You Got to Run to the City of Refuge"
"Jesus Rides the Milk-White Horse"
"All My Sins Done Taken Away"
"Lead Me to the Rock that Is Higher than High"
"Don't You Have Everybody for Your Friend"

"Some Gone Love You, Some Gone Hate You"
"Stay in the Field"
"Lawd Have Mercy on Me"
"I'm Gonna Sing a New Song"
"Sweet Honey in the Rock"
"Stand the Storm It Won't Be Long"
"I Got A Mother Over Yonder"
"Anchor the Chariot, Trouble Along"
"The Ole Sheep Done Know the Way"

The shouting spirituals that Garfield sang are below:

"Too Late Sinner"
"Can't Hide Sinner"
"This House Gonna Fall"
"I Saw the Light from Heaven Come Down"
"My Mind Done Changed"

Garfield is leader of the Croft Praise House, which has traditionally belonged to members of Bethesda Christian Fellowship. However, Croft Praise House had been in disrepair for a number of years, forcing Garfield to oversee the services at nearby Jenkins Praise House. In his capacity as pray's house leader, Garfield holds a position of great authority in the community, and he was duly elected through a church conference and subsequent majority vote.

To be considered as a pray's house leader, a candidate must meet the following qualifications: (1) hold membership in the plantation where the pray's house stands, (2) hold membership in the pray's house, and (3) be a resident on the plantation where the pray's house is located.[27] After being elected, pray's house leaders collect money from their members, oversee worship services, officiate at sessions of the religious court, and speak at the funerals of deceased members.[28] These leaders usually cannot hold the office of deacon or minister, but Garfield's respect within the community allows him to serve jointly as Jenkins Praise House leader and Bethesda Christian Fellowship deacon.[29]

In discussing his family background, Garfield remembers going to stay with his grandparents, on Saxonville Road on the island, who instilled in him the importance of attending church services. On one occasion, Garfield recalls, "It rained, and we had to hitch our big old oxen named Brandy to a cart. We had to go cross in a cart because the water was too deep to go to prayer service. At the church service this fellow named Vickie Holmes, a big tall man, sang this song:

If you been in the howling wilderness
Don't turn back, don't turn back
If you turn back, you make my leader shame.[30]

Garfield carefully explained the meaning of this spiritual:

> That song had a great meaning because during that time you had to seek
> your soul salvation. You didn't go up there to tell the preacher you wanted
> to join church, and they pray . . . and baptize you. You had to start from
> your praise house in your community. They had leaders and committee
> there.[31]

This spiritual discusses the seekin' experience and the isolation a young convert
encounters during this time. Ultimately, these early experiences from his grandparents and church leaders contributed to Garfield's unchanging commitment to
remain involved in church and pray's house services.

Garfield's individual perception of the younger singers on the island greatly
affects his singing of the spirituals. He admits that he sings fewer spirituals today
because "Most of the people now in the church they can't sing the old time spirituals like maybe I would sing it."[32] Garfield asserts that these singers are unable
to stick to the spiritual's tune long enough to initiate a true shouting experience;
hence, the singing lacks the emotionalism so indispensable to African American
worship. Garfield further expresses concern for the lack of adequate background
singers or basers who are pivotal for the song leader. He states:

> If you got the right people to set 'em you can shout 'em. But you set the
> song with your feet and your hands and whosoever sits down with you
> that's your background. You got to have background.[33]

Art Rosenbaum agrees, stating, "If the basers do not support the leader suf-
ficiently, there is a breakdown in shared community energy."[34] Ultimately, Garfield relies on a small corpus of songs that do not require complicated musical
accompaniments.

Both Gracie and Garfield continue to sing the old songs despite the many
economic, social, and environmental changes affecting all of the island's spirituals. Through the use of Joyner's folklore model, I have identified two common
factors responsible for these singers' retention of the island's songs. First, both
Gracie and Garfield received an early indoctrination in the pray's house service
that imparted to each the importance of this tradition. Consequently, they
continue to remain active in pray's house services. Second, Garfield and Gracie
are recognized within the community as song leaders and are expected to raise
"their" songs during pray's house services, evening services, watch night services,
and devotional periods. Therefore they maintain an extensive song repertoire of
baptismal, communion, shouting, and general use songs.

Yet there are important differences between these two singers. First, the
more formal musical training Garfield received from the Penn School and Saint
Joseph Baptist Church is responsible for his adherence to strict part singing and

his reluctance in using the 3+3+2 clapping pattern. Conversely, Gracie's musical training, received from the pray's house and older singers, allows her to retain many of the Gullah words in the island's spirituals and the 3+3+2 characteristic clapping.

Second, Bethesda Christian Fellowship's more contemporary service limits Garfield's ability to sing many of his spirituals. This means that many of the songs known only to him go unheard. In contrast, Ebenezer Baptist Church's more traditional church provides many opportunities for Gracie to raise her songs, and these spirituals will undoubtedly continue to survive.

Conclusion

Despite the ability of these songs to survive the World Wars, economic depression, and natural disasters, I have shown that the greatest threat to their active cultural longevity was suppression by well-meaning Whites and even by those islanders who saw little value in their own culture. Beginning with Penn School, Laura Towne and Rossa Cooley devalued the use of the Gullah language and insisted on standard English even when students sang their own music. Yet their approach led to academic successes, and their legacy is seen today in the impressive accomplishments of Penn School alumni, who speak and sing with impeccable diction and adherence to standard English.

Cooley was especially effective in using house blessings, chapel services, and the famed Saint Helena Quartet to redirect the islanders from the shouting spirituals she deemed too barbaric. As seen throughout this book, shouting songs, with their characteristic stomping and 3+3+2 handclapping patterns, virtually disappeared on the island. In their place, Cooley introduced Hampton Institute's imported spirituals and the less emotional island spirituals she favored. However, the school's Community Sings was her redeeming musical legacy. This event served to organize the community through the singing of the islanders' more emotional music, and it is no coincidence that it still survives today.

Another important discussion in this book was the mutual influence between Saint Helena Island and Hampton Institute, now known as Hampton University. Cooley's Hampton-trained faculty brought their music to the island and gradually altered or replaced preexisting songs. In this process, many of Hampton's songs were interwoven into the island's musical fabric. In turn, Penn School graduates, who attended Hampton Institute, brought their own spirituals, such as "Ride On, Jesus" and "God's a-gwineter Move All de Troubles Away," to Hampton's campus, thus introducing the unique Gullah texts and singing approaches to its faculty and students. From this mutual textual and melodic exchange, the islanders' singing became more formal and less emotional, while Hampton's students experienced to some degree West African textual elements and the overt emotionalism of slave culture.

The imposing presence of Joshua Blanton dominated my examination of the island's songs during the Great War. His success as song leader for the US Army made him a true ambassador for race relations, and he proved the readiness of African American soldiers for war. Through his efforts, Black and White troops

Rossa B. Cooley. From the Penn School Collection at the
UNC-Chapel Hill Wilson Library. Permission granted by
Penn Center Archives, St. Helena Island, SC.

found common ground and brotherhood in the poignant melodies and texts of
the island's spirituals. Natalie Burlin's anthem "Hymn of Freedom" proved to be
extremely effective at garnering support for the war effort, and her use of the
"Ride on, Jesus" melody helped this old spiritual to survive.

In the early part of the twentieth century, a series of natural disasters brought
economic hardship to the island, causing many islanders to engage in illegal
whiskey production. To curtail skirmishes with police and increased incidents
of public intoxication, church leaders added new verses to the old songs that discouraged alcohol consumption for those hoping to go to heaven. Instead of being
reserved solely for church and work use, these songs assumed a greater role in
addressing social issues. Later, the island's music gained great popularity during
the civil rights movement; however, few realized their origins on Saint Helena
Island. Guy Carawan and Bessie Jones played a pivotal role in their utilization as
the soundtrack for the movement. Rebranded as freedom songs, the island songs
gave nonviolent protest its greatest weapon in diffusing hatred and bigotry.

FINAL OBSERVATIONS

As the oldest published Negro spirituals, the Saint Helena Island songs provide
one of the last remaining glimpses of slave life in America. Through the singing
of these songs one is immediately exposed to the strange patios of Gullah, the hip
jerking of the ring shout, portamento vocal singing, the 3+3+2 hand clapping,

foot stamping and, most important, the hopes, desires, and suffering of those in bondage. The Saint Helena Island spirituals give us a rare opportunity to follow their retentions and alterations in printed and recorded sources through three centuries of usage. While some scholars question the validity of using transcriptions in the examination of folk life, I have shown that, when used in conjunction with previous audio recordings, field research, and secondary sources, they are an effective representation of a culture's music. Thus, I am deeply indebted to the commitment of William Allen, Charles P. Ware, Lucy McKim Garrison, Thomas Higginson, Thomas Fenner, Carl Diton, N. G. J. Ballanta-Taylor, and Guy Johnson.

My Introduction recalled my first visit to the island's pray's house, where I heard Deacon Smalls raise one of his spirituals. The singing that night was an encounter I will never forget, for I felt a spiritual connection with the old slaves who had come before. I suddenly remembered seeing my paternal grandmother Marjorie Adams Crawford singing and playing old gospel songs, my family attending church services in small white churches in the country, and watching church members jumping in response to the Holy Spirit. Thanks to the Saint Helena Island spirituals, I connected to my ancestral past and for this gift I am truly grateful.

These songs, however, are not exclusive to a specific nationality but are universal in their reach. Regardless of our individual backgrounds, these spirituals connect to our roots on common ground, and in doing so, they demand that we partake and rejoice in the discovery of the similarities we all share instead of the differences. I hope this book will become more than a history of Gullah Geechee music and will bring much needed attention to an important art form that is still being performed. Finally, we need to educate the younger generation of islanders about the important legacy of their music and, in process, reintroduce them to their ancestral past and present in Deacon James Garfield Smalls, Minnie (Gracie) Gadson, Rosa and Joseph Murray.

Appendix

This Gullah Songbook contains fifty-five Saint Helena Island spirituals that are classified within five main categories: shouting songs, seekin' songs, Christmas songs, communion and Easter songs, and general use songs. Of the more than three hundred island songs in extant song collections, I selected a representative sampling of spirituals containing the strongest evidence of use within these sacred areas. To this end, I relied heavily on the collective cultural memories of Minnie (Gracie) Gadson, James Garfield Smalls, and Rosa and Joseph Murray, who confirm a specific repertory of spirituals used in pray's houses and churches on the island since the 1920s. These performers can be heard singing many of these songs on the compact disc *Gullah: The Voice of an Island* released by the Athenaeum Press at Coastal Carolina University (2014). Further insight into song usage can be found in the editorial notes made by William Allen, Charles Ware, and Lucy McKim Garrison in *Slave Songs of the United States* and in Henry Spaulding's article "Under the Palmetto" in the 1863 *Continental Monthly*.[1]

In 1942, Lydia Parrish presented a similar categorization of Sea Islands songs in her compilation *Slave Songs of the Georgia Sea Islands*. She divided the spirituals on Saint Simon's Island into four categories: Afro-American Shout Songs; Ring Play, Dance, and Fiddle Songs; Religious Songs; and Work Songs.[2] Unlike Parrish's inclusion of secular songs, I focus exclusively on Saint Helena Island's sacred repertory of spirituals to highlight the often-overlooked liturgical functions of Negro spirituals. Much more attention is usually paid to the analyses of secret codes, structural form, and song texts while the highly organized nature of the slaves' service is all too often characterized as being governed only by emotion.

The organization of the slave church on Saint Helena Island came to maturity during the antebellum period when slaves combined the Judeo-Christian symbols, myths, and values of Whites with their own West and Central African rhythms and trance-like worship.[3] During secret hush harbor evening services held in the woods, they fashioned a prescribed order of service that contained specific types of hymns and spirituals. Historian Janet Cornelius explains:

It was common for a secret service to begin with the European hymns and turn to the spirituals to initiate the movements toward trance and ecstasy. After the first hymn or spiritual came prayer, a major focus of the hush-harbor service. Prayer was lengthy and, like the "sperchul," supported members of the group by name. The preacher based his folk sermon on biblical phrases and whole passages he knew by heart. . . . The sermon would begin with normal prose and build to a rhythmic cadence, regularly marked by the exclamations of the congregation. . . . After the sermon came the shout. The shout incorporated the rhythm and the dance, which moved worshippers into trance possession and communion with the spiritual world.

Following the shout, members would pass one another shaking hands, and bidding each other farewell. . . . As they separated, they sang a parting hymn of praise.[4]

The required song repertoire for the hush harbor service was an opening hymn, which was read and sung in a responsorial manner (lined), Negro spirituals, shouting songs to heighten the emotional level of the worshipers, and a closing hymn. With the passage of slave codes forbidding such secret gatherings, White masters allowed their slaves to worship openly within the religious structure known as the pray's house, bringing more formality to the islanders' religious experience. Pray's house leaders and deacons set forth strict rules for membership and closely monitored worshippers' etiquette during the sacred services, especially the ring shout. Anyone crossing their feet or lifting their leg during its performance was removed from the circle.

I begin this songbook with those Saint Helena Island spirituals containing the greatest degree of West and Central African retentions—shouting songs. Integral to their performance were the basers, who clapped and sang the accompaniment; shouters, who shuffled around in a counterclockwise circle; and the soloist, who sang the verses and freely improvised. In his study of the shouting songs performed by the McIntosh County Shouters in Georgia, musicologist Johann Buis finds no versification in their song structure. He states, "No verses exist in any songs. Rather, the call-and-response structure makes responses fairly easy and predictable." Earlier I discussed refrain-only shout songs that had lost connections to their former verses. For example, "Satan's Camp A-Fire" (no. 10) contains only a refrain within its ABAB textual structure:

> Fier, my Saviour, fier,
> Satan's camp a-fire;
> Fier, believer, fier,
> Satan's camp a-fire.

However, there are examples of shouting songs containing more of a two-part verse/chorus form. Buis's transcription of "Pharaoh's Host Got Lost" offers an example:

Leader:
Moses, Moses lay your rod

Basers:
In that Red Sea

Leader:
Lay your rod, let the children cross

Basers:
In that Red Sea

Chorus:
Ol' Pharaoh's hos' got los', los, los'
Ol' Pharaoh's hos' got los'
In that Red Sea
They shout when the hos' got los', los', los
They shout when the hos' got los', los', los
In that Red Sea

The ABAB textual form of the first section (A') is in marked contrast to the AAB repeated textual form of the second section (B') or chorus. In addition, the everchanging texts in section A' differ from the generally fixed texts in section B'. Last, the first section (A') features the soloist's various melodic motifs while in the second section (B') the same melody or harmonization is repeated by the group. Although the first section is highly improvisatory, it does appear to function as a verse, albeit in a nontraditional manner. Seven of fifteen shouting songs contain the ABAB and AAB verse/chorus structure: "No Man Can Hinder Me" (no. 8), "Rock O' Jubilee" (no. 9), "Dere's a Meeting Here Tonight" (no. 5), "This Old House Gonna Fall" (no. 12), "Turn Sinner, Turn O'" (no. 13), "Way Down in Egypt Land" (no. 14), and "Yo' Better Run, Run, Run" (no. 15).

Songs associated with the religious experience known as seekin' make up the second category of spirituals. The seekin' experience involved a religious rite of passage for teenage boys and girls who underwent tests of faith as a prerequisite for membership into a pray's house or church. It was in essence an amalgamation of the retained ancestral initiation rites of West African secret societies and the slaves' newly adopted Christian teachings of Jesus Christ's wilderness experience. Included in this songbook are five seekin' songs: "Ef Ye Want to See Jesus" (no. 16), "Go in the Wilderness" (no. 17), "Hunting for a City" (no. 18), "I'm Leaning on the Lawd" (no. 19), and "The Lonesome Valley" (no. 20). These spirituals contain words such as "valley," "hunting," and "wilderness," which allude to the physical and mental challenges involved in this spiritual journey.

The culminating event in seekin' was baptism, but Minnie (Gracie) Gadson and Rosa and Joseph Murray confirm the usual performance of "Wade in de Water" or "Take Me to de Water." Thus, the islanders probably sang seekin' songs after the sermon, when the pastor invited nonmembers to join the church, which was commonly known as "opening up the doors of the church." The song texts "come backslider" and "you want to get religion" in the spiritual "Hunting for a City" are suggestive of such liturgical usage. Furthermore, Charlotte Forten, the first African American teacher at Penn School, encountered a similar placement of these seekin' songs when the islanders sang "The Lonesome Valley" after she read to them the Sermon on the Mount.[5]

Four Christmas songs constitute the third category in the songbook. They include "Go Tell It on the Mountain" (no. 21), the Marian songs "Mary Had a Baby, Aye Lawd" (no. 22) and "Mary Had a Baby, Sing Hallelu" (no. 23), and "Rise up, Shepherd an' Foller" (no. 24). In the 1920s, Rosa Cooley brought many of these spirituals to the island for use in her Mystery Play at Penn School; consequently, they represent a newer song tradition on the island in comparison to other spiritual types. The short texts in the Marian songs made them ideal for soloists to raise during the offering or as a quiet response to a prayer. The more formal "Rise up, Shepherd an' Foller" was usually reserved for the Mystery Play, but most of the Penn School teachers attended Brick Baptist, the mother church on the island, so they may have introduced this spiritual to the membership.

By far, the most popular Christmas song is "Go Tell It on the Mountain." This spiritual's verses contain a 7, 6, 7, 6, poetic meter and rhyme scheme that closely resemble the meters of popular Dr. Watts hymns lined at the beginning of each church service. They include Charles Wesley's "Father, I Stretch My Hands to Thee" (8, 6, 8, 6,), Horatius Bonar's "I Heard the Voice of Jesus Say" (8, 6, 8, 6,), and Isaac Watt's "I Love the Lord; He Heard My Cries" (8, 6, 8, 6,). Still performed today, "Go Tell It on the Mountain" functions as both an opening hymn and spiritual selection.

Ten communion and Easter songs make up this songbook's fourth category of spirituals. I combine these services because of the crossover usage for spirituals such as "All My Sins Done Taken Away" (no. 25) and "Looka How Dey Done Muh Lord" (no. 31). Those songs closely associated with Easter are "De Angel Roll de Stone Away" (no. 26), "Happy Morning" (no. 29), and Stars Begin to Fall" (no. 33), commonly known as "My Lord, What a Morning." Unfortunately, these songs are rarely performed on the island.

"De Blood Done Sign My Name" (no. 27), "Drinkin' of the Wine" (no. 28), and "Let Us Break Bread Together" (no. 30) are the standard Gullah spirituals for the communion service. In my fieldwork throughout the South Carolina Lowcountry, I found these spirituals to be among the most popular Gullah Geechee songs. Their monthly performance within the long communion service and their enduring melodies contribute to their continued use in many churches. Although some clergymen on the island objected to the singing of "Drinkin' of the Wine" because its lyrics seemed to condone alcohol consumption, this song is still remembered by church members throughout the Sea Islands region.

I categorize the final twenty-one songs as general use songs because of their suitability as opening music for the devotional service, lead-in songs raised by a member giving a testimony, or fill-in selections during a momentary stoppage in the church service. As a deacon, James Garfield Smalls is often called upon to begin a devotional service with the songs "Ev'ry Time I Feel the Spirit" (no. 41) or "En dat Great Gittin-up Mornin'" (no. 40). These spirituals are considered "his" songs, and they never fail to lift the spirits of the congregants.

Minnie (Gracie) Gadson and Rosa Murray often open devotional services with "Just Keep on Praying" or "Glory, Glory Hallelujah" and use these spirituals as introductions to their testimonials about "How good the Lord has been." The tradition of testifying allows the individual to express their most immediate concerns within the safety of the communal sacred experience. Often, the number of members giving testimonials exceeds the allotted time for the devotional period, and many a deacon has been forced to bring it to an end so the church service may begin.

I conclude the songbook with a transcription of the hymn "Father, I Stretch My Hands to Thee" in the highly ornamental long meter style. This hymn lining tradition is quickly disappearing on Saint Helena Island, but it is still performed during pray's house services, where I transcribed this version, or in special prayer services during the Heritage Days Festival at Penn Center. I must recognize the laudable efforts of James Abbington to include metered hymns in the popular *African American Heritage Hymnal* (2001). William Dargan's *Lining the Word: Dr. Watts Hymn Singing in the Music of Black Americans* remains the seminal study of the hymn lining tradition.

Rhythm

My transcriptions of Gullah songs adhere to a meter in 2 or 4, which is consistent with previous studies by the *Slave Songs* editors Ballanta-Taylor, Carl Diton, and Johann Buis. However, song leaders often employ a run-on singing approach that shortens ending cadences and prematurely begins each new verse, thus shifting the accentuation. This singing style is quite challenging for musicians who are unfamiliar with this unique performance practice.

Another feature of Gullah music is the use of triplet rhythms for patterns of eighth notes. In measures 5 and 7 of the spiritual "Bell da Ring" (no, 2), the four eighth notes would have a triplet swing feel in performance as opposed to a strict eighth note rhythmic interpretation. Later musical styles, such as blues and jazz, routinely applied this triplet swing feel to eighth-note patterns.

46. BELL DA RING.

I know member, know Lord, I know I yed - de de bell da ring. 1. Want to go to meet - ing, Bell da ring, Want to go to meet-ing, Bell da ring. 2. (Say) Road so storm-y,* Bell da ring, (Say) Road so storm - y, Bell da ring.

Allen, McKim, Ware.

One of the strongest West and Central African rhythmic retentions is the 3+3+2 handclapping pattern still used on Saint Helena Island. This tresillo rhythm is an additive pattern after performers had established the basic pulse by clapping or stomping their feet. I chose not to include the handclapping and stomping patterns in my transcriptions because the singers I recorded performed alone and did not have basers to provide the rhythmic accompaniment.

Melody

This songbook contains a mixture of two-part and four-part harmonizations and single-line melodic transcriptions. In general, the four-part harmonizations captured the singing of the Saint Helena Quartet, who were former singers at Hampton Institute and later teachers at Penn School. A main characteristic of their singing, especially in slow spirituals, was their portamento or vocal sliding approach. In the spiritual "Nobody Knows de Trouble I've Seen," the vocal slides occur in the last measure on the word "Jesus."

Among the fifty-five spirituals in this songbook are twenty-six transcriptions based on my personal field recordings conducted on the island from 2007 through 2013 and audio recordings obtained from the Folklife Center at the Library of Congress. Although it is impossible to capture all of the subtle melodic nuances of the islanders' singing, especially the bent notes and vocal

Silver, *To Live As Free Men*, "Nobody Knows de Trouble I've Seen."
Transcription by author.

slides, I include altered tones when possible. For example, there are flatted thirds throughout "Adam in the Garden Pickin' Up Leaves" (no. 1) and a flatted seventh in "Father, Praise Father" (no. 42). These accidentals result in an ambiguous major/minor tonality so characteristic of Negro spirituals and the blues. When possible, I present multiple versions of spirituals such as "De Lonesome Valley," "Ev'ry Time I Feel the Spirit," "Glory, Glory Hallelujah," "What Side Do You Leanin' On," and "Nobody Knows de Trouble I've Seen" to highlight melodic and textual changes made to these songs over time.

Song Texts

Ron Daise, noted actor, educator, Gullah Geechee cultural expert, and native of Saint Helena Island, provides a pronunciation guide for the Gullah texts in each song and gives contextual information to help readers understand this West and Central African-derived language. The song texts range from a mixture of Gullah and English to English-only examples such as "Let Us Break Bread

Together." His linguistic notes are aimed at the general reader and musical artists endeavoring to perform these songs. A special feature is Daise's complete Gullah translation of the first spiritual in each of the five liturgical categories. Readers interested in hearing this language should listen to Daise's *Gullah Tings fa Tink Bout* CD. When asked to explain Geechee speech, Rosa Murray stated jokingly, "We weren't raised up on fresh water like in Philadelphia or New York. We were raised up in salt water!"[6]

These spirituals first gained attention because their Gullah texts so fascinated White visitors; however, there is often little interest in hearing them as they were originally composed. Europeanized versions of spirituals, with an occasional word in dialect, are the usual norm. It is my hope that this songbook will motivate readers to reexamine the importance of reconnecting Negro spirituals to the language of the slave past. Some will argue that Gullah lacks the beauty of standard English, but there was nothing beautiful about the slave experience. We commonly hear the slaves' melodies and rhythms in various renditions of spirituals. I believe we should finally hear their language!

GULLAH SONGBOOK

Shouting Spirituals

1. Adam in the Garden Pickin' Up Leaves
2. Bell da Ring
3. Cyan' Hide Sinner
4. Dere's a Meeting Here Tonight
5. De Trouble ob de World
6. Give Up de World
7. Lord, Remember Me
8. No Man Can Hinder Me
9. Rock O' Jubilee
10. Satan's Camp A-Fire
11. This Old House Gonna Fall
12. Too Late Sinner
13. Turn Sinner, Turn O!
14. Way Down in Egypt Land
15. Yo' Better Run, Run, Run

1. Minnie (Gracie) Gadson, "Adam in the Garden Pickin' Up Leaves." Transcription by author.[1]

GULLAH VERSION

Oh, Eve, weh Adam, Oh, Eve
Adam een de gaardin pickin up de leave
Pickin up, pickin up, picken up de leave
Adam een de gaardin pickin up de leave
Satan mad an me so glad
Adam een de gaardin pickin up de leave
E miss de soul dat e tink e done had
Adam een de gaardin pickin up de leave, Say

2. "Bell Da Ring," from Allen, Ware, and Garrison, 1867, *Slave Songs of the United States.*[2]

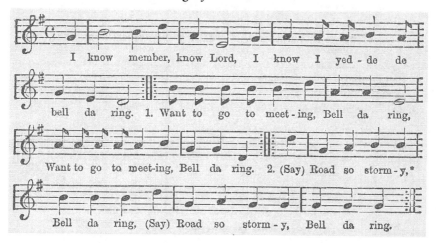

GULLAH TEXTUAL NOTES:

Present time is made definite by the auxiliary *do* or *da* ("Bell is ringing")

"de" is pronounced as "duh" and means "the"

In the Gullah lexicon, a "d" is substituted for "t" at the beginning of many words

"Lord" is pronounced as "Lawd"

"yedde" means hear

"meeting" is pronounced as "meetin."

3. "Cyan' Hide Sinner, from Ballanta-Taylor, 1925, *Saint Helena Island Spirituals.*[3]

GULLAH TEXTUAL NOTES:

"Cyan'" is the Gullah word used for "cannot"

"Cyan' hide liar" is a declarative statement; in the Gullah lexicon, the subject
"you" in this statement is understood.

4. "Dere's a Meeting Here Tonight," from Allen, Ware, and Garrison, 1867,
Slave Songs of the United States.[4]

11. THERE'S A MEETING HERE TO-NIGHT.

1. I take my text in Mattew, and by de Re-ve - la - tion, I

know you by your gar-ment, Dere's a meet-ing here to - night.   Dere's a

Oh !

meet-ing here to- night, (Brudder Tony,) Dere's a meet-ing here to -

Oh !

- night, (Sister Rina,) Dere's a meeting here to-night, I hope to meet a - gain.

GULLAH TEXTUAL NOTES:

"dere" is used for "there" and is often pronounced as "deh"; in the Gullah
lexicon, a "d" is substituted for "t" at the beginning of many words

brudder is pronounced as brudduh; in the Gullah lexicon, word endings of "er,"
"ar," and "or" are substituted with "a," "ah," or "uh"

5. De Trouble ob de World," from Allen, Ware, and Garrison, 1867,
Slave Songs of the United States.[5]

10. THE TROUBLE OF THE WORLD.

1. I want to be* my Fa-der's chil'-en, I want to be

my Fa-der's chil'-en, I want to be my Fa-der chil'-en,

Roll, Jor-dan, roll. O say,†ain't you done wid de

trou-ble ob de world, Ah!.... trou-ble ob de world, Ah!

Say ain't you done wid de trou-ble ob de world, Ah Roll, Jor-dan, roll.

GULLAH TEXTUAL NOTES:

"de" is pronounced as "duh" and means "the"; in the Gullah lexicon, a "d" is
substituted for "t" at the beginning of many words

Fader is pronounced as fadduh; in the Gullah lexicon, word endings of "er," "ar,"
and "or" are substituted with "a," "ah," or "uh"

"ob" means "of"

6. "Give Up de World," from Allen, Ware, and Garrison, 1867,
Slave Songs of the United States.[6]

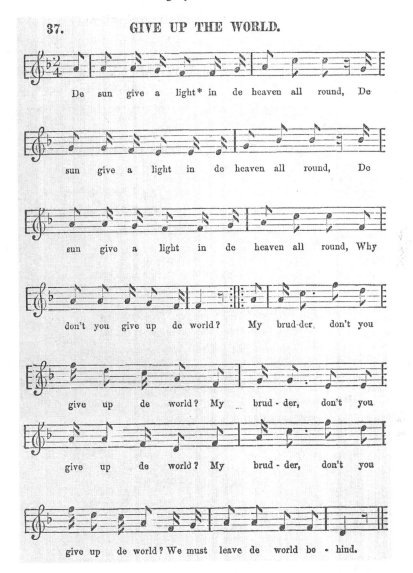

37.   GIVE UP THE WORLD.

De sun give a light* in de heaven all round, De
sun give a light in de heaven all round, De
sun give a light in de heaven all round, Why
don't you give up de world? My brud-der, don't you
give up de world? My brud-der, don't you
give up de world? My brud-der, don't you
give up de world? We must leave de world be-hind.

GULLAH TEXTUAL NOTES:

"de" is pronounced as "duh" and means "the"; in the Gullah lexicon, a "d" is
substituted for "t" at the beginning of many words

brudder is pronounced as brudduh; in the Gullah lexicon, word endings of "er,"
"ar," and "or" are substituted with "a," "ah," or "uh"

7. "Lord, Remember Me," from Allen, Ware, and Garrison, 1867,
Slave Songs of the United States.[7]

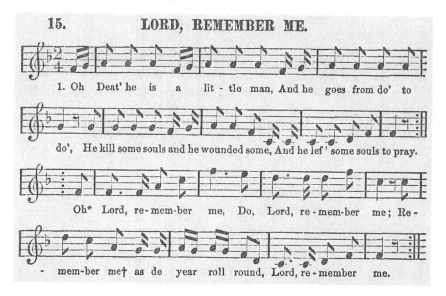

GULLAH TEXTUAL NOTES:

"Remember" is often pronounced as "rememba"; in the Gullah lexicon, word
   endings of "er," "ar," and "or" are substituted with "a," "ah," or "uh"

"Lord" is pronounced as "Lawd"

"Jesus" is pronounced as "Jedus"

8. "No Man Can Hinder Me," from Allen, Ware, and Garrison, 1867, *Slave Songs of the United States.*[8]

14.   NO MAN CAN HINDER ME.

Walk in, kind Sa - viour, No man can hin - der me ! Walk in, sweet Je - sus, No man can hin - der me !2. See what won - der Je - sus done, O no man can hin - der me ! See what won-der Je - sus done, O no man can hin-der me ! O no man, no man, no man can hin - der me ! O no man, no man, no man can hin-der me !

GULLAH TEXTUAL NOTES:

"walk" is pronounced as "waak;" "Savior" is pronounced as "Sabior"

"hinder" is pronounced as hinduh; in the Gullah lexicon, word endings of "er," "ar," and "or" are substituted with "a," "ah," or "uh"; "Jesus" is pronounced as "Jedus"

"the" is pronounced as "duh" and means "the"; in the Gullah lexicon, a "d" is substituted for "t" at the beginning of many words

9. "Rock O' Jubilee," from Allen, Ware, and Garrison, 1867, *Slave Songs of the United States.*[9]

Penn Center 1973 recording, "Jubilee." Transcription by author.

GULLAH TEXTUAL NOTES:

"poor" is pronounced as "po'"

"Lord" is pronounced as "Lawd"

"Thank" is pronounced as "tank"

10. "Satan's Camp A-Fire," from Allen, Ware, and Garrison, 1867,
Slave Songs of the United States.[10]

36.   **SATAN'S CAMP A-FIRE.**

Fi - er, my Sav - iour, fi - er, Sa - tan's camp a -

fire; Fi - er, be - lie - ver, fi - er, Sa - tan's camp a - fire.

GULLAH TEXTUAL NOTES:

"Satan's camp a-fire" is a declarative statement

In the Gullah lexicon, using "a-" with the noun "fire" denotes "on fire" and
the verb "is" is understood

"Fier" is the pronunciation used for "fire" stated expressively

11. Deacon James Garfield Smalls, "This Old House Gonna Fall."
Transcription by author.[11]

This old house,   this old house,   this old house,   a - gon na   fall!

This old house,   this old house,   this old house   gon na   fall!

GULLAH TEXTUAL NOTES:

"this" is often pronounced as "dis"

"old" is often pronounced as "ol"; in the Gullah lexicon, final word consonants
are silent

12. "Too Late Sinner," from Ballanta-Taylor, 1925, *Saint Helena Island Spirituals.*[12]

GULLAH TEXTUAL NOTES:

"ah" is the Gullah word used for "I"; in the Krio language of Sierra Leone, the West African country from where numerous Gullah people are descended, "A" is the word for "I"

"de" is pronounced as "duh" and means "the"; in the Gullah lexicon, a "d" is substituted for "t" at the beginning of many words

13. "Turn, Sinner, Turn O!," from Allen, Ware, and Garrison, 1867,
Slave Songs of the United States.[13]

48.   TURN, SINNER, TURN O!

1. Turn, sin - ner, turn to - day, Turn, sin - ner, turn O!
2. Turn, O sin - ner, de worl' da gwine, Turn, sin - ner, turn O!

Turn, sin - ner, turn to - day, Turn, sin - ner, turn O!
Turn, O sin - ner, de worl' da gwine, Turn, sin - ner, turn O!

1ST VAR.

3. Wait not for to - morrow's sun, Turn, sin - ner, turn O!
4. To-morrow's sun will sure to shine, Turn, sin - ner, turn O!

Wait not for to - morrow's sun, Turn, sin - ner, turn O!
To-morrow's sun will sure to shine, Turn, sin - ner, turn O!

2D VAR.

5. The sun may shine, but on your grave, Turn, sinner, turn O! The

sun may shine, but on your grave, Turn, sin - ner, turn O!

3D VAR.

6. Hark! I hear dem sin - ner say, Turn, sin - ner, turn O!
7. If you get to heaven I'll get there too, Turn, sin - ner, turn O!

GULLAH TEXTUAL NOTES:

"sinner" is often pronounced as "sinna"; in the Gullah lexicon, word endings of
"er," "ar," and
"or" are substituted with "a," "ah," or "uh"

"hear dem sinner say" is a descriptive expression for "hear those sinners say"

14. Minnie (Gracie) Gadson, "Way Down in Egypt Land." Transcription by author.[14]

GULLAH TEXTUAL NOTES:

"Egypt" is pronounced without ending "t" sound; in the Gullah lexicon, final consonants on words are silent

"mother" is pronounced as "mudduh"; in the Gullah lexicon, word endings of "er," "ar," and "or" are substituted with "a," "ah," or "uh"

15. "Yo' Better Run, Run, Run," from Ballanta-Taylor, 1925, *Saint Helena Island Spirituals.*[15]

GULLAH TEXTUAL NOTES:

"de" is pronounced as "duh" and means "the"; in the Gullah lexicon, a "d" is substituted for "t" at the beginning of many words

"better" sometimes is pronounced as "bedduh"; in the Gullah lexicon, a "b" in the middle of words is substituted with a "d" and word endings of "er" are substituted with "a," "ah," or "uh"

Seekin' Spirituals

16. Ef Ye Want to See Jesus
17. Go in de Wilderness
18. Hunting for a City
19. I'm Leaning on the Lawd
20. The Lonesome Valley

16. "Ef Ye Want to See Jesus," from Armstrong, Ludlow, Fenner, *Hampton and Its Students.*[16]

Ef ye want to see Jesus.—*Concluded.*

come out de wil - der-ness, Lean- in' on de Lord. Oh lean - in'
come out de wil - der-ness, Lean- in' on de Lerd.

on de Lord, Lean - in' on de Lord, Oh lean - in' up -

- on de Lamb of God, who was slain on Cal - va - ry.

GULLAH VERSION

Ef hunnah wanfa see Jedus, Go een de wildaness, Go een de wildaness,
    Go een de wildaness,
Ef hunnah wanfa see Jedus, Go een de wildaness, Leanin on de Lawd.

Oh, bruddah, how ya feel wen ya come out de wildaness, come out de
    wildaness, come out de wildaness.
Oh, bruddah, how ya feel wen ya come out de wildaness, Leanin on de
    Lawd.

A been feel so happy wen A come out de wildaness, come out de wilda-
    ness, come out de wildaness.
A been happy happy wen A come out de wildaness, Leanin on de Lawd.

Oh, leanin on de Lawd, Leanin on de Lawd, Oh, leanin on de Lam a
    Gawd, wa been slay on Calbary

17. "Go in de Wilderness," from Allen, Ware, and Garrison, 1867,
Slave Songs of the United States.[17]

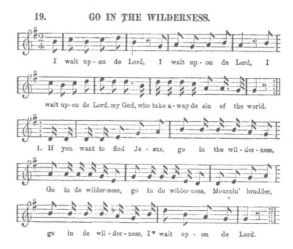

19.   GO IN THE WILDERNESS.

I wait up-on de Lord, I wait up-on de Lord, I

wait up-on de Lord, my God, who take a-way de sin of the world.

1. If you want to find Je-sus, go in the wil-der-ness,

Go in de wilder-ness, go in de wilder-ness, Mournin' brudder,

go in de wil-der-ness, I* wait up-on de Lord.

GULLAH TEXTUAL NOTE:

"de" is pronounced as "duh" and means "the"; in the Gullah lexicon, a "d" is substituted for "t" at the beginning of many words

18. "Hunting for a City," from Allen, Ware, and Garrison, 1867,
Slave Songs of the United States.[18]

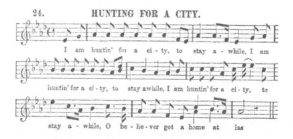

24.   HUNTING FOR A CITY.

I am huntin' for a ci-ty, to stay a-while, I am

huntin' for a ci-ty, to stay awhile, I am huntin' for a ci-ty, to

stay a-while, O be-lie-ver got a home at las

GULLAH TEXTUAL NOTES:

"hunting" is pronounced as "huntin'"
"for" is pronounced as "fo"

19. Silver, *To Live As Free Men*, "I'm Leaning on the Lawd." Transcription by author.[19]

GULLAH TEXTUAL NOTES:

"de" is pronounced as "duh" and means "the"; in the Gullah lexicon, a "d" is substituted for "t" at the beginning of many words

"mother" is pronounced as "mudduh"; in the Gullah lexicon, word endings of "er," "ar," and "or" are substituted with "a," "ah," or "uh"

20. "The Lonesome Valley," from Allen, Ware, and Garrison, 1867, *Slave Songs of the United States.*[20]

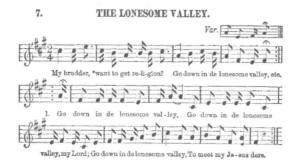

The Lonesome Valley

GULLAH TEXTUAL NOTES:

"de" is pronounced as "duh" and means "the"; in the Gullah lexicon, a "d" is substituted for "t" at the beginning of many words

"Jesus" is pronounced as "Jedus"

"want" is pronounced as "wahn"

"brudder" is pronounced as "mudduh"; in the Gullah lexicon, word endings of "er," "ar," and "or" are substituted with "a," "ah," or "uh"

The Lonesome Valley

De Lonesome Valley

Christmas Spirituals

21. "Go Tell It On de Mountain," from Ballanta-Taylor, 1925, *Saint Helena Island Spirituals.*[21]

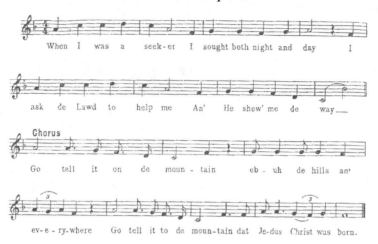

When I was a seek-er I sought both night and day I
ask de Lawd to help me An' He show' me de way___

Chorus

Go tell it on de moun-tain ob - uh de hills an'

ev- e - ry-where Go tell it to de moun-tain dat Je-dus Christ was born.

GULLAH VERSION:

Wen A been a seeka
A been seek bot night an day
A aks de Lawd fa hep me
An Him show me de way—
Go tell em on de mountain, oba de hill, an ebryweh
Go tell em on de mountain dat dat Jedus Chris da bon
Him tell me A da a watchman
An sit me on de wall
An ef A da a Christian
Fa true, A da de leas ob all
Een de time ob Dabid
Some say Him beena King
An ef a chile da bon fa tru

22. "Mary Had a Baby, Aye Lawd," from Ballanta-Taylor, 1925,
Saint Helena Island Spirituals.[22]

GULLAH TEXTUAL NOTES:

"de" is pronounced as "duh" and means "the"; in the Gullah lexicon, a "d" is
   substituted for "t" at the beginning of many words

"him" often is pronounced "em"

"manger" often is pronounced "manga"; in the Gullah lexicon, word endings of
   "er," "ar," and "or" are substituted with "a," "ah," or "uh"

23. "Mary Had a Baby, Sing Hallelu," from Ballanta-Taylor," 1925,
Saint Helena Island Spirituals.[23]

GULLAH TEXTUAL NOTES:

"de" is pronounced as "duh" and means "the"; in the Gullah lexicon, a "d" is
   substituted for "t" at the beginning of many words

"him" often is pronounced "em"

"manger" often is pronounced "manga"; in the Gullah lexicon, word endings of
   "er," "ar," and "or" are substituted with "a," "ah," or "uh"

24. "Rise Up, Shepherd an' Foller," from Ballanta-Taylor, 1925, *Saint Helena Island Spirituals.*[24]

1. Dere's a star in de Eas' on Christ - mas morn

Rise up Shep-herd an' fol - ler It 'll lead to de place where de

Sav - ious born ____ Rise up Shep-herd an' fol - ler.

Chorus

Leave yo' sheep an' leave yo' lams Rise up shep-herd an'

fol - ler Leave yo' lives an' leave yo' rams Rise up shep-herd an'

fol-ler Fol - ler fol-ler rise up shep-herd an' fol - ler

fol - ler de star of Beth- le- hem __ Rise up shep-herd an' fol - ler.

GULLAH TEXTUAL NOTES:

"dere's a star" is used for "there's a star" and often is pronounced as "deh a staar"; in the Gullah lexicon, a "d" is substituted for "t" at the beginning of many words, the verb "to be" is omitted from sentence construction, and words similar in sound to "star" are pronounced similarly as "staar"

"de" is pronounced as "duh" and means "the"; in the Gullah lexicon, a "d" is substituted for "t" at the beginning of many words

"foller" is used for "follow" and sometimes is pronounced as "folla"; in the Gullah lexicon, word endings of "ow" are substituted with "a," "ah," or "uh"

Communion and Easter Spirituals

25. Silver, *To Live As Free Men,* "All My Sins Done Taken Away."
Transcription by author.[25]

GULLAH TEXTUAL NOTES:

"All my sins done taken away" means "All of my sins have been taken away";
in the Gullah lexicon, present perfect tense is constructed by placing "done"
before the past tense of the verb and past tense is constructed without adding
"ed," therefore, "have been taken away" also could be constructed as "done
git take way"

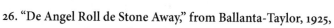

26. "De Angel Roll de Stone Away," from Ballanta-Taylor, 1925,
Saint Helena Island Spirituals.[26]

GULLAH TEXTUAL NOTES:

"de" is pronounced as "duh" and means "the"; in the Gullah lexicon, a "d" is
substituted for "t" at the beginning of many words

27. "De Blood Done Sign My Name," from Ballanta-Taylor, 1925,
Saint Helena Island Spirituals.[27]

GULLAH TEXTUAL NOTES:

"de" is pronounced as "duh" and means "the"; in the Gullah lexicon, a "d" is
substituted for "t" at the beginning of many words

"done sign" means "has signed"; in the Gullah lexicon, present perfect tense
is constructed by placing "done" before the past tense of the verb and past
tense is constructed without an "ed"

28. Minnie (Gracie) Gadson, "Drinkin' of the Wine." Transcription by author.[28]

GULLAH TEXTUAL NOTES:

"of" is pronounced with "uh" sound

"the" is pronounced with "duh" sound; in the Gullah lexicon, a "d" is substituted for "t" at the beginning of many words

29. "Happy Morning," from Allen, Ware, and Garrison, 1867, *Slave Songs of the United States.*[29]

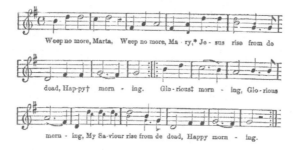

GULLAH TEXTUAL NOTES:

"de" is pronounced as "duh" and means "the"; in the Gullah lexicon, a "d" is substituted for "t" at the beginning of many words

"Jesus" is pronounced as "Jedus"

"morning" is pronounced as "mornin'"

30. Deacon James Garfield Smalls, "Let Us Break Bread Together."
Transcription by author.[30]

GULLAH TEXTUAL NOTES:

"together" is pronounced as "togeda"

"knees" would be singular "knee"

"de" is pronounced as "duh" and means "the"; in the Gullah lexicon, a "d" is
  substituted for "t" at the beginning of many words

"Lord" is pronounced as "Lawd"

31. "Looka How Dey Done Muh Lord," Ballanta-Taylor, 1925,
Saint Helena Island Spirituals.[31]

GULLAH TEXTUAL NOTES:

"Look-a how dey dun muh Lawd" means "Look at how they did my Lord"; in
   the Gullah lexicon, "do" is present tense and "done" is past tense

"dey" is used for "they"; in the Gullah lexicon, a "d" is substituted for "t" at the
   beginning of many words

Pray's House Service. "See How They Done My Lord,"
transcription by author.

GULLAH TEXTUAL NOTES:

"see how they done" means "see how they did"; in the Gullah lexicon, "do" is
   present tense and "done" is past tense

32. Penn Center recording, "Somebody Touched Me." Transcription by author.[32]

GULLAH TEXTUAL NOTES:

"Lord" is pronounced as "Lawd"

"must" will have silent "t" sound

33. "Stars Begin to Fall," from Allen, Ware, and Garrison, 1867, *Slave Songs of the United States.*[33]

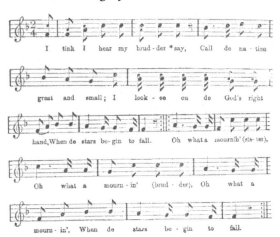

GULLAH TEXTUAL NOTES:

"de" is pronounced as "duh" and means "the"; in the Gullah lexicon, a "d" is substituted for "t" at the beginning of many words

"brudder" is pronounced as "brudduh"; in the Gullah lexicon, word endings of "er," "ar," and "or" are substituted with "a," "ah," or "uh"

34. Penn Center recording, "We Are Climbing Jacob's Ladder." Transcription by author.

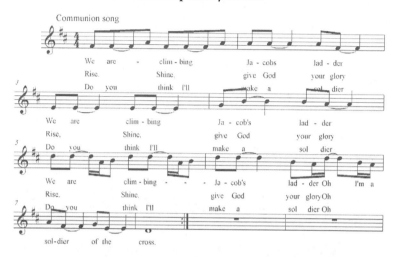

GULLAH TEXTUAL NOTE:

Very few Gullah texts would be used in this Penn School song.

General Use Songs

35. A Great Campmeetin' in de Promised Land
36. De Ole Sheep Done Know de Road
37. De Ole Ship Marie
38. Don't Let de Wind Blow Here No More
39. Don't You Take Everybody for Your Friend
40. En dat Great Gittin-up Mornin'
41. Ev'ry Time I Feel the Spirit
42. Father, Praise Father
43. Glory, Glory Hallelujah
44. I've Got a Home in the Rock, Don't You See
45. I Know I Been Changed
46. I Shall Not Be Moved
47. Just Keep On Praying
48. Nobody Knows de Trouble I've Had

35. "A Great Campmeetin' in de Promised Land," from Armstrong, Ludlow, Fenner, *Hampton and Its Students*.[34]

A great Camp-meetin'.—*Concluded.*

tire,...... Mourn an' neb-ber tire, Mourn an' neb-ber

tire, Dere's a great camp-meet-in' in de Promised Land.

Oh, waak tagedda, chirren, dohncha git weary
Waak tagedda, chirren, dohncha git weary
Waak tagedda, chirren, dohncha git weary
Deres a great camp meetin een de Promis Lan

Gwinna moan an neba tyad
Moan an neba tyad
Moad an neba tyad
Deres a a great camp meetin een de Promis Lan

Oh, taak tagedda, chirren, dohncha git weary
Taak tagedda, chirren, dohncha git weary
Taak tagedda, chirren, dohncha git weary
Deres a great camp meetin een de Promis Lan

Oh, sing tagedda, chirren, dohncha git weary
Sing tagedda, chirren, dohncha git weary
Sing tagedda, chirren, dohncha git weary
Deres a great camp meetin een de Promis Lan

36. "De Ole Sheep Done Know de Road," from Armstrong, Ludlow, Fenner, *Hampton and Its Students.*[35]

De ole Sheep done know de Road.

CHORUS.

Oh de ole sheep done know de road, De ole sheep done know de road, De ole sheep done know de road, De young lambs mus' find de way.

Oh, soon-er in de mornin' when I rise, De young lambs mus' find de way.
My brudder aint ye got yer counts all sealed, De young lambs, &c.

Wid crosses an' tri-als on eb - ry side, De young lambs mus' find de way.
You'd bet-ter go get em 'fore ye leave dis field, De young lambs, &c.

GULLAH TEXTUAL NOTES:

"De ole sheep done know" means "The old sheep has known"; in the Gullah lexicon, present perfect tense is constructed by placing "done" before the past tense of the verb and past tense is constructed without an "ed"

"de" is pronounced as "duh" and means "the"; in the Gullah lexicon, a "d" is substituted for "t" at the beginning of many words

37. "De Ole Ship Marie," from Ballanta-Taylor, 1925, *Saint Helena Island Spirituals.*[36]

GULLAH TEXTUAL NOTES:

"de" is pronounced as "duh" and means "the"; in the Gullah lexicon, a "d" is substituted for "t" at the beginning of many words

"hebby loaded" means "heavy loaded"; in the Gullah lexicon, a "v" in the middle of a word is substituted with a "b"

38. "Don't Let de Wind Blow Here No More," from Ballanta-Taylor, 1925, *Saint Helena Island Spirituals.*[37]

GULLAH TEXTUAL NOTE:

"de" is pronounced as "duh" and means "the"; in the Gullah lexicon, a "d" is
substituted for "t" at the beginning of many words

39. Deacon James Garfield Smalls, "Don't You Take Everybody for Your Friend." Transcription by author.[38]

GULLAH TEXTUAL NOTES:

"don't is pronounced without final "t" sound

"every" is pronounced as "ev'ry" and on occasion is pronounced as "ebry"; in
the Gullah lexion, a "v" in the middle of a word is substituted with a "b"

"for" is pronounced without ending "r" sound and on occasion is pronounced
as "fa"; in the Gullah lexicon, word endings of "or" are substituted with "a,"
"ah," or "uh"

⌢

40. "En dat Great Gittin-up Mornin,'" from Armstrong, Ludlow, Fenner, *Hampton and Its Students.*[39]

En dat great gittin=up Mornin'.

THIS song is a remarkable paraphrase of a portion of the Book of Revelations, and one of the finest specimens of negro "Spirituals." The student who brought it to us, and who sings the Solos, has furnished all that he can remember of the almost interminable succession of verses, which he has heard sung for half an hour at a time, by the slaves in their midnight meetings in the woods. He gives the following interesting account of its origin :

"I have heard my uncle sing this hymn, and he told me how it was made. It was made by an old slave who knew nothing about letters or figures. He could not count the number of rails that he would split when he was tasked by his master to split 150 a day. But he tried to lead a Christian life, and he dreamed of the General Judgment, and told his fellow-servants about it, and then made a tune to it, and sang it in his cabin meetings."

J. B. TOWE.

I'm a gwine to tell you bout de comin' ob de Sav-iour; Fare-you-well,

Fare-you-well. I'm a gwine to tell you 'bout de com-in ob de Saviour;

Fare-you-well, Fare-you-well. Dar's a bet-ter day a comin'; Fare-you-well,

Fare-you-well; When my Lord speaks to His Fa-der; Fare-you-well,

Fare-you-well. Says Fa-der, I'm tired o' bear-in', Fare-you-well,

GULLAH TEXTUAL NOTES:

"dat" means "that" and "de" is pronounced as "duh" and means "the"; in the

Gullah lexicon, a "d" is substituted for "t" at the beginning of many words

"for" is pronounced as "fo'"

41. "Ev'ry Time I Feel the Spirit," from Ballanta-Taylor, 1925, *Saint Helena Island Spirituals.*[40]

spoke,   out of His mouth came____ fire and smoke.   All ar

Ooh Ooh Ooh   Ooh Ooh Ooh   Ooh____   Ooh

Ooh Ooh Ooh   Ooh   Ooh

round me   look so shine.   I ask my God if____ all were

Ooh Ooh Ooh   Ooh Ooh Ooh

Ooh Ooh Ooh   Ooh Ooh Ooh

mine.   Yes ev' - ry

mine.

mine.

GULLAH TEXTUAL NOTE:

"Eb-ry time" means "every time"; in the Gullah lexicon, a "v" in the middle of a word is substituted with a "b"

42. Silver, *To Live As Free Men*, 1942, "Father, Praise Father." Transcription by author.[41]

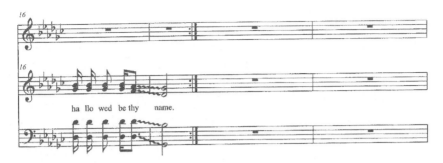

ha llo wed be thy   name.

GULLAH TEXTUAL NOTE:

"Father" is pronounced as "Fadduh"; in the Gullah lexicon, word endings of
    "er" are substituted with "a," "ah," or "uh"

43. Pray's House Service, "Glory, Glory Hallelujah."
    Transcription by author.[42]

Glo-ry, Glo-ry - Ha-lle - lu-jah Since I laid my   burden

down.   Glo-ry, Glo-ry   Ha-lle - lu jah   Since I

laid   my   bur den down.

Verse 2. I feel better so much better
Verse 3. Burden down Lord

GULLAH TEXTUAL NOTES:

"better is pronounced as "bedduh"; in the Gullah lexicon, a "t" in the middle of
words is substituted with a "d" and word endings of "er" are substituted with
"a," "ah," or "uh"

"Lord" is pronounced as "Lawd"

Ballanta-Taylor, "Glory, Glory Hallelujah,"
Saint Helena Island Spirituals, 53.

44. "I've Got a Home in the Rock, Don't You See," from Diton, 1928, *Thirty-Six South Carolina Spirituals.*[43]

GULLAH TEXTUAL NOTES:

"the" is pronounced as "duh" and means "the"; in the Gullah lexicon, a "d" is substituted for "t" at the beginning of many words

"Saviour' is pronounced as "Sabior"

45. Minnie (Gracie) Gadson, "I Know I Been Changed."
Transcription by author.[44]

GULLAH TEXTUAL NOTES:

"the" is pronounced as "de"; in the Gullah lexicon, a "d" is substituted for "t" at the beginning of many words

"heaven" is pronounced as "heben"; in the Gullah lexicon, a "v" in the middle of words is substituted with a "b"

"there" is pronounced as "dere"; in the Gullah lexicon, a "d" is substituted for "t" at the beginning of many words

"friends" is pronounced without ending "s" sound; "Lord" is pronounced as "Lawd"

"fire" is pronounced as "fiah"

46. Silver, *To Live As Free Men*, "I Shall Not Be Removed."
Transcription by author.[45]

GULLAH TEXTUAL NOTES:

"the" is pronounced as "de"; in the Gullah lexicon, a "d" is substituted for "t" at the beginning of many words

"water" is pronounced as "wadduh"; in the Gullah lexicon, a "t" in the middle of words is substituted with a "d" and word endings of "er" are substituted with "a," "ah," or "uh"

47. Minnie (Gracie) Gadson, "Just Keep on Praying."
Transcription by author.[46]

Just keep on pra-ying the Lord is nigh, Just keep on-
pra-ying he'll hear your cry. The Lord has pro-mised and His word is
true. Just keep on pra-ying He'll an - swer you.

GULLAH TEXTUAL NOTES:

"praying" is pronounced without the ending "g" sound

"Lord" is pronounced as "Lawd"

48. "Nobody Knows de Trouble I've Had," from Allen, Ware, and
Garrison, 1867, *Slave Songs of the United States*.[47]

No - bod - y knows de trouble I've had,* No - bod - y knows but
Je - sus, No - bod - y knows de trouble I've had, (Sing)
Glo - ry hal - le - lu! 1. One morning I was a - walking down,
O yes, Lord! I saw some ber - ries a - hanging down,
Variation on St. Helena Id.
O yes, Lord! O yes, Lord! I saw some berries hanging down.

GULLAH TEXTUAL NOTES:

"de" is pronounced as "duh" and means "the"; in the Gullah lexicon, a "d" is
substituted for "t" at the beginning of many words

"Lord" is pronounced as "Lawd"

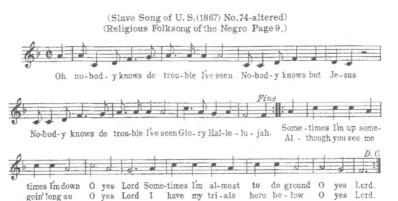

(Slave Song of U. S.(1867) No.74-altered)
(Religious Folksong of the Negro Page 9.)

Oh. no-bod-y knows de trou-ble I've seen No-bod-y knows but Je-sus

Fine

No-bod-y knows de trou-ble I've seen Glo-ry Hal-le-lu-jah.

Some-times I'm up some-
Al-though you see me

D. C.

times I'm down   O yes Lord   Some-times I'm al-most   to de ground   O yes Lord.
goin' long so   O yes Lord   I have my tri-als   here be-low   O yes Lord.

Ballanta-Taylor, "Nobody Knows de Trouble I've Seen,"
Saint Helena Island Spirituals, 89.

Largo

Transcribed by
E. S. Crawford

Glo-ry Hal-le-lu-jah.   No-bo-dy knows de trou-ble I've seen.

No-bo-dy knows but Je-sus,   No-bo-dy knows de trou-ble I've seen.

Glo-ry Hal-le-lu-jah.   Some-times I'm up some-times I'm down.   O yes

Lord.   Some-times I'm al-most to de ground,   Oh yes Lord.

From *To Live As Free Men,* directed by John Silver, 1942,
"Nobody Knows de Trouble I've Seen." Transcription by author.

49. Silver, *To Live As Free Men,*
"Ride on Jesus." Transcription by author.[48]

GULLAH TEXTUAL NOTES:

"heaven" is pronounced as "heben"; in the Gullah lexicon, a "v" in the middle of words is substituted with a "b"

"river" is pronounced as "ribuh"; in the Gullah lexicon, a "v" in the middle of words is substituted with a "b" and word endings of "er" are substituted with "a," "ah," or "uh"

"Jesus" is pronounced as "Jedus"

"morning" is pronounced as "mornin'"

50. "Ring the Bells," from Diton, 1928, *Thirty-Six South Carolina Spirituals.*[49]

GULLAH TEXTUAL NOTES:

"de" is pronounced as "duh" and means "the"; in the Gullah lexicon, a "d" is
   substituted for "t" at the beginning of many words

"Savior" is pronounced as "Sabior"

51. James Garfield Smalls, "Some Gone Love You, Some Gone Hate You." Transcription by author.[50]

GULLAH TEXTUAL NOTE:

"don't" is pronounced without the ending "t" sound

52. Deacon James Garfield Smalls, "Stay in the Fiel." Transcription by author.[51]

GULLAH TEXTUAL NOTES:

"the" is pronounced as "duh"; in the Gullah lexicon, a "d" is substituted for "t"
   at the beginning of many words

"mother" is pronounced as "muddah"; in the Gullah lexicon, a "t" in the middle of words is substituted with a "d" and word endings of "er" are substituted with "a," "ah," or "uh"

53. Deacon James Garfield Smalls, "Sweet Honey in the Rock." Transcription by author.[52]

Sweet ho-ney in the rock, Sweet ho-ney in the rock, and it

tastes like ho-ney in the rock. Why don't you taste and see if it's

sweet e-nough for you, and it's tastes like ho-ney in the rock.

GULLAH TEXTUAL NOTE:

"the" is pronounced as "duh"; in the Gullah lexicon, a "d" is substituted for "t" at the beginning of many words

54. Brick Church Anniversary, "What Side Do You Leanin' On." Transcription by author.[53]

What side - do you lea-nin' on, lea-nin' on - the Lord's side. What side - do you

lea - nin' on, - lea-nin' on - the Lord's side.

GULLAH TEXTUAL NOTES:

"the" is pronounced as "de"; in the Gullah lexicon, a "d" is substituted for "t" at
  the beginning of many words

"Lord" is pronounced as "Lawd"

75.   WHO IS ON THE LORD'S SIDE.

Let me tell you what is nat'-ral-ly de fac'

Who is on de Lord's side, None o' God's chil-'n

neb-ber look back, Who is on de Lord's side.

1. Way in de wal-ley, Who is on de Lord's side,

Way in de wal-ley, Who is on de Lord's side.

Allen, Ware, and Garrison, 1867, *Slave Songs of the United States*, 56.

GULLAH TEXTUAL NOTES:

"the" is pronounced as "de"; in the Gullah lexicon, a "d" is substituted for "t" at
  the beginning of many words

"Lord" is pronounced as "Lawd"

55. "Father, I Stretch My Hands to Thee," (long-meter).
Transcription by author.[54]

GULLAH TEXTUAL NOTE:

"Father" is pronounced as "Fadduh"; in the Gullah lexicon, word endings of
"er" are substituted with "a," "ah," or "uh"

NOTES

INTRODUCTION

1. For a complete discussion of the Gullah language, see Lorenzo D. Turner, *Africanisms in the Gullah Dialect* (Ann Arbor: University of Michigan Press, 1974). See also Patricia Ann Jones Jackson, "The Status of the Gullah: An Investigation of Convergent Processes" (PhD diss., University of Michigan, 1978). She identifies African, as well as creole influences in the Gullah language and shows a propensity for the Sea Islanders to adhere to the creole unmarked verb structure. Jones Jackson also includes story texts in a word-for-word translation which correspond with each line of phonetic script.

2. Orville Burton, *Penn Center: A History Preserved* (Athens: University of Georgia Press, 2014), 4.

3. Thomas Fenner, *Religious Folk Songs of the Negro as Sung on the Plantations* (Hampton, VA: Institute Press, 1909), 124 and 181.

4. Lawrence Schenbeck, "Representing America, Instructing Europe: The Hampton Choir Tours Europe," *Black Music Research Journal* 25, 1/2 (Spring–Fall 2005): 11.

5. Thomas Fortune, ed., "Two Views of Negro Music," *The New York Age,* January 25, 1919.

6. Bernice Johnson Reagon, "Music in the Civil Rights Movement," interviewed by Maria Daniels, WGBH Boston, July 2006.

7. Bob Darden, *Nothing but Love in God's Water: Black Sacred Music from the Civil War to the Civil Rights Movement,* vol. 1 (University Park: Penn State University Press, 2014), 126.

8. Reiland Rabaka, *Civil Rights Music: The Soundtracks of the Civil Rights Movement* (Lanham, MD: Lexington Books, 2016), 17. Michael Castellini, "Sit In, Stand Up and Sing Out!: Black Gospel Music and the Civil Rights Movement" (PhD diss., Georgia State University, 2013), 2.

9. William Francis Allen, Charles Pickard Ware, and Lucy McKim Garrison, *Slave Songs of the United States* (New York: A. Simpson, 1867); Carl Diton, *Thirty-Six South Carolina Spirituals* (New York: G. Schirmer, 1928); Nicholas George Ballanta-Taylor, *Saint Helena Island Spirituals* (New York: G. Schirmer, 1925); Society for the Preservation of Spirituals, *The Carolina Low-Country* (New York: Macmillan, 1931); Guy B. Johnson, *Folk Culture on St. Helena Island* (Chapel Hill: University of North Carolina, 1930); Samuel Miller Lawton, "The Religious Life of the South Carolina Coastal and Sea Island Negroes" (PhD diss., George Peabody College for Teachers, 1939).

10. Lucy McKim, "Songs of the Port Royal Contrabands," *Dwight's Journal of Music* 21 (November 1862): 254–55. See Allen, Ware, and Garrison, *Slave Songs,* vi. Allen describes the islanders' ability to maintain impeccable time while setting any text.

11. Henry George Spaulding, "Under the Palmetto," *Continental Monthly* 4 (August 1863): 188–203.

12. Thomas Wentworth Higginson, "Negro Spirituals," *Atlantic Monthly* (June 1867): 685–94.

13. Allen, Ware, and Garrison, *Slave Songs*, x.

14. David Frankenburger and William F. Allen, *Essays and Monographs* (Boston: G. H. Ellis, 1890), 6–7. Frankenburger cites a letter Allen wrote to a classmate while on vacation in the summer of 1849 that expresses the importance of western art music, specifically the music of Haydn, Mozart, and Beethoven. Allen states, "I have been employed in manual labor (rather homeopathic), reading novels, visiting, singing, and playing. We have got hold of some fine music of Mozart, Haydn, etc. . . , and I enjoy a perfect Elysium in raising my voice to unheard of pitch and sinking it beneath gloomy Acheron." See also Epstein, *Sinful Tunes,* 312. Epstein references Ware's letter from Saint Helena Island in which he complains, "I should be perfectly satisfied, in a musical way, if I had someone to sing with. I do pine for musical food; even my own playing is as water to the thirsty, or a sea breeze to the people of this region after a still morning with the mercury at 92°."

15. Epstein, *Sinful Tunes,* 315. In the fall of 1857, fifteen-year-old Lucy began teaching piano at home, but later she returned to Eagleswood to study and teach, remaining there through 1860–61. At Eagleswood, she studied violin with a fine émigré musician, Frederick Mollenhauer.

16. Barbara Bellows, *A Talent for Living: Josephine Pinckney and the Charleston Literary Tradition* (Baton Rouge: Louisiana State University Press, 2006), 68.

17. Carl Diton, "Biography," accessed July 26, 2017, http://credo.library.umass.edu/view /pageturn/mums312-b153-i399/#page/1/mode/1up.

18. Ronald Radano, "Denoting Difference: The Writing of the Slave Spirituals," *Critical Inquiry* 22, no. 3 (Spring 1996): 538, 542.

19. Christopher Waterman and Adebis Adeleke, *Jùjú: A Social History and Ethnography of an African Popular Music* (Chicago: University of Chicago Press, 1990), 6.

20. Bruno Nettl, *The Study of Ethnomusicology: Thirty-Three Discussions,* 3d ed. (Urbana: University of Illinois Press, 2015), 82.

21. Guy Carawan, Candie Carawan, Bob Yellin, and Ethel Raim, *Ain't You Got a Right to the Tree of Life?: The People of Johns Island, South Carolina—Their Faces, Their Words, and Their Songs* (New York: Simon and Schuster, 1966). The Carawans chronicle the music on Johns Island through their civil rights efforts on the island. See also Art Rosenbaum, *Shout Because You're Free: The African American Ring Shout Tradition in Coastal Georgia,* contributor Johann S. Buis (Athens: University of Georgia Press, 1998). Rosenbaum examines the shout tradition that has been retained in McIntosh County, Georgia. His study contains valuable transcriptions of twenty-five shouting songs by musicologist Johann Buis.

CHAPTER 1

1. William F. Allen Family Papers, State Historical Society of Wisconsin, 1863–65.

2. Peter Wood, *Black Majority; Negroes in Colonial South Carolina from 1670 Through the Stono Rebellion* (New York: Knopf, 1974), 114–17.

3. William Roberts, "To be Sold by Private Contract, Eight as Valuable Boat Negroes," *The South Carolina Gazette,* October 8, 1772.

4. John Biggers, *The Web of Life in Africa* (Austin: University of Texas Press, 1996), 35–36.

5. John George Wood, *The Natural History of Man; Being an Account of the Manners and Customs of the Uncivilized Races of Men* (London: G. Routledge and Sons, 1868), 546, 589. See also Edward Salo, "Crossing the Rivers of the State: The Role of the Ferry in the Development of South Carolina, Circa 1680–1920s" (PhD diss., Middle Tennessee State University, 2009), 143. Native Americans in the Sea Islands region also constructed their canoes by burning and carving them from large trees.

6. Pete Seeger and Toshi Seeger, *Singing Fishermen of Ghana,* accessed January 1, 2018, http://www.folkstreams.net/film-detail.php?id=123.

7. Cited in Epstein, *Sinful Tunes,* 172. The sorrowful and sad strains of Negro spirituals are described in Spaulding's ("Under the Palmetto," 200) personal observations of the Negro songs, in which he finds that "a tinge of sadness pervaded all their melodies." Frederick Douglass, in *Narrative of the Life of Frederick Douglass* (Boston: Anti-slavery Office, 1845, 26), writes that, upon hearing the spirituals, he was filled with ineffable sadness. See also Harry Burleigh, *Negro Spirituals arr. for solo voice* (New York: G. Ricordi & Co., 1917–25), foreword. Harry T. Burleigh, a grandson of a former slave, discusses the sorrowful nature of Negro spirituals, and he often infuses his song arrangements with accompaniments suggesting both major and minor harmonies. In the *The Power of Black: Interpreting Its History from Africa to the United States* (New York: Oxford University Press, 1996), 41–42, Samuel Floyd divides the song texts of Negro spirituals into sorrow songs and jubilee songs.

8. Samuel G. Stoney, ed., "The Autobiography of William John Grayson," *South Carolina Historical and Genealogical Magazine* 49, 1 (January 1948): 23–40.

9. Fanny Kemble, *Journal of a Residence on a Georgian Plantation in 1838–1839* (New York: Harper & Bros, 1863), 128.

10. Ibid., 129.

11. James Scott, *Domination and the Arts of Resistance: Hidden Transcripts* (New Haven, CT: Yale University, 1992), x.

12. Castellini, "Sit In, Stand Up and Sing Out!" 5.

13. Bartholomew Rivers Carroll, "An Editorial Trip to Edisto Island," *Chicora* I (1842): 42, 63.

14. William Howard Russell, *My Diary, North and South, by William Howard Russell* (London: Bradbury and Evans, 1863), 140.

15. Allen, Ware, and Garrison, *Slave Songs,* xvi.

16. Thomas Higginson, *Army Life in a Black Regiment* (Boston: Fields, Osgood & Co, 1870), 203–4.

17. Cited in James Hester, *A Yankee Scholar in Coastal South Carolina: William Francis Allen's Civil War Journals* (Columbia: University of South Carolina, 2015), 106.

18. Ray Allen Billington, "A Social Experiment: The Port Royal Journal of Charlotte L. Forten, 1862–1863," *Journal of Negro History* 35, 3 (July 1950): 233–264.

19. Wendell Garrison, "Slave Songs of the United States," *The Nation,* November 21, 1867, 411.

20. Allen, Ware, and Garrison, *Slave Songs,* xvi.

21. Aldine Kieffer, *The Musical Million* (Rockingham County, Virginia, ca. 1873), 354.

22. Janet Duitsman Cornelius, *Slave Missions and the Black Church in the Antebellum South* (Columbia, SC: University of South Carolina Press, 1999), 88. Cornelius discusses White plantation owners who were concerned about evangelist Daniel Baker's series of revivals that targeted the religious welfare of their slaves.

23. Cited in Epstein, *Sinful Tunes*, 189.

24. Allen, Ware, and Garrison, *Slave Songs*, 102.

25. Guy Carawan, *Ain't You Got a Right to the Tree of Life?: The People of Johns Island, South Carolina—Their Faces, Their Words, and Their Songs* (Athens: University of Georgia Press, 1994), 15.

26. Pete Seeger, Bob Reiser, Guy Carawan, and Candie Carawan, *Everybody Says Freedom* (New York: Norton, 1989), 163.

27. Lawrence Gellert, *Me and My Captain* (Chain Gang Songs) (New York: Hours Press, 1939), 5.

28. William Pollitzer, *The Gullah People and Their African Heritage* (Athens: University of Georgia Press, 1999), 89.

29. Charles Kovacik and Robert Mason, "Changes in the South Carolina Sea Island Cotton Industry," *Southeastern Geographer* 25, 2 (November 1985): 78. See also Guion Griffis Johnson, *A Social History of the Sea Islands* (Chapel Hill: University of North Carolina, 1930), 36.

30. Sterling Stuckey, *Slave Culture: Nationalist Theory and the Foundations of Black America* (New York: Oxford University Press, 1987), 11.

31. Marimba Ani, *Let the Circle Be Unbroken: The Implications of African Spirituality in the Diaspora.* (Trenton, NJ: Red Sea Press, 1980), 12. Ani introduced this Swahili term in her book to describe the atrocities inflicted on enslaved Africans.

32. Vicente Rossi, *Cosas De Negros* (*Los Oríjenes Del Tango Y Otros Aportes Al Folklore Rioplatense. Rectificaciones* Históricas, 1926), 283.

33. Allen, Ware, and Garrison, *Slave Songs*, xiii.

34. Ibid., xiv.

35. Cited in Albert Raboteau, *Slave Religion: The Invisible Institution in the Antebellum South* (Oxford: Oxford University Press, 1980), 215. See also Charles Colcock Jones, *Religious Instruction of Negroes. An Address Delivered Before the General Assembly of the Presbyterian Church, at Augusta, Ga.,* December 10, 1861 (Richmond: Presbyterian Committee of Publication, 1862), 70–72, 77–79.

36. Robert F. Thompson, *The Four Moments of the Sun* (Washington, DC: National Gallery of Art, 1981), 54, 28. Other examples of the use of counterclockwise movement in Western Africa are found in Marion Kilson, "The Ga Naming Rite," *Anthropos* 64/64 (1968/1969): 904–20. Kilson discusses the counterclockwise movement during the libation portion of the Ga naming rite; and Arthur Powell and Oshon Temple, "Seeding Ethnomathematics with Oware: Sankofa," *Teaching Children Mathematics* 7, no. 6 (February 2001): 369–75. Powell and Temple reveal the counterclockwise movement of seeds in the Oware game from Ghana.

37. Thompson, *Four Moments*, p. 28.

38. Herb Frazier, "Sisters in Song," *Chicago Tribune*, May 9, 1997.

39. California Newsreel, "The Language You Cry In," accessed in February 28, 2015, http://newsreel.org/video/THE-LANGUAGE-YOU-CRY-IN.

40. Ibid.

41. Allan Austin, *African Muslims in Antebellum America: Transatlantic Stories and Spiritual Struggles* (New York: Routledge, 1997), 6–12.

42. Michael Gomez, Exchanging Our Country Marks: The Transformation of African Identities in the Colonial and Antebellum South (Chapel Hill: University of North Carolina Press, 1998), 75.

43. Corey Stayton, "The Kongo Cosmogram: A Theory in African American Literature" (master's thesis, Clark Atlanta University, 1997), 25.

44. Laura Towne, *Letters and Diary, 1862–1888,* edited by Rupert Sargent Holland (Cambridge: Riverside, 1912), 20.

45. James Weldon Johnson, J. Rosamond Johnson, and Lawrence Brown, *The Book of American Negro Spirituals* (New York: Viking Press, 1925), 33–34.

46. Allen, Ware, and Garrison, *Slave Songs,* xiii.

47. Mary Twining, "Movement and Dance in the Sea Islands," *Journal of Black Studies* 15, no. 4 (June 1985): 471.

48. Cited in Epstein, *Sinful Tunes,* 284. William Allen, "Diary," MS, State Historical Society of Wisconsin, entry for December 25, 1863.

49. Lawton, "The Religious Life," 54–56.

50. Art Rosenbaum, *Shout Because You're Free: The African American Ring Shout Tradition in Coastal Georgia* (Athens: University of Georgia Press, 1998), 20, 21.

51. Allen, Ware, and Garrison, 41.

52. Stuckey, *Slave Culture,* 29.

53. See Allen, Ware, and Garrison, *Slave Songs,* v. Allen gives an insightful description of each participant's role in the ring shout.

54. PSP, "Spring Festival," Southern Historical Collection, University of North Carolina at Chapel Hill, T-3615/163 LC, May 5, 1973.

55. See W. K. McNeil, *Encyclopedia of American Gospel Music* (New York: Routledge, 2005), 312; Rosenbaum, *Shout Because You're Free,* 2; Wilbur Cross, *Gullah Culture in America* (Westport, CT: Praeger, 2007), 217. See also Allen, Ware, and Garrison, *Slave Songs,* v. Allen provides the first extensive discussion of the role of the song leader and the basers in a ring shout.

56. McIntosh County Shouters, *Slave Shout Songs from the Coast of Georgia,* custom compact disc series (Washington, DC: Smithsonian Folkways Recordings, 2003).

57. See Allen, Ware, and Garrison, *Slave Songs,* 25. Rosenbaum seems to have overlooked the earlier version found in *Slave Songs.*

58. Gunther Schuller, *Early Jazz: Its Roots and Musical Development* (New York: Oxford University Press, 1968), 19–20.

59. Samuel Floyd, "Black Music in the Circum-Caribbean," *American Music* 17, no. 1 (Spring 1999): 1–38.

60. A. M. Jones, *Studies in African Music* (London: Oxford University Press, 1959), 20.

61. Johnson, Johnson, and Brown, *American Negro Spirituals,* 33.

62. Boyer, Horace Clarence, "Roberta Martin: Innovator of Modern Gospel Music," in Berniece Reagan, ed., *We'll Understand It Better By and By: Pioneering African American Gospel Composers* (Washington, DC: Smithsonian Institute Press, 1992), pp. 275–86.

63. Stuckey, 27.

CHAPTER 2

1. "Annual Reports of the Penn Normal, Industrial, and Agricultural School, 1862–1978," [03615] Penn School Papers, Southern Historical Collection, University of North Carolina at Chapel Hill (hereafter cited as PSP). These documents contain precise reports of donations given to the Penn School during its existence. Along with these records are correspondences from the Penn School administrators thanking specific donors or requesting additional funds.

2. Clyde Vernon Kiser, *Sea Island to City: A Study of St. Helena Islanders in Harlem and Other Urban Centers* (New York: Athenaeum, 1932), 74. Rossa Cooley, Penn School principal, often used the New Testament text regarding "more abundant life" (John 10:10) to describe the school's ultimate mission on Saint Helena Island.

3. Elizabeth Jacoway, *Yankee Missionaries in the South: The Penn School Experiment* (Baton Rouge: Louisiana State University Press, 1980), 30. See Marc C. David, "The Penn School of St. Helena: Breaking the Shackles of Illiteracy on the Sea Islands of South Carolina, 1862–1922" (PhD. diss., Syracuse University, 1999), 13. David attributes the initial low student enrollment to a rumor that the missionaries had come to sell the islanders to Cuba. After a Black man from Frogmore, Columbus Brown, insisted the Yankees had come to help them in their time of need, enrollment quickly increased. See also David, "The Penn School of St. Helena," 14. David cites an observer's account of a visit on March 1862 to the Penn School in which 131 students were counted as opposed to the eighty in this citation.

4. Henry Wilder Foote, "The Penn School on St. Helena Island," *The Southern Workman* 31 (1902): 266. These Black instructors were Penn School graduates who were assigned to the more elementary work.

5. Ibid., 11. See also David, "The Penn School of St. Helena,"15. David discusses the delay until January 6, 1865, of the school's opening.

6. Patricia Jones-Jackson and Charles Joyner, "Contemporary Gullah Speech: Some Persistent Linguistic Features," *Journal of Black Studies* 13, no. 3 (March, 1983): 289–303.

7. Ibid., 292–94.

8. Cooley, *School Acres,* 11.

9. James McPherson, *The Abolitionist Legacy: From Reconstruction to the NAACP* (Princeton: Princeton University, 1975), 207. See David, "The Penn School of St. Helena," 17. Despite the vocational training offered at the school, David emphasizes Towne's commitment to an academic education equal to their White counterparts. Later, Towne added carpentry, nursing, sewing, and printing to the school's academic offerings in an effort to improve the quality of living on the island.

10. Gerald Robbins, "Laura Towne: White Pioneer in Negro Education, 1862–1901," *Journal of Education* 143 (April 1961): 40–64. See also United States. Department of the Treasury, *The Negroes at Port Royal.* "Report of E. L. Pierce, Government Agent to the Hon. Salmon P. Chase, Secretary of the Treasury" (Boston: R. F. Wallcut, 1862).

11. E. L. Pierce, "The Freedmen at Port Royal," 303–4.

12. Patricia Howell Michaelson, *Speaking Volumes: Women, Reading, and Speech in the Age of Austen* (Stanford: Stanford University, 2004), 189. Michaelson describes the Samuel B. Morse anthology *School Dialogues . . . Calculated to Promote an Easy and Elegant Mode of Conversation Among the Young Masters and Mistresses of the United States* (1797). This

popular nineteenth-century resource contained elocution lessons designed to improve a student's communication and conversational skills.

13. Robbins, "Laura Towne," 46.

14. See Louise Ware, *George Foster Peabody: Banker, Philanthropist, Publicist* (Athens: University of Georgia, 1951), 115. Ware discusses Cooley's visit to Peabody's summer home and his invitation for her to assume leadership of Penn School. Frissell's position as head trustee for Penn School and his steadfast support of Cooley's administration confirm his involvement in the choice of Cooley.

15. Ibid., 15. In defense of Towne and the Penn School faculty, there was a shortage of qualified teachers in the Sea Islands region that prompted the school to assume leadership in teacher preparation.

16. Cooley, *School Acres,* 36.

17. Ibid.

18. Ibid. See also Michael Wolfe, *The Abundant Life Prevails: Religious Traditions of Saint Helena Island* (Waco: Baylor University Press, 2000), 63. Wolfe references a quote by Frissell, who envisioned Penn School as an opportunity to develop a "plan for industrial education that would benefit the entire rural South." See also W. E. B. Du Bois, "The Browsing Reader," *Crisis* (November 1930): 378. Du Bois, who originally was a supporter of the Penn School, criticizes the Penn School's economic and social programs that were more focused on vocational training.

19. Cooley, *School Acres,* 82–83.

20. Ibid.

21. "The Forty-Third Report of the Principal of the Penn Normal, Industrial, and Agricultural School, 1906," in PSP.

22. Cooley, *School Acres,* 151.

23. Elizabeth Pearson, ed., *Letters from Port Royal, 1862–1868* (Boston: W. B. Clarke, 1906), 15, 25, 125. See also Wolfe, *The Abundant Life Prevails,* 56.

24. Ron Daise "Biography," *Metacritic,* accessed September 2, 2015, http://www.meta critic.com/person/ron-daise?filter-options=tv.

25. Ralph Robert Middleton, interview by author Eric Crawford, Saint Helena Island, SC, April 20, 2009.

26. Towne, *Letters and Diary,* 79, 80, 144, 256, 296. In later years, the Penn School offered a band class.

27. Ibid., 114. Towne recalls the presence of Colonel Robert Gould Shaw and the Fifty-Fourth Massachusetts (Colored) Regiment in the audience during the Fourth-of-July program in 1863.

28. James Greenleaf, Library of Congress, Rare Book and Special Collections Division, *America Singing: Nineteenth-Century Song Sheets.*

29. Ira Sankey, *Sacred Songs and Solos, Sung by I. D. Sankey, etc . . .* (London: Morgan and Scott, 1873). In April 1862 Towne discusses the addition of new lyrics to "John Brown's Song," which may refer to the new words published in the February 1862 edition of the *Atlantic Monthly* by Julia Ward Howe. These words came from Howe's poem, "Battle Hymn of the Republic," which became the title of the new song. See Merrill Peterson, *John Brown: The Legend Revisited* (Charlottesville: University of Virginia Press, 2004), 34.

30. Charlotte Forten (Grimké), *The Journal of Charlotte L. Forten* (New York: Dryden,

1953), 132–37. Charlotte Forten discusses the complexity of Thomas Moore's 1816 hymn "Sound the Loud Timbrel," her difficulty in learning to play the hymn on the organ, and the success of the performance.

31. M. R. S., "Visitor's Account," cited in Epstein, *Sinful Tunes*, 275.

32. Towne, *Letters and Diary*, 237.

33. James Blake, Letter to "Miss Stevenson," *The Freedmen's Record* 1 (February 1865): 28.

34. "The Mystery Play for St. Helena Island, 1950," in PSP.

35. Cooley, *Homes of the Freed*, 154.

36. Raboteau, *Slave Religion*, 224. Raboteau states that traditionally Christmas had been more of a holiday than a holy day for many slaves. Slaves were more celebratory of the time off from work than of Christ's birth.

37. Rossa Cooley, *School Acres: An Adventure in Rural Education* (New Haven, CT: Yale University Press, 1930), 97.

38. Ibid.

39. Cited in Jacoway, *Yankee Missionaries*, 151. See also Cooley, *Homes of the Freed*, xiii; Cooley, *School Acres*; Johnson, *Folk Culture on St. Helena Island*, 171; Woofter, *Black Yeomanry*, 111. See also Hebert Covey, *African American Slave Medicine: Herbal and Non-Herbal Treatments* (Lanham: Lexington Books, 2007), 52–54. Covey includes several interviews of slave midwives which reveal varying levels of obstetric training. See also Elsie Parsons, *Folk-Lore of the Sea Islands, South Carolina* (New York: American Folk-Lore Society, 1969), 197. Parsons includes folktales that give graphic details of home remedies for childbirth and childhood illnesses.

40. Michael Haines, "Fertility and Mortality in the United States," EH.Net Encyclopedia, edited by Robert Whaples, http://eh.net/encyclopedia/article/haines.demography (accessed March 19, 2008). See also Kiser, *Sea Island to City*, 72–73. Kiser confirms the annual number of deaths of children under the age of one to be 48 per 1,000 births during the period of 1920 to 1928.

41. Midwives "Christmas Party" on December 15, 1955, AFS 11303–1134, Penn Community Services/Religious Songs and Services Collection, The American Folklife Center, The Library of Congress, Washington, DC. During this Christmas party, the spiritual "Mary Had a Baby, Aye Lawd" was performed.

42. Ruth Crawford Seeger, *American Folk Songs for Children in Home, School and Nursery School; A Book for Children, Parents and Teachers*. Garden City (New York: Doubleday & Co, 1948), 48. See also Ruth Crawford Seeger, *American Folk Songs for Christmas; Illustrated by Barbara Cooney* (Garden City, NY: Doubleday, 1953).

43. Minnie (Gracie) Gadson, telephone interview by author Eric Crawford, August 13, 2010.

44. Towne, *Letters and Diary*, 35. Towne described this spiritual as one of the most touching she had ever heard.

45. Allen, Ware, and Garrison, *Slave Songs*, 7.

46. Charles Nordhoff, *The Freedmen of South-Carolina Some Account of Their Appearance, Character, Condition, and Peculiar Customs* (New York: Charles T. Evans, 1863), 10. Cited in Epstein, *Sinful Tunes*, 276.

47. Cited in Willie Lee Rose, *Rehearsal for Reconstruction* (Indianapolis: The Bobbs-Merrill Company Inc., 1964), 168.

48. W. E. B. Du Bois, *The Souls of Black Folk. Essays and Sketches . . . Second Edition* (A. C. McClurg & Co: Chicago, 1903), 255.

49. Forten and Stevenson, *The Journals of Charlotte Forten Grimké*, 391.

50. Wolfe, *The Abundant Life Prevails*, 46.

51. "Album of Native Sea Island Spiritual Recordings," produced by John Silver, Penn Normal, Industrial, and Agricultural School Collection, American Folklife Center, Library of Congress, Washington, DC, [22,485] CD, 1942. See also *To Live as Free Men*, directed by John Silver, Saint Helena Island, SC: Castle Films, 1942..

52. *To Live as Free Men*, directed by Silver. Cooley expressed these sentiments throughout this movie sponsored by Penn School.

53. Jacoway, *Yankee Missionaries*, 108.

54. Hampton Institute, *Hampton Normal and Agricultural Institute* (Hampton, VA: Normal School Steam Press, 1888), 89.

55. Samuel Chapman Armstrong and Helen Lou James, "Why Penn School Is Needed On St. Helena Island," *The Southern Workman* 37 (1908): 93. See Lawton, "The Religious Life," 76. Lawton interviewed twelve ministers who did not feel that the shout had a religious function. See also G. R. Wilson, "The Religion of the American Negro Slave: His Attitude Toward Life and Death," *The Journal of Negro History* 8 (1923): 57.

56. Cooley, *School Acres*, 151.

57. Ibid.

58. Eleanor Barnwell, ed., *Memories of Penn School* (St. Helena Island, SC: Penn Center, 2002).

59. See Ray Allen, "Shouting the Church: Narrative and Vocal Improvisation in the African American Gospel Quartet Performance," *The Journal of American Folklore* 104, no. 413 (Summer 1991): 299–300. Allen provides a transcription of an African American quartet's performance that includes vocal interjections such as "Oh Lordy" and "Yeah" that are in parentheses and separated from the melody's primary text.

60. Allen, Ware, and Garrison, *Slave Songs*, xxii. Allen discusses his inability, in some instances, to separate the "interjaculatory" words from the melody. Ballanta-Taylor referred to these interjections as "exclamatory words" and cited the leader's texts "O Sinner, O Gambler" and "O Hypocrite" as representative examples. These vocal interjections stand apart from the melodic line and, unlike Allen's version, are not part of the song's melody.

61. I recorded this pray's house performance at Jenkins Praise House, Saint Helena Island, SC, on May 10, 2009. This spiritual was led by the pray's house leader James Garfield Smalls and is considered by other islanders to be his song.

62. The "Echoes of Penn" singers normally choose four or five of these Penn favorites to sing for each Community Sings program.

CHAPTER 3

1. Jacoway, *Yankee Missionaries*, 74.

2. Rossa Cooley, *Homes of the Freed* (New York: Negro Universities Press, 1926), 108.

3. Ibid., 153.

4. Ibid., 84.

5. Rosa Cooley, *School Acres: An Adventure in Rural Education* (New Haven, CT: Yale University Press, 1930), 94–95.

6. Guy B. Johnson, *Folk Culture on St. Helena Island, South Carolina* (Chapel Hill: University of North Carolina, 1930), 71.

7. Cooley, *Homes of the Freed,* 100, 101.

8. Laura Towne, "Pioneer Work on the Sea Islands," *Southern Workman* 30 (July 1901): 397–401.

9. Towne, "Pioneer Work"; also see Cooley, *Homes of the Freed* (New York: Negro Universities Press, 1926), 125.

10. Cooley, *Homes of the Freed,* 130–31.

11. Janet Hutchison, "Better Homes and Gullah," *Agricultural History* 67, 2 (Spring 1993): 105. Hutchison discusses Saint Helena Island's loss of half of its population between 1900 and 1930. The island population in 1900 was 9,000, but it had decreased to 4,625 by 1930.

12. Janet Hutchison, "The Cure for Domestic Neglect: Better Homes in America, 1922–1935," *Perspectives Vernacular Architecture* 2 (1986): 168–78.

13. Cooley, *Homes of the Freed,* 156. Cooley discusses the $50.00 third prize award and the $200.00 second prize award. See Jacoway, *Yankee Missionaries,* 149. Jacoway references a special first prize Saint Helena received without providing details on the special designation of the prize and the award dollar amount.

14. Minnie (Gracie) Gadson, telephone interview by author Eric Crawford, February 3, 2010. Minnie (Gracie) Gadson refers to this service as a housewarming.

15. "Listing of spirituals from house blessing programs," PSP.

16. Minnie (Gracie) Gadson, singer, telephone interview by author Eric Crawford, February 3, 2010.

17. Cooley, *School Acres,* 103.

18. Cooley, *Homes of the Freed,* 150.

19. Ibid. Cooley recalls the beautiful tenor voice of Joshua E. Blanton that will always be remembered on the island.

20. Courtney Siceloff, "Negro Religious Songs and Services," [AFS 11,303–11,304] reel to reel, American Folklife Center, Library of Congress, Washington, DC, ca. 1955.

21. Rev. Dr. Kenneth Doe, telephone interview by author Eric Crawford, February 1, 2010.

22. Wolfe, *The Abundant Life Prevails,* 123.

23. Ibid, 124. See also National Parks Service. "Low Country Gullah Culture: Special Resource Study and Final Environmental Impact Statement," accessed February 8, 2010, www.nps.gov/sero/planning/gg_srs/ggsrs_section2.

24. Rev. Dr. Kenneth Doe, telephone interview by author Eric Crawford, February 1, 2010. Rev. Dr. Kenneth Doe explains that most churches assign a deacon to a specific community on the island, and often they are present for a house blessing in that community.

25. Cooley, *School Acres,* 103. Cooley uses the plural form "Sings" when referring to this event, and this will be the preferred spelling used. See also Jacoway, *Yankee Missionaries,*

125. It should be noted that the Historic Penn Center identifies the event as a Community Sing.

26. Jacoway, *Yankee Missionaries*, 125. See also "America Sea Islands," PSP. See also Cooley, *School Acres*, 101. The Community Sings were also used to disseminate important information to the community. During one service, Cooley read a letter from President Hoover's wife in thanks to the islanders for bestowing on her the title of First Lady of the Island.

27. Courtney Siceloff to Mrs. Rae Korson, Folklore Division Reference Librarian, March 31, 1956.

28. "Pre-Thanksgiving Program," Community Sings, November 18, 1973, PSP. This spiritual is believed to have originated in the Sea Islands.

29. Although the Community Sings program was included in church announcements, many of the congregation members I talked with were not going to the Community Sings. Moreover, church officials did not place any emphasis on church members attending this event.

30. "Penn School Founders' Day" program, Community Sings service held on Sunday April 19, 2009, Frissell Community House, Saint Helena Island, SC.

31. Lawton, "The Religious Life," 48.

32. Jacoway, *Yankee Missionaries*, 166. George Peabody used the Saint Helena Quartet in the summer of 1926 to garner support for the financially strapped Penn School. However, the Saint Helena Quartet's northern tour followed on the heels of the Hampton Quartet's successful tour, resulting in the meager sum of $382.98 in tour net dollars. See also Jacoway, *Yankee Missionaries*, 126.

33. Arthur Hayes, *Souvenir of the Class of 1902* (Hampton: Hampton Institute, 1902), 13. Vernon Smith, "The Hampton Institute Choir" (PhD diss., Florida State University, 1985): 78. Smith discusses Bessie Cleaveland's directorship of the Hampton Choir from 1892 through 1903.

34. Bessie Cleaveland comments in *Hampton Institute Catalog*, 1899–1900. See also Bessie Cleaveland, "Music in the Public Schools," *The Southern Workman* 30, no. 1 (January 1901): 208–10. The Holt system of sight reading was formally known as *The Normal Music Course*. See John Tufts and Hosea Holt, *The Normal Music Course: A Series of Exercises, Studies, and Songs* (Boston: W. Ware & Co., 1885). Considered to be the most significant sight-singing series of the late nineteenth century, this method consisted of five books that focused on contrapuntal two- and three-part singing exercises.

35. J. E. Smith, "Hampton at Penn School," *The Southern Workman* 46 (January-December 1917): 85–86.

36. Ibid. Carolyn Sampson, daughter of Anthony Watson, stated that her father played the clarinet in Hampton Institute's band. Carolyn Sampson, phone interview by author Eric Crawford, January 19, 2011.

37. J. E. Davis, "Hampton at Penn School," 46.

38. Ibid., 87–88.

39. Although Dett assumed direction of the Hampton Institute choirs, Drew remained at the university to direct the school's glee club.

40. Vernon Smith, 91.

41. Allen, Ware, and Garrison, *Slave Songs,* v.

42. The only harmony parts in the *Slave Songs* collection were occasional alto notes in spirituals nos. 27, 31, 32, 39, 44, and 76.

43. Ballanta-Taylor presented four-part harmonizations for seventy-eight of the 103 spirituals in his collection *Saint Helena Island Spirituals.*

44. Natalie Curtis Burlin, *Hampton Series Negro Folk-Songs* (New York: G. Schirmer, 1918–19), 47. Burlin describes the vocal peculiarities in Negro spirituals that are impossible to transcribe.

45. Barnwell, ed., *Memories of Penn School,* 9.

46. Louis Harlan and Raymond Smock, *Booker T. Washington Papers,* vol. 2 (University of Illinois University Press, 1972), 45.

47. See Federal Writer's Project, *Virginia: A Guide to the Old Dominion* (New York: US History Publishers, 1952), 152. Hampton Institute's seventeen singers gave their first concert at Lincoln Hall, Washington, DC, on February 15, 1873, to raise money for the school's Virginia Hall. See also Fenner, *Religious Folksong,* 144. Fenner provides the concert schedule for the 1874 choir tour. Notably, the November concert schedule contained twenty-six days of performances and only four days off for the singers.

48. Fenner, *Religious Folksongs,* 144.

49. Allen, Ware, and Garrison, *Slave Songs,* 55.

50. This listing of spirituals was amassed from the PSP and Ballanta-Taylor's *Saint Helena Island Spirituals.*

51. I interviewed several Penn School graduates who felt that these spirituals originated on the island.

52. Ronald Daise, *Reminiscences of Sea Island Heritage* (Orangeburg, SC: Sandlapper, 1986), 36.

53. I. M. A. Meyers, "Two Hundred Thousand for New Building Program at Denmark," *The Palmetto Leader,* June 27, 1931. See also "$159,000 Voted by Episcopals for Colored Schools," *The Baltimore Afro-American,* October 27, 1934; "Voorhees Singers in Atlantic City," *New Journal and Guide,* October 13, 1934; and "Happenings at Voorhees," *The Palmetto Leader,* June 21, 1928. The latter citation discusses the six-week trip through St. Louis, Minneapolis, Milwaukee, and South Dakota, which required traveling 500 miles each day.

54. "Voorhees Singers Make Hit at Episcopal Convention," *New Journal and Guide,* October 26, 1940.

55. "Voorhees College Gets a Junior Rating," *New Journal and Guide,* May 4, 1946.

CHAPTER 4

1. John Lovell, *Black Song: The Forge and the Flame: The Story of How the Afro-American Spiritual Was Hammered Out* (New York: Macmillan; London: Collier-Macmillan, 1972), 533. Lovell discusses Curtis's views in 1913 regarding the effectiveness of Negro music. After a performance at Carnegie Hall of the spiritual "O Freedom," Curtis felt that Negro music had led to an improved understanding between Whites and Blacks. In addition, Lovell offers examples of Negro spirituals being adapted for labor singing and for freedom songs.

2. Ibid.

3. Ibid.

4. Frances Grant, "Negro Patriotism and Negro Music," *New Outlook,* February 26, 1919, 343–47. See also "A Wartime Spiritual," *The New York Times* December 7, 1919.

5. NAACP, "The Looking Glass," *The Crisis* 17, no. 2 (December 1918): 76.

6. Grant, *New Outlook,* 343–46.

7. Ibid., 346.

8. Mr. Blanton was referenced earlier as an accomplished singer and Penn School teacher.

9. Grace Bigelow House, "Origin of the Hymn," *The Southern Workman* 47 (1918): 476. Although the majority of Burlin's text is new, she does include a reference to the spiritual's original chorus with the words "O Ride On, Leaders," "Ride on, Leaders."

10. Alfred Smith, *New Outlook,* 347.

11. Burlin, *Hampton Series Negro Folk-Songs,* 71.

12. Ibid., 71–72. The original text also included the biblical stories of Nicodemus and Samson.

13. John J. Niles and Margaret Thorniley Williamson, *Singing Soldiers* (New York: Scribner, 1927), 50, 60, 61.

14. See Robert Ferrell, *America's Deadliest Battle: Meuse-Argonne, 1918* (Lawrence: University Press of Kansas, 2007).

15. Ibid., 152.

16. Ibid., 42.

17. Andrew Huebner, *The Warrior Image: Soldiers in American Culture from the Second World War to the Vietnam Era* (Chapel Hill: University of North Carolina, 2008), 12.

18. Guy Benton Johnson Papers #3826, [Box 75, 1101, Series 5.5] Southern Historical Collection, The Wilson Library, University of North Carolina at Chapel Hill.

19. Horace Clarence Boyer, *How Sweet the Sound: The Golden Age of Gospel* (Washington, DC: Elliott & Clark, 1995), 23. Boyer refers to "Soldier in the Army of the Lord" as a shout song.

20. Grace Bigelow House, "The Hymn in the Camps," *The Southern Workman* 47 (1918): 477. See Emmett Scott, *Scott's Official History of the American Negro in the World War: A Complete and Authentic Narration, from Official Sources, of the Participation of American Soldiers of the Negro Race in the World War for Democracy: A Full Account of the War Work Organizations of Colored Men and Women and Other Civilian Activities, Including the Red Cross, the Y.M.C.A., the Y.W.C.A. and the War Camp Community Service, with Official Summary of Treaty of Peace and League of Nations Covenant* (Chicago: Victory Pub., 1919), 105. See also Jessie Smith, ed., *Notable Black Women* (Detroit: Gale Research, 1996), 270. Helen Hagan, a concert pianist, and Hugh Henry Proctor, a minister, accompanied Blanton on his trip to France.

21. House, "The Hymn in the Camps," 477.

22. "Martin Luther King Program," Community Sings, January 16, 1977, T-3615/89 LC, PSP.

23. Guy Benton Johnson Papers #3826 [1117].

24. House, "The Hymn in the Camps," 477.

25. Joshua Blanton, "Men in the Making," *The Southern Workman* 48 (November 1919): 17.

26. Ibid., 18.

27. Unknown author, "Folk Song in the Camps," *New York Times,* September 19, 1918.

28. Ibid., 38. Eight songs from the *Army Song Book* were identified as basic repertoire for every army soldier to learn. These were "The Star-Spangled Banner," "America," "The Battle Hymn of the Republic," "Old Black Joe," "Swanee River," "My Old Kentucky Home," "Roll, Jordan Roll," and the French national anthem "La Marseillaise."

29. Blanton, "Men in the Making," 21.

30. Samuel Floyd, *The Power of Black: Interpreting Its History from Africa to the United States* (New York: Oxford University Press, 1996), 100–131. Floyd discusses the Harlem Renaissance and the lesser known Chicago Renaissance that were responsible for the growth of ragtime, blues, jazz, and gospel.

31. Ralph Ellison, *Shadow and Act* (New York: Vintage Books, 1972), xiv.

32. United States of America, *Army Song Book,* 41.

33. Lauren Sklaroff, "Variety for the Servicemen: The Jubilee Show and the Paradox of Racializing Radio during World War II," *American Quarterly* 56, no. 4 (December 2004): 945. Sklaroff discusses the radio program "Jubilee" that featured Black jazz entertainers such as Duke Ellington and Lena Horne.

34. "The Enlisted Soldiers" was actually a text taken from the second verse of the hymn "They Look Like Men of War."

35. See R. Nathaniel Dett, *Religious Folk-Songs of the Negro as Sung at Hampton Institute* (Hampton, VA: Hampton Institute, 1927), 180. It was Armstrong who named this song the "Negro Battle Hymn" and presumably brought the hymn to Hampton Institute. See also Francis Trevelyan Miller, Robert Sampson Lanier, and Henry Wysham Lanier, *The Photographic History of the Civil War* (New York: The Review of Reviews Co., 1911), 352.

36. Carl Diton, *Thirty-Six South Carolina Spirituals* (New York: G. Schirmer, 1928), 6.

37. The word "wish" in the spiritual's text is interpreted to mean "faith" in this context.

38. Cornelia Bailey and Christena Bledsoe, *God, Dr. Buzzard, and the Bolito Man: A Saltwater Geechee Talks About Life on Sapelo Island* (New York: Doubleday, 2000), 318.

39. Ibid.

40. Bill Marscher and Fran Marscher, *The Great Sea Island Storm of 1893* (Macon, GA.: Mercer University Press, 2004), preface. The authors cite an estimated property loss of 32 billion dollars if the 1893 storm occurred today.

41. Rossa Cooley, letter to the editor, *The New York Times,* October 5, 1911.

42. Johnson, *Folk Culture on St. Helena Island,* 67. According to Johnson, this spiritual originated in Charleston, South Carolina, or Savannah, Georgia.

43. Jacoway, *Yankee Missionaries,* 139–40. Despite the devastation from the boll weevil, Jacoway found little migration away from the island. She credits the low numbers of islanders leaving the island to Penn School's attempts to get farmers to grow alternative crops like peanuts, soybeans, sweet potatoes, and lettuce.

44. International Trade Centre, "Cotton Exporter's Guide," 2009–10, accessed April 9, 2010, www.cottonguide.org/chapter-5/extra-long-staple-cotton. Extra long staple cotton was referred to as Sea Island cotton in the 1600s and 1700s because of its almost exclusive cultivation in this region. See Jacoway, *Yankee Missionaries,* 140. Jacoway discusses the long staple cotton's characteristic fine, long fibers that made it the world's most beautiful cotton cloth.

45. See Paul Oliver, *Songsters and Saints: Vocal Traditions on Race Records* (Cambridge: Cambridge University Press, 1984), 250. Oliver gives the lyrics of "The Ballad of the Boll Weevil" song. There is no evidence of the boll weevil song ever being a part of the Saint Helena Island repertoire of spirituals.

46. "The Boll Weevil Song," The University of Illinois at Chicago, accessed February 12, 2015, http://www.uic.edu/educ/bctpi/historyGIS/greatmigration/gmdocs/boll_weevil _song.html.

47. Pierre McGowan, *The Gullah Mailman* (Raleigh, NC: Pentland Press, 2000), 71.

48. Cynthia Gregory Smalls, "Elements that Impact the Retentions of the Gullah Culture on the Sea Islands" (PhD diss., Walden University, 2004), 65.

49. Beaufort County Court, *Report of the Clerk of General Sessions*, Beaufort County, South Carolina, 1931–44.

50. McGowan, 33.

51. Beaufort County Court, *Report of the Clerk of Court of General Sessions*, Beaufort County, South Carolina, 1956. There were a total of nineteen cases of driving under the influence in 1956 in Beaufort County with a majority of them involving African Americans on Saint Helena Island.

52. Courtney Siceloff, "Negro Religious Songs and Services mid-1950s" (sound recording) AFS 11,303–11,304, Library of Congress, Washington, DC.

53. Ibid.

54. For a discussion of the use of the sea islands' songs in the civil rights movement, see Guy Carawan, Candie Carawan, Bob Yellin, and Ethel Raim, *Ain't You Got a Right to the Tree of Life?: The People of Johns Island, South Carolina, Their Faces, Their Words, and Their Songs* (New York: Simon and Schuster, 1966). In the early days of the Southern Christian Leadership Conference, Martin Luther King Jr. held important organizational meetings at the Penn Center.

CHAPTER 5

1. Guy Carawan, Candie Carawan, Julian Bond, and Florence Reece, *Sing for Freedom: The Story of the Civil Rights Movement Through Its Songs* (Montgomery, AL: NewSouth Books, 2007), xvii.

2. Kristen Turner, "Guy and Candie Carawan: Mediating the Music of the Civil Rights Movement" (PhD diss., University of North Carolina at Chapel Hill, 2011), 16.

3. Ibid., 17.

4. Julius Lester, interview by author Eric Crawford, May 24, 2017.

5. Ronald Cohen and Rachel Clare Donaldson, *Roots of the Revival: American and British Folk Music in the 1950s* (Urbana: University of Illinois Press, 2014), 141. Josh Dunson, music journalist, is recalling his discussions with Carawan. See Henry Hampton, *Voices of Freedom: An Oral History of the Civil Rights Movement from the 1950s Through the 1980s* (New York: Bantam, 2011), 30. During the bus boycotts, Coretta Scott King confirmed hearing hymns such as "What a Friend We Have in Jesus" and "What a Fellowship" as well as the spirituals "Lord, I Want to Be a Christian in My Heart," "Oh Freedom," and "Go Down Moses."

6. Cohen and Donaldson, *Roots of Revival*.

7. John Glen, *Highlander: No Ordinary School* (Knoxville: University of Tennessee

Press, 1996), 164–65. Glen suggests that Horton may have died from kidney aggravation caused by drinking moonshine and not typewriter cleaning fluid.

8. Josh Dunson, *Freedom in the Air: Song Movement of the Sixties* (New York: International Publishers, 1965), 29. See Ronald Cohen, "Agnes 'Sis' Cunningham and Labor Songs in the Depression South," in *Radicalism in the South since Reconstruction,* edited by Chris Green, Rachel Rubin, and James Smethurst (New York: Palgrave Macmillan, 2006), 90. The author of "Strange Things Happening in This Land" was the African American sharecropper-organizer John Handcox. Handcox was active in Monroe County, Arkansas, and was a singer in the Southern Tenant Farmers' Union (STFU). His most popular song was "We're Gonna Roll the Union On."

9. Labor Union Songs, undated, MSS 265 B70 F7 Part 2, Highlander Research and Education Center Records, Wisconsin Historical Society, Library-Archives Division.

10. Society for the Preservation of Spirituals, *Gullah Lyrics to Carolina Low Country Spirituals* (Charleston, SC: Society for the Preservation of Spirituals, 2007), 37.

11. Allen, Ware, and Garrison, *Slave Songs,* 3.

12. Bernice Johnson Reagon, "Let the Church Say Freedom," *Black Music Research Journal* 7 (1987): 110. "We Shall Not Be Moved" was equally popular as a civil rights song. For example, the great civil rights composer and singer Matthew Jones sang this spiritual during a mass meeting in Greenwood, Mississippi, not long after the death of Medgar Evers. In his adaptation, he directly addresses Mississippi "Governor Johnson."

13. Eric Thomas Chester, *The Wobblies in Their Heyday: The Rise and Destruction of the Industrial Workers of the World during the World War I Era* (Santa Barbara, CA: Praeger Publishers, 2014), xii. The IWW was a powerful union in the 1910s and 1920s that reached a membership of 150,000 members in 1917.

14. Dorian Lynskey, *33 Revolutions Per Minute* (London: Faber, 2013), 33–34. See also Carawan, *Sing for Freedom: The Story of the Civil Rights Movement,* 8. Guy Carawan lists some of the former texts of "We Shall Overcome" and the additional verses provided by Zilphia Horton and Pete Seeger.

15. David Spener, *We Shall Not Be Moved/No Nos Moverán: Biography of a Song of Struggle* (Philadelphia, Temple University, 2016), 41.

16. Lee Hays and Robert S. Koppelman, *"Sing Out, Warning! Sing Out, Love!": The Writings of Lee Hays* (Amherst, MA: University of Massachusetts Press, 2010), 70. Hays's use of the term country refers to the Cotton Belt, which encompasses the mountain system from Virginia through the Carolinas and Georgia into Alabama, northward through Tennessee, Kentucky, and Missouri. See Congressional Documents of the House of Representatives for the Second Session of the Forty-Ninth Congress, *Statistics of Norfolk* (Washington, DC: Government Printing Office, 1886–87), 93.

17. Carawan, *Sing for Freedom,* 8.

18. Archie Green, *Sing for Freedom: In the Community, on the Campus* (Monteagle, TN: Highlander Folk School, 1960).

19. Waldemar Hille, "Way Down in Egypt Land." (Labor Union Songs, undated, MSS 265 B70 F7 Part 2, Highlander Research and Education Center Records, Wisconsin Historical Society, Library-Archives Division.)

20. The use of the designation "adaptation of a traditional song" gives copyright to this arrangement although this spiritual is considered public domain. See also Joanne Grant,

"Freedom Songs," *Sing Out! The Folk Song Magazine* 14, no. 2 (April–May 1964): 68. In her book review of the Carawan's publication *We Shall Overcome*, Grant is concerned about Carawan's use of "traditional" for the source of their spirituals. She finds it of value to know "the original words of the songs as it helps demonstrate the inventiveness of the young students who are, in the main, responsible for the new songs created out of the old."

21. John Robb, Jack Loeffler, and Enrique R. Lamadrid, *Hispanic Folk Music of New Mexico and the Southwest A Self-Portrait of a People* (Albuquerque, NM: University of New Mexico Press, 2014), 4. The authors argue that folk songs tend to revert to a cultural norm as part of their evolution. A culture will prune away difficult or artsy elements in an attempt to achieve perfect simplicity. See Cecil Sharp, *English Folk-Song: Some Conclusions* (London: Simpkin, 1907), 14. According to Sharp, musical elements within a folk song that express the taste and feeling of a community will survive; whereas, aspects of a more personal nature will be eliminated.

22. Josh Dunson, "Slave Songs at the 'Sing for Freedom,'" *Broadside* 46 (May 30, 1964).

23. Ibid.

24. Guy Carawan, Candie Carawan, and Ethel Raim, *We Shall Overcome!: Songs of the Southern Freedom Movement* (New York: Oak Publications, 1963).

25. Guy Carawan, Candie Carawan, and Ethel Raim, *Freedom Is a Constant Struggle: Songs of the Freedom Movement* (New York: Oak Publications, 1968).

26. Peter Seeger, Bob Reiser, Guy Carawan, and Candie Carawan, *Everybody Says Freedom* (New York: Norton & Company, 2009), 29.

27. Ibid., 29.

28. The Mississippi Summer Project of 1964 also brought in such artists as Bob Dylan, Pete Seeger, Barbara Dane, Julius Lester, and Jackie Washington to sing in concerts and mass meetings. Julius Lester, email message to author Eric Crawford, July 20, 2017.

29. Dave Dennis, interview by author Eric Crawford, February 1, 2017.

30. Martin Luther King Jr., "The Birth of a Nation" (sermon, Montgomery, Alabama, April 7, 1957), The Martin Luther King Jr. Papers Project, http://kingencyclopedia .stanford.edu/primarydocuments/Vol4/7-Apr-1957_BirthOfANewNation.pdf.

31. Student Nonviolent Coordinating Committee, "Report on the Conference for Southern Community Cultural Revival," 1965, MSS 265 B71 folder 3, Highlander Research and Education Center Records, Wisconsin Historical Society, Library-Archives Division.

32. Alan Lomax, "Description of Sea Island Festivals," *News and Courier* (Charleston, SC), January 19, 1964.

33. Student Nonviolent Coordinating Committee, "Report on the Conference for Southern Community Cultural Revival," October 1965, Highlander Research and Education Center Archives, 65:2.

34. Ibid.

35. Ibid.

36. Willis Laurence James and Jon Michael Spencer, *Stars in de Elements Study of Negro Folk Music* (Durham, NC: Duke University Press, 1995), 148.

37. Eleanor Walden, interviewed by author Eric Crawford, May 13, 2017.

38. See Dunson, *Freedom in the Air*, 105. The Blacks in the audience were more receptive to Len Chandler's song "Time of the Tiger," Tom Paxton's "Ramblin' Boy," and Phil Ochs song "What's That I Hear Now?" Walden's song repertoire consisted mostly of satires

on popular songs and IWW songs such as "They Go Wild Over Me," The Preacher and the Slave," and "Pie in the Sky."

39. Dunson, *Freedom in the Air*, 105.

40. Ibid.

41. Guy Carawan, "Drinking of the Wine," *Sing Out! The Folk Song Magazine* 14, no. 2 (April–May 1964): 31.

42. Leon Friedman, *The Civil Rights Reader: Basic Documents of the Civil Rights Movement* (New York: Walker, 1968), 46. John Lewis was revered by civil rights leaders because of his over twenty arrests and several beatings. Lewis served as chairman of SNCC.

43. Unknown author, "Go Tell It on the Mountain," *Broadside the National Topical Magazine* 51 (October 20, 1964).

44. Ibid.

45. Robert Moses was beaten when he accompanied farmer Curtis Dawson and Reverend Alfred Knox as they tried to register to vote. Although he filed charges and the case went to trial, an all-White jury acquitted Sheriff E. L. Caston. Historian Taylor Branch asserts that Moses achieved a Christlike name within the SNCC organization. See Laura Visser-Maessen, *Robert Parris Moses: A Life in Civil Rights and Leadership at the Grassroots* (Chapel Hill: University of North Carolina, 2017), 71–73.

46. Kenneth Clark, *The Reminiscences of Kenneth B. Clark* (Alexandria, VA: Alexander Street Press, 2003), 158.

47. Peniel Joseph, *The Black Power Movement Rethinking the Civil Rights-Black Power Era* (Florence: Taylor and Francis, 2013), 3. Joseph classifies this period as the beginning of the demise of legal segregation and the attainment of voting rights. See also Elizabeth Hinton and Manning Marable, *The New Black History Revisiting the Second Reconstruction* (New York: Palgrave Macmillan, 2011), 158. The authors connect the heroic period to international developments in Cuba, Asia, and Africa, which provided Black American radicals with a glimpse of alternative political and world historic realities.

48. Julius Lester, "The Angry Children of Malcolm X," *Sing Out! The Folk Song Magazine* 16, no. 5 (October–November 1966): n.p.

49. Bernice Johnson Reagon, "Movement Songs that Moved the Nation," *Perspectives: The Civil Rights Quarterly* 15, no. 3 (Summer 1983): 28.

50. Rob Rosenthal and Richard Flacks, *Playing for Change: Music and Musicians in the Service of Social Movements* (Boulder, CO: Paradigm Publishers, 2011), 127–28.

CHAPTER 6

1. Charles Joyner, *Shared Traditions: Southern History and Folk Culture* (Urbana: University of Illinois, 1999), 257.

2. Ibid.

3. Ibid., 258.

4. Regula Qureshi, "Music Sound and Contextual Input: A Performance Model for Musical Analysis," *Ethnomusicology* 31 (1987), 71. See also Helen Myers, *Ethnomusicology: An Introduction* (New York: W. W. Norton, 1992), 103.

5. Frank Mitchell, *Navajo Blessingway Singer: The Autobiography of Frank Mitchell, 1881–1967* (Tucson: University of Arizona Press, 1980). Virginia Danielson, *The Voice of Egypt: Umm Kulthūm, Arabic Song, and Egyptian Society in the Twentieth Century*

(Chicago: University of Chicago Press, 2008). See also Bruno Nettl, *The Study of Ethno-musicology: Thirty-One Issues and Concepts* (Urbana: University of Illinois Press, 2006), 240–41.

6. Patricia Guthrie, "Catching Sense: The Meaning of Plantation Membership Among Blacks on St. Helena, South Carolina" (PhD diss., The University of Rochester, 1977), 91. Guthrie discusses the pray's house on Hopes Plantation that no longer holds services and is in a rapid state of decay.

7. See Kiser, *Sea Island to City*, 113. Kiser explains that friends and relatives in large cities stimulate interest among young islanders to leave the island.

8. Heritage Days is a three-day event celebrating the Gullah culture on Saint Helena Island. During Heritage Days on November 12–14, 2009, I was strongly encouraged to attend the Ebenezer Baptist Church services by the Penn Center staff.

9. Minnie (Gracie) Gadson, in-person interview with the author.

10. Ibid.

11. Guthrie, "Catching Sense," 90–92.

12. Ibid.

13. Minnie (Gracie) Gadson, August 11, 2009, interview.

14. Joyner, *Shared Traditions*, 258–59.

15. Minnie (Gracie) Gadson, August 11, 2009, interview.

16. Joyner, *Shared Traditions*, 259.

17. Minnie (Gracie) Gadson, August 11, 2009, interview.

18. In the eight services I observed at Ebenezer Baptist Church, Gracie sang at least one spiritual in each one.

19. James Garfield Smalls, in-person interview by author Eric Crawford, Saint Helena Island, SC, August 12, 2009.

20. Ibid.

21. This schism among the Brick Baptist membership is briefly discussed on Bethesda Christian Fellowship's website, accessed October 13, 2010, http://welcome2bethesda.org /Church%20History.html.

22. Garfield is the leader of the Senior Choir, an ensemble whose repertoire is mainly hymns.

23. There is acknowledgment that the emotionalism could be traced to the schism that led former Ebenezer members to form Bethesda.

24. The Bethesda Christian Fellowship services are almost entirely devoid of any spirituals.

25. Smalls, August 12, 2009, interview.

26. There is a more detailed discussion of the Penn School policy toward formal speech in chapter 2.

27. Guthrie, "Catching Sense," 92.

28. Ibid., 92–93.

29. Ibid.

30. Smalls, August 12, 2009, interview.

31. Ibid.

32. Ibid.

33. Ibid.

34. Art Rosenbaum, *Shout Because You're Free: The African American Ring Shout Tradition in Coastal Georgia* (Athens: University of Georgia Press, 1998), 71.

APPENDIX: NOTE ON GULLAH SONGBOOK

1. Allen, Ware, and Garrison, *Slave Songs*, 3. See also Spaulding, "Under the Palmetto," 188–203.

2. Lydia Parrish, *Slave Songs of the Georgia Sea Islands* (Athens: University of Georgia Press, 1942).

3. Raboteau, *Slave Religion,* 213.

4. Ibid., 217. Raboteau quotes this passage given by a former slave named Peter Randolph from Prince George County, Virginia.

5. Charlotte Forten and Brenda E. Stevenson, *The Journals of Charlotte Forten Grimké* (New York: Oxford University Press, 2011), 398.

6. Rose Murray, in-person interview with the author, December 12, 2020.

APPENDIX: GULLAH SONGBOOK

1. Minnie (Gracie) Gadson recorded this spiritual on Saint Helena Island, SC, August 11, 2009. See Art Rosenbaum, Margo Newmark Rosenbaum, and Johann S. Buis, *Shout Because You're Free: The African American Ring Shout Tradition in Coastal Georgia* (Athens: University of Georgia Press, 2013, 144). Rosenbaum discusses the pantomime involved in the shouting song "Eve and Adam."

2. William Francis Allen, Charles Pickard Ware, and Lucy McKim Garrison, *Slave Songs of the United States* (New York: A. Simpson, 1867), 32. Allen references this spiritual as being a shout song.

3. Nicholas George Ballanta-Taylor, *Saint Helena Island Spirituals* (New York: G. Schirmer, 1925), 35. This spiritual was confirmed by Gracie Gadsen, noted Saint Helena singer, as a shouting song.

4. Allen, Ware, and Garrison, *Slave Songs*, 9. See Henry George Spaulding, "Under the Palmetto," *Continental Monthly*, IV (August 1863): 198–99. Spaulding classified "There's A Meeting Here Tonight" as a shouting song.

5. Allen, Ware, and Garrison, *Slave Songs*, 8. Allen's description of this spiritual indicates its usage in the pray's house as a shouting song.

6. Allen, Ware, and Garrison, *Slave Songs*, xvi, 27–28. Allen cites this song as a rowing song and shouting song.

7. Allen, Ware, and Garrison, *Slave Songs*, 12. See Spaulding, "Under the Palmetto," 198–99. Spaulding cites this spiritual as being a shouting song and describes a recitative performance style for each verse.

8. Allen, Ware, and Garrison, *Slave Songs*, xvi, 10. Allen cites this spiritual as being a rowing and shouting song.

9. Allen, Ware, and Garrison, *Slave Songs*, 25. Allen cites this spiritual as being a shouting song. See also McIntosh County Shouters, *Slave Shout Songs from the Coast of Georgia,* custom compact disc series (Washington, DC: Smithsonian Folkways Recordings, 2003). On August 20, 1983, folklorist Art Rosenbaum recorded singers from McIntosh County, Georgia, performing a similar version of "Jubilee."

10. Allen, Ware, and Garrison, *Slave Songs*, xvi, 27. Allen cites this spiritual as being a rowing and shouting song. Minnie (Gracie) Gadson performed this shouting song for me.

11. James Garfield Smalls performed this spiritual on Saint Helena Island, SC, August 12, 2009.

12. Ballanta-Taylor, *Saint Helena Island Spirituals*, 32. This spiritual was confirmed as a shouting song by pray's house leader Deacon James Garfield Smalls. See also Lydia Parrish, *Slave Songs of the Georgia Sea Islands* (Athens: University of Georgia Press, 1942), 225. Lydia Parrish also discusses this spiritual's use as a work song during rice making.

13. Allen, Ware, and Garrison, *Slave Songs*, 36. Allen cites this spiritual as being a shouting song.

14. Minnie (Gracie) Gadson recorded this spiritual on Saint Helena Island, SC, August 11, 2009. Gadson cites "Way Up in Egypt Land" as being a shouting spiritual.

15. Ballanta-Taylor, *Saint Helena Island Spirituals*, 45. Deacon James Garfield Smalls cites this spiritual as a shouting song.

16. Mary Armstrong, Helen Wilhelmina Ludlow, and Thomas Fenner, *Hampton and Its Students* (New York: G. P. Putnam's sons, 1874), 184. Allen, Ware, and Garrison, *Slave Songs*, xii. One of the Gullah customs, often alluded to in the songs, is that of wandering through the woods and swamps, when under religious excitement. To get religion is with them to "fin' dat ting."

17. Allen, Ware, and Garrison, *Slave Songs*, xii.

18. Ibid.

19. *To Live as Free Men*, directed by John Silver, Saint Helena Island, SC: Castle Films, 1942. Allen, Ware, and Garrison, *Slave Songs*, xii.

20. Allen, Ware, and Garrison, *Slave Songs*, xii.

21. Ballanta-Taylor, *Saint Helena Island Spirituals*, 90. See also Rossa Cooley, *School Acres: An Adventure in Rural Education* (New Haven, CT: Yale University Press, 1930), 147. Cooley cites this spiritual's use during the Christmas Mystery Play.

22. Ballanta-Taylor, *Saint Helena Island Spirituals*, 40. Refer to "The Nativity," Community Sings, T-3615/91, CD, PSP, December 13, 1971, and Midwives "Christmas Party," AFS 11303–1134, CD, PSP, December 15, 1955. This spiritual was popular on the island during the Christmas season.

23. Ballanta-Taylor, *Saint Helena Island Spirituals*, 41. Refer to "The Nativity," Community Sings, T-3615/91, CD, PSP, December 13, 1971 and Midwives "Christmas Party," AFS 11303–1134, CD, PSP, December 15, 1955. This spiritual was popular on the island during the Christmas season.

24. Ballanta-Taylor, *Saint Helena Island Spirituals*, 91. See also Cooley, *School Acres*, 146. Cooley cites this spiritual's use during the Christmas Mystery Play.

25. *To Live as Free Men*, directed by Silver. This spiritual's text implies usage during the communion service.

26. Ballanta-Taylor, *Saint Helena Island Spirituals*, 80. This spiritual's text strongly suggests its use during the Easter season.

27. Ballanta-Taylor, *Saint Helena Island Spirituals*, 65. On August 19, 2009, Pastor Kenneth Doe led his Bethesda Christian Fellowship Church congregation in the singing of this spiritual during a communion service.

28. Minnie (Gracie) Gadson recorded this spiritual on Saint Helena Island, SC, August 11, 2009. Gadson cites "Drinkin' of the Wine" as a communion song. See also Society for the Preservation of Spirituals, *Gullah Lyrics to Carolina Low Country Spirituals* (Charleston, SC: Society for the Preservation of Spirituals, 2007), 18.

29. Allen, Ware, and Garrison, *Slave Songs*, 10. See also Allen, *Diary, 1863–1866*. Cited in Epstein, *Sinful Tunes*, 354. Allen comments on hearing this (new) spiritual on April 7, 1864, near Easter. The text of this composition confirms usage for the Easter season.

30. "Let Us Break Bread Together," sung by James Garfield Smalls, Saint Helena Island, SC, August 12, 2009. This spiritual remains a favorite communion song during worship services on Saint Helena Island.

31. Ballanta-Taylor, *Saint Helena Island Spirituals*, 56. "Looka How Dey Done Muh Lord" was sung on March 19, 1978, during a pre-Easter service held on the Penn School campus.

32. Minnie (Gracie) Gadson recorded this spiritual on Saint Helena Island, SC, August 11, 2009. Gadson cites this spiritual's use during baptism.

33. Allen, Ware, and Garrison, *Slave Songs*, 25. This spiritual's text indicates its usage during the Easter season.

34. Armstrong, Ludlow, and Fenner, *Hampton and Its Students*, 222–23. As a Penn School favorite, this spiritual was often sung at the school using the slightly altered title "Work Together Children."

35. "De Ole Sheep Done Know de Road" is used in sacred and secular settings and is one of the most popular spirituals on the island. See Armstrong, Ludlow, and Fenner, *Hampton and Its Students*, 198; and Ronald Daise, *Reminiscences of Sea Island Heritage*, 36. Saint Helena Island native Daise discusses this song in his book.

36. Ballanta-Taylor, *Saint Helena Island Spirituals*, 34.

37. Ibid., 39. See Guy Benton Johnson, *Folk Culture on St. Helen Island* (Chapel Hill: University of North Carolina Press, 1930), 60. Guy Johnson states that the spiritual "Don't Let the Wind Blow Here No More" was written in response to the devastation done by the Great Sea Island Hurricane of 1893. It was used in sacred or secular settings.

38. "Don't You Take Everybody for Your Friend," sung by James Garfield Smalls, Saint Helena Island, SC, August 12, 2009. Deacon Smalls confirm this spiritual's general use during the island's church services.

39. Armstrong, Ludlow, and Fenner, *Hampton and Its Students*, 235–36. Deacon Smalls sings this spiritual as an opening song or offering song during a church service and during prayer and pray's house services.

40. Ballanta-Taylor, *Saint Helena Island Spirituals*, 88. Deacon Smalls confirms this spiritual's general use during church services.

41. *To Live as Free Men*, directed by Silver. This spiritual's unique use of the opening lines of the "Lord's Prayer" and rhyming biblical couplets make its liturgical use unclear.

42. Community Sings, "Glory, Glory, Hallelujah," Southern Historical Collection University of North Carolina at Chapel Hill, T-3615, recorded in 1973 on Saint Helena Island, SC. This spiritual was performed in a Community Sings in May 1973 and is considered a Penn School favorite. According to Gracie Gadson, this spiritual had general usage in a church service.

43. Diton, *Thirty-Six South Carolina Spirituals,* 16. This spiritual was a popular song during house blessing services on the island.

44. Minnie (Gracie) Gadson in-person interview by author, Saint Helena Island, SC, August 11, 2009. Gracie confirms this spiritual's general usage in island church services.

45. *To Live as Free Men,* directed by Silver. This spiritual was a favorite during Arbor Day celebrations.

46. Minnie (Gracie) Gadson recorded this spiritual on Saint Helena Island, SC, August 11, 2009. During my visits to the island in 2009 and 2010, I often heard this spiritual performed during the devotional period of a church service.

47. Allen, Ware, and Garrison, *Slave Songs,* 55. Allen references this spiritual's plaintive melody that moved General Howard to tears during a formal ceremony. See M. R. S. "A Visitor's Account of Our Sea Island Schools," *Pennsylvania Freedman's Bulletin* (October 1866): 6. An account given by a visitor to the Sea Islands known as M. R. S. cites this spiritual's usage as a shouting song.

48. *To Live as Free Men,* directed by Silver. See also Burlin, *Hampton Series Negro Folk-Songs,* 4–5. Burlin used the melody of this spiritual for her World War I anthem "Hymn of Freedom."

49. Diton, *Thirty-Six South Carolina Spirituals,* 40. PSP, "Spring Festival," Southern Historical Collection, University of North Carolina at Chapel Hill, T-3615/163 LC, May 5, 1973. The Saint Helena Group recorded this spiritual in 1973 during a dramatization of yester-year spirituals.

50. "Some Gone Love You, Some Gone Hate You," sung by James Garfield Smalls, Saint Helena Island, SC, August 12, 2009. Smalls cites this spiritual's general usage in the island's church services. See Charlotte L. Forten and Brenda Stevenson, *The Journals of Charlotte Forten Grimké: The Schomburg Library of Nineteenth-Century Black Women Writers* (New York: Oxford University Press, 1988), 136. Forten's entry in her diary references this spiritual's use as a shouting song.

51. "Stay In the Fiel,'" sung by James Garfield Smalls, Saint Helena Island, SC, August 12, 2009. Although rarely performed today, Smalls cites this spiritual's general usage in the island's church services.

52. "Sweet Honey in the Rock," sung by James Garfield Smalls, Saint Helena Island, SC, August 12, 2009. Although rarely performed today, Smalls confirms this spiritual's general usage in the island's church services.

53. PSP, "Brick Church Anniversary," Southern Historical Collection, University of North Carolina at Chapel Hill, T-3615/176 LC pt. 1, CD recording, 1973. This spiritual is used in sacred and secular settings.

54. "Father, I Stretch My Hands to Thee" sung by pray's house congregation, Saint Helena Island, SC, Thursday, July 16, 2009.

BIBLIOGRAPHY

MANUSCRIPTS

Bennett, John, Papers. [1176.00] South Carolina Historical Society, Charleston, SC, 1865–1956.

Coffin Point Plantation Journals. [9426] South Carolina Historical Society, Charleston, SC, 1800–1816.

Dabbs, Edith M., Collection of Papers Relating to Saint Helena Island, SC. [04285] Southern Historical Collection, University of North Carolina at Chapel Hill, 1791; 1860–1963.

Fripp, John Edwin, Papers. [00869] Southern Historical Collection, University of North Carolina at Chapel Hill, 1817–1944.

Highlander Research and Education Center Records. Wisconsin Historical Society, Library Archives Division.

Johnson, Guion Griffis, Papers. [04546] Southern Historical Collection, University of North Carolina at Chapel Hill, 1873–1987.

Johnson, Guy Benton, Papers. [03826] Southern Historical Collection, University of North Carolina at Chapel Hill, 1830–82, 1901–87.

Kester, Howard, Papers. [03834] Southern Historical Collection, University of North Carolina at Chapel Hill, 1923–72.

Odum, Howard Washington, Papers. [3167] Southern Historical Collection, University of North Carolina at Chapel Hill, 1908–82.

Penn School Papers (cited as PSP). [#3615] Southern Historical Collection, University of North Carolina at Chapel Hill, 1862–1978.

———. "Aiken Trip." Southern Historical Collection, University of North Carolina at Chapel Hill.

———. "Ballanta-Taylor to J. P. King." Southern Historical Collection, University of North Carolina at Chapel Hill, July 9, 1924.

———. "Chapel Service." Southern Historical Collection, University of North Carolina at Chapel Hill, April 25, 1932.

———. "Forty-Third Report of the Principal of the Penn School." Southern Historical Collection, University of North Carolina at Chapel Hill, 1906.

———. "Grace Bigelow House to Northern Sponsors." Southern Historical Collection, University of North Carolina at Chapel Hill.

———. "History of the Penn School." Southern Historical Collection, University of North Carolina at Chapel Hill.

———. "Listing of Spirituals from House Blessing Programs." Southern Historical Collection, University of North Carolina at Chapel Hill.

———. "The Mystery Play." Southern Historical Collection, University of North Carolina at Chapel Hill.

———. "Negro Folklore Evening Program." Southern Historical Collection, University of North Carolina at Chapel Hill. April 12, 1930.

———. Rossa Cooley's Syllabus for Bible Course at Hampton Institute." Southern Historical Collection, University of North Carolina at Chapel Hill, 1906.

Thorpe, David Franklin, Papers. [4262] Southern Historical Collection, University of North Carolina at Chapel Hill, 1854–1944 (bulk 1854–70).

Tombee Plantation Journal. [9390] South Carolina Historical Society, Charleston, SC, 1845–86.

FIELD RECORDINGS

Dougherty, Park. "Singing by the Society for the Preservation of Spirituals." [AFC 1982/015] CD, American Folklife Center, Library of Congress, Washington, DC, 1937–38, 1952–54, and 1988.

Johnson, Guy B. "Guy Benton Johnson Papers." [03826] wax cylinders. Southern Historical Collection, University of North Carolina at Chapel Hill, 1928–39.

———. "St. Helena Island Collection." [AFC 1990/025] CD. American Folklife Center Library of Congress, Washington, DC, 1928.

Penn Community Services. "Religious Songs and Services." [AFC 1957/006] CD. American Folklife Center, Library of Congress, Washington, DC, January 15, 1956.

Penn School Papers. "Brick Church Anniversary." [03615] CD. Southern Historical Collection, University of North Carolina at Chapel Hill, 1973.

———. "Community Sings." [03615] CD. Southern Historical Collection, University of North Carolina at Chapel Hill, November 1976.

———. "Community Sings, Pre-Easter Program." [03615] CD. Southern Historical Collection, University of North Carolina at Chapel Hill, March 1978.

———. "Interview of Charles Daniel Watson conducted by Agnes Sherman and Susan Caprich." [03615] CD. Southern Historical Collection, University of North Carolina at Chapel Hill, January 11, 1974.

———. "Martin Luther King Program." [03615/89] CD. Southern Historical Collection, University of North Carolina at Chapel Hill, January 16, 1977.

———. "Orange Grove Baptist Church at Brick Church." [03615] CD. Southern Historical Collection, University of North Carolina at Chapel Hill, September 17, 1971.

———. "Spring Festival." [03615] CD. Southern Historical Collection, University of North Carolina at Chapel Hill, May 1973.

Siceloff, Courtney. "Collection of Gullah Folk Music and Spirituals." [AFS 10,899] CD. American Folklife Center, Library of Congress, Washington, DC, ca. 1955.

———. "Negro Religious Songs and Services." [AFS 11,303–11,304] reel to reel. Library of Congress, Washington, DC, ca. 1955.

Silver, John A. "Album of Native Sea Island Spiritual Recordings." [AFS 22,485] CD. American Folklife Center, Library of Congress, Washington, DC, 1942.

PUBLISHED SOURCES

Abbington, James. *Readings in African American Church Music and Worship.* Chicago, IL: GIA, 2001.

Afrika, Llaila O. *The Gullah*. Beaufort, SC: Published by the Author, 1989.

Allen, Elizabeth. *Memorial of Joseph and Lucy Clark Allen: (Northborough, Mass.)*. Wisconsin: G. H. Ellis, 1891.

Allen, Irving. *The City in Slang: New York Life and Popular Speech*. New York: Oxford University Press, 1993.

Allen, Joseph. *The Centennial Celebration of the Town of Northborough, Mass., August 22, 1866*. Northborough, Mass., s.n., 1866.

Allen, Ray. "Shouting the Church: Narrative and Vocal Improvisation in the African American Gospel Quartet Performance." *The Journal of American Folklore* 104, no. 413 (Summer 1991): 295–317.

Allen, William. "Diary." MS, State Historical Society of Wisconsin, entry for December 25, 1863.

Allen, William Francis, Charles Pickard Ware, and Lucy McKim Garrison. *Slave Songs of the United States*. New York: A. Simpson, 1867.

American Bible Society. *De Good Nyews Bout Jedus Christ Wa Luke Write: The Gospel According to Luke in Gullah Sea Island Creole with Marginal Text of the King James Version*. New York: American Bible Society, 1994.

Anderson, Paul. "My Lord, What A Morning: The Sorrow Songs In Harlem Renaissance Thought." In *Symbolic Loss: The Ambiguity of Mourning and Memory at Century's End*, edited by Peter Homans, 83–100. Charlottesville: University of Virginia, 2000.

Ani, Marimba. *Let the Circle Be Unbroken: The Implications of African Spirituality in the Diaspora*. Trenton, NJ: Red Sea Press, 1980.

Armstrong, Mary Francis, Helen Wilhelmina Ludlow, and Thomas Fenner. *Hampton and Its Students*. New York: G. P. Putnam's Sons, 1874.

Armstrong, Samuel Chapman, and Helen Lou James. "Why Penn School Is Needed On St. Helena Island." *The Southern Workman* 37 (1908): 90–94.

Arrowood, Mary, and Thomas Hamilton. "Nine Negro Spirituals: 1850–1861, from Lower South Carolina." *Journal of American Folklore* 41, no. 162 (October–December 1928): 579–84.

Austin, Allan. *African Muslims in Antebellum America: Transatlantic Stories and Spiritual Struggles*. New York: Routledge, 1997.

Bailey, Ben. "The Lined-Hymn Tradition in Black Mississippi Churches." *The Black Perspective in Music* 6, no. 1 (Spring 1978): 3–17.

Bailey, Cornelia Walker, and Christina Bledsoe. *God, Dr. Buzzard, and the Bolito Man: A Saltwater Geechee Talks about Life on Sapelo Island*. New York: Doubleday, 2000.

Baird, Keith. "Guy B. Johnson Revisited: Another Look at Gullah." *Journal of Black Studies* 10, no. 4 (1980): 425–35.

Ball, Charles. *Slavery in the United States*. Miami, FL: Mnemosyne, 1969.

Ballanta-Taylor, Nicholas George Julius. *Saint Helena Island Spirituals*. New York: G. Schirmer, 1925.

Baraka, Amiri Imamu. *Black Music*. New York: W. Morrow, 1967.

Baring-Gould, Sabine. "Now the Day Is Over," *Lutheran Hymnal*. St. Louis: Concordia, 1865.

Barnwell, Eleanor, ed. *Memories of Penn School*. St. Helena Island, SC: Penn Center, 2002.

Barton, William E. *Old Plantation Hymns: A Collection of Hitherto Unpublished Melodies of the Slave and Freedman, with Historical and Descriptive Notes.* Boston: Lamson, Wolffe, 1899.

Bascom, William R. "Acculturation Among the Gullah Negroes." *American Anthropologist* 43 (January–March 1941): 43–50.

Bass, Robert Duncan. "Negro Songs from the Pedee County." *The Journal of American Folklore* 44, no. 174 (October–December 1931): 418–36.

Bayard, Samuel. "Prolegomena to the Study of the Principal Melodic Families of British-American Folksong." *Journal of American Folklore* 63, no. 247 (January–March 1950): 1–44.

———. "Two Representative Tune Families of British Tradition." *Midwest Folklore* 4, no. 1 (1954): 13–34.

Beaufort County Court. *Report of the Clerk of General Sessions.* Beaufort County, SC, 1931–44 and 1956.

Béhague, Gerard H. *Music and Black Ethnicity: The Caribbean and South America.* New Brunswick, NJ: Transaction Publishers, 1994.

Bellinger, Lucius. *Stray Leaves from the Port-Folio of a Methodist Local Preacher.* Macon, GA: J. W. Burke, 1870.

Bellows, Barbara. *A Talent for Living: Josephine Pinckney and the Charleston Literary Tradition.* Baton Rouge: Louisiana State University Press, 2006.

Benjamin, S. C. "The Sea Islands." *Harpers New Monthly Magazine* 57 (November 1878): 839–61.

Benmaman, Virginia Doubchan. "An Investigation of Reading Comprehension Ability of Black Fourth and Fifth Grade Students Who Are Reading Below Grade Level Utilizing Materials Written in Gullah and Standard English." Master's thesis, University of South Carolina, 1975.

Bennett, John. "Gullah: A Negro Patois, Part 1." *South Atlantic Quarterly* 7, no. 4 (October 1908): 332–47.

———. "Gullah: A Negro Patois, Part 2." *South Atlantic Quarterly* 8, no. 4 (January 1909): 39–52.

Beoku-Betts, Josephine. "We Got Our Way of Cooking Things: Women, Food, and Preservation of Cultural Identity among the Gullah." *Gender and Society* 9 (October 1995): 535–55.

Bickerton, Derek. *Roots of Language.* Ann Arbor, MI: Karoma, 1981.

Biggers, John. *The Web of Life in Africa.* Austin: University of Texas Press, 1996.

Billington, Ray Allen. "A Social Experiment: The Port Royal Journal of Charlotte L. Forten, 1862–1863." *The Journal of Negro History* 35, no. 3 (July 1950): 233–64.

Black, Gary. *My Friend the Gullah: A Collection of Personal Experiences.* Columbia, SC: R. L. Bryan, 1974.

Blake, James. Letter to "Miss Stevenson." *The Freedmen's Record* 1 (February 1865): 28

Blanton, Joshua. "One Man's Life Story." *Southern Workman* 52, no. 8 (August 1923): 405–8.

Blassingame, James. *The Slave Community: Plantation Life in the Antebellum South.* New York: Oxford University Press, 1979.

Bliss, Philip, and Emily Oakey. "What Shall the Harvest Be?" In *Gospel Hymns No. 2,* edited by Phillip Bliss and Ira Sankey, 90–91. New York: Biglow and Main, 1876.

Bost, Dolores. "Using Gullah in Public Life: The Life and Work of a Pastor in the Sea Islands." PhD diss., Columbia University, 2001.

Bostick, Douglass. *A Brief History of James Island: Jewel of the Sea Islands.* Charleston, SC: History Press, 2008.

Botkin, B. A. "Review: Untitled." *American Speech* 7, no. 1 (October 1931): 64–66.

Botume, Elizabeth Hyde. *First Days Amongst the Contrabands.* Boston: Lee and Shephard, 1893.

Bourdieu, Pierre, and Jean Claude Passeron. *Reproduction in Education, Society and Culture.* London: Sage, 1977.

Boyer, Horace Clarence. *How Sweet the Sound: The Golden Age of Gospel.* Washington, DC: Elliott & Clark, 1995.

Branch-Haislip, Grace C. "Haines Normal and Industrial Institute and Penn Normal and Industrial School: A Prospective on Black and White Educational Involvement." PhD diss., Rutgers University, 1982.

Breen, T. H., ed. *Shaping Southern Society: The Colonial Experience.* New York: Oxford University Press, 1976.

Bresee, Clyde. *Sea Island Yankee.* Chapel Hill, NC: Algonquin Books of Chapel Hill, 1986.

Brown, Alphonso. *A Gullah Guide to Charleston: Walking Through Black History.* Charleston, SC: History Press, 2008.

Brown, John Mason. "Songs of the Slave." *Lippincott's Magazine* 2 (December 1868): 617–23.

Brown, Sterling. "Negro Folk Expression: Spirituals, Seculars, Ballads and Work Songs." *Phylon* 14, no. 1 (1st Qtr., 1953): 45–61.

Bullock, Henry Allen. *A History of Negro Education in the South.* Cambridge, MA: Harvard University Press, 1967.

Burchard, Peter. *Charlotte Forten: A Black Teacher in the Civil War.* New York: Crown, 1995.

Burkholder. J. Peter. "Borrowing." In *Grove Music Online. Oxford Music Online,* accessed September 6, 2010, http://o-www.oxfordmusiconline.com.library.nsu.edu/subscriber /article/grove/music/5291 8pg14.

Burleigh, Harry. *The Spirituals of Harry T. Burleigh for High Voice.* Miami, FL: Belwin Mills, 1984.

Burlin, Natalie Curtis. *Hampton Series Negro Folk-Songs.* New York: G. Schirmer, 1918.

———. "Negro Music at Birth." *The Musical Quarterly* 5, no. 1 (January 1919): 86–89.

———. "The Negro's Contribution to the Music of America." *The Craftsman* 23 (1913): 660–69.

Burn, Billie. *An Island Named Daufuskie.* Spartanburg, SC: The Reprint Company, 1991.

Burnim, Mellonee V., and Portia K. Maultsby, eds. *African American Music: An Introduction.* New York: Routledge, 2006.

Burns, Debra Brubaker, Anita Jackson, and Connie Arrau Sturm. "Contributions of Selected British and American Women to Piano Pedagogy and Performance." *Journal of the International Alliance for Women in Music* 8, nos. 1–2 (March 2002): 1–9.

Burton, Orville. *Penn Center: A History Preserved.* Athens: University of Georgia Press, 2014.

Butler, David. *Jazz Noir: Listening to Music from the Phantom Lady to The Last Seduction.* Westport, CT: Greenwood Publishing, 2002.

Campbell, Emory S. *Gullah Cultural Legacies: A Synopsis of Gullah Traditions, Customary Beliefs, Artforms and Speech on Hilton Head Island and Vicinal Sea Islands in South Carolina and Georgia*. Hilton Head, SC: Gullah Heritage Consulting Services, 2002.

Capers, William. *A Catechism for Little Children (and for Use on) the Missions to the Slaves in South Carolina*. Charleston, SC: J. S. Burges, 1833.

———. *A Catechism for the Use of Methodist Missions*. Charleston, SC: J. S. Burges, 1833.

Carawan, Guy, and Candie Carawan. *Ain't You Got a Right to the Tree of Life? The People of Johns Island, South Carolina—Their Faces, their Words, and Their Songs*. Athens: University of Georgia Press, 1988.

———. *Sea Island Folk Festival: Moving Star Hall Singers*, Folkways Records, FS#3841, 1966.

———. *Sing for Freedom: The Story of the Civil Rights Movement Through Its Songs*. Bethlehem, PA: Sing Out Corp., 1990.

———. "Singing and Shouting in Moving Star Hall." *Black Music Research Journal* 15, no. 1 (Spring 1995): 17–28.

Carney, Judith. *Black Rice: The African Origins of Rice Cultivation in the Americas*. Cambridge, MA: Harvard University Press, 2001.

Carrington, Bolton, H. "Decoration of Graves of Negroes in South Carolina." *Journal of American Folklore* 4, no. 14 (July–September 1891): 214.

Carroll, Bartholomew. "An Editorial Trip to Edisto Island." *Chicora* I (1842): 42, 63.

Carter, Harold. *The Prayer Tradition of Black People*. Valley Forge, PA: Judson, 1976.

Castellini, Michael. "Sit In, Stand Up and Sing Out!: Black Gospel Music and the Civil Rights Movement." PhD diss., Georgia State University, 2013.

Chang, E. Christina. "The Singing Program of World War I: The Crusade for a Singing Army." *Journal of Historical Research in Music Education* 23, no. 1 (October 2001): 19–45.

Charters, Samuel Barclay. *A Language of Song: Journeys in the Musical World of the African Diaspora*. Durham, NC: Duke University Press, 2009.

Chase, Gilbert. *America's Music: From Pilgrims to the Present*. New York: McGraw-Hill, 1956.

Chenu, Bruno. *The Trouble I've Seen: The Big Book of Negro Spirituals*. Valley Forge, PA: Judson Press, 2003.

Chester, Eric. *The Wobblies in Their Heyday: The Rise and Destruction of the Industrial Workers of the World during the World War I Era*. Santa Barbara, CA: Praeger Publishers, 2014.

Childs, St. Julien Ravenel. "Cavaliers and Burghers in the Carolina Low-Country." In *Historiography and Urbanization: Essays in American History in Honor of W. Stull Holt*, edited by Eric Goldman, 1–20. Baltimore, MD: Johns Hopkins, 1941.

Christensen, Abigail M. Holmes. "Spirituals and 'Shouts' of Southern Negroes." *Journal of American Folklore* 7, no. 25 (April 1894): 154–55.

Christensen, Niels. "The Negroes of Beaufort County, South Carolina." *Southern Workman* 32 (October 1903): 481–85.

Clarana, Jose. "The Schooling of the Negro." *Crisis* 6 (July 1913): 132–36.

Clark, Erskine. *Wrestlin' Jacob: A Portrait of Religion in the Old South*. Atlanta, GA: John Knox Press, 1979.

Clark, Kenneth. *The Reminiscences of Kenneth B. Clark*. Alexandria, VA: Alexander Street Press, 2003.

Cleaveland, Bessie. "Music in the Public Schools." *The Southern Workman* 30, no. 1 (January 1901): 208–10.

Clements, William. "The 'Offshoot' and the 'Root': Natalie Curtis and the Black Expressive Culture in Africa and America." *Western Folklore* 54, no. 4 (October 1995): 277–301.

Cleveland, J. Jefferson, and Verolga Nix. *Songs of Zion*. Nashville, TN: Abington, 1981.

Coakley, Joyce V. *Sweetgrass Baskets and the Gullah Tradition*. Charleston, SC: Arcadia, 2005.

Cohen, Norm, and Ann Cohen. "Tune Evolution as an Indicator of Traditional Musical Norms." *The Journal of American Folklore* 86, no. 339 (January–March 1973): 37–47.

Cohen, Ronald, and Rachel Clare Donaldson. *Roots of the Revival: American and British Folk Music in the 1950s*. Urbana: University of Illinois Press, 2014.

Cole, Jean Lee, and Charles Mitchell. *Zora Neale Hurston Collected Plays*. New Brunswick, NJ: Rutgers University Press, 2008.

Coleridge-Taylor, Samuel. *Twenty-Four Negro Melodies for Solo Piano; op. 59*. Boca Raton, FL: Masters Music, 1999.

Cone, James. *The Spirituals and the Blues: An Interpretation*. New York: Seabury Press, 1972.

Conroy, Pat. *The Water Is Wide*. Boston: Houghton Mifflin, 1972.

Cooley, Rosa B. "America's Sea Islands." *The Outlook* (April 30, 1919): 739–41.

———. "Education in the Soil." *Progressive Education* 8 (December 1933): 448–55.

———. *Homes of the Freed*. New York: Negro Universities Press, 1926.

———. *School Acres: An Adventure in Rural Education*. New Haven, CT: Yale University Press, 1930.

———. "Service to Penn School." *Southern Workman* 46 (October 1917): 605–6.

———. "Tribute to a Faithful Nurse." *Southern Workman* 64 (March 1935): 70–71.

Cornelius, Janet Duitsman. *When I Can Read My Title Clear: Literacy, Slavery, and Religion in the Antebellum South*. Columbia: University of South Carolina Press, 1991.

Costen, Melva. *In Spirit and in Truth: The Music of African American Worship*. Louisville, KY: Westminster John Knox, 2004.

———. "Singing Praise to God in African American Worship Contexts." In *African American Religious Studies: An Interdisciplinary Anthology*, edited by Gayraud Wilmore, 392–404. Durham: Duke University Press, 1989.

Courlander, Harold. *Negro Folk Music, U.S.A.* New York: Columbia University Press, 1963.

Covey, Hebert. *African American Slave Medicine: Herbal and Non-Herbal Treatments*. Lanham, MD: Lexington Books, 2007.

Cowdery, James. "A Fresh Look at the Concept of Tune Family." *Ethnomusicology* 28, no. 3 (September 1984): 495–504.

———. *The Melodic Tradition of Ireland*. Kent, OH: Kent State University Press, 1990.

Cowdery, James, and Stanley Scott. *Exploring the World of Music: An Introduction to Music from a World Music Perspective*. Princeton, NJ: Recording for the Blind & Dyslexic, 2008.

Creel, Margaret Washington. *A Peculiar People: Slaves, Religion, and Community-Culture Among the Gullahs*. New York: New York University Press, 1989.

———. "Gullah Attitudes Toward Life and Death." In *Africanisms in American Culture*, edited by Joseph E. Holloway, 69–97. Bloomington: Indiana University Press, 1991.

Cross, Wilbur. *Gullah Culture in America.* Westport, CT: Praeger, 2007.

Crum, Mason. *Gullah: Negro Life in the Carolina Sea Islands.* New York: Negro Universities Press, 1968.

Cruz, Jon. *Culture on the Margins: The Black Spiritual and the Rise of American Cultural Interpretation.* Princeton, NJ: Princeton University Press, 1999.

Cunningham, Irma Ewing. *A Syntactic Analysis of Sea Island Creole.* Tuscaloosa: University of Alabama Press, 1992.

Cutler, Judy Goffman. *Maxwell Parrish: A Retrospective.* San Francisco: Pomegranate Artbooks, 1995.

Dabbs, Edith M. *Face of an Island.* South Carolina: R. L. Bryan, 1970.

———. *Sea Island Diary: A History of St. Helena Island.* Spartanburg, SC: Reprint Co., 1983.

———. *Walking Tall: A Brief Sketch of Penn School, a Forerunner of Penn Community Services, Frogmore, South Carolina.* Frogmore, SC: Penn Community Services, 1964.

Dabney, Charles William. "Penn School, St. Helena Island." *Southern Workman* 60 (June 1931): 277–81.

Daise, Ronald. *De Gullah Storybook: (fa laarn fa count from 1–10).* Beaufort, SC: GOG Enterprises, 1986.

———. *Reminiscences of Sea Island Heritage.* Orangeburg, SC: Sandlapper Pub., 1986.

Danielson, Virginia. *The Voice of Egypt: Umm Kulthūm, Arabic Song, and Egyptian Society in the Twentieth Century.* Chicago: University of Chicago Press, 2008.

Darden, Bob. *Nothing but Love in God's Water: Black Sacred Music from the Civil War to the Civil Rights Movement*, vol. 1. University Park: Penn State University Press, 2014.

———. *People Get Ready.* New York: Continuum, 2004.

Dargan, William T. "Congregational Singing Traditions in South Carolina." *Black Music Research Journal* 15, no. 1 (Spring 1995): 29–73.

———. *Lining out the Word: Dr. Watts Hymn Singing in the Music of Black Americans.* Berkeley: University of California Press, 2006.

Dash, Julie. *Daughters of the Dust.* New York: Dutton, 1997.

David, Marc C. "The Penn School of St. Helena: Breaking the Shackles of Illiteracy on the Sea Islands of South Carolina, 1862–1922." PhD diss., Syracuse University, 1999.

Davis, Darién J. *Slavery and Beyond: The African Impact on Latin America and the Caribbean.* Wilmington, DE: SR Books, 1995.

Davis, J. E. "A Unique People's School." *Southern Workman* 43 (April 1914): 217–28.

———. "Hampton at Penn School." *Southern Workman* 46, (January–December 1917): 81–89.

Del Negro, Giovanna P. *The Passeggiata and Popular Culture in an Italian Town: Folklore and the Performance of Modernity.* Montreal: McGill-Queen's Press, 2005.

Dennis, Rutledge. "Social Darwinism, Scientific Racism, and the Metaphysics of the Race." *The Journal of Negro Education* 64, no. 3 (Summer 1995): 243–52.

Dett, R. Nathaniel. *Religious Folk-Songs of the Negro as Sung at Hampton Institute.* Hampton, VA: Hampton University Press, 1927.

Deveaux, Scott, and Scott Knowles Deveaux. *The Birth of Bebop: A Social and Musical History.* Berkeley: University of California Press, 1997.

Dewey, John. *Democracy and Education.* New York: MacMillan, 1916.

Dibble, Jerry. *John Stainer: A Life in Music.* Suffolk: Boydell, 2007.

Diton, Carl. *Thirty-Six South Carolina Spirituals.* New York: G. Schirmer, 1928.

Doe, Kenneth C. "The Praise House Tradition and Community Renewal at St. Joseph Baptist Church." D. min. thesis, Erskine Theological Seminary, 1991.

Dorson, Richard Mercer. *American Folklore: With Revised Bibliographical Notes,* Volume 4 of Chicago History of American Civilization. Chicago: University of Chicago Press, 1977.

———. *Handbook of American Folklore.* Bloomington: Indiana University Press, 1983.

Doster, S. M. G. *Voices from St. Simons: Personal Narratives of an Island's Past.* Winston-Salem, NC: John F. Blair, 2008.

Douglass, Frederick. *Narrative of the Life of Frederick Douglass.* Boston: Anti-Slavery Office, 1845.

Du Bois, W. E. B. "The Browsing Reader." *Crisis* (November 1930): 378.

———. *The Souls of Black Folk.* New York: The New American Library, 1982.

Dudley, Shannon. "Judging by the Beat: Calypso versus Soca." *Ethnomusicology* 40, no, 2 (Spring–Summer 1996): 269–298.

Dunson, Josh. *Freedom in the Air: Song Movement of the Sixties.* New York, International Publishers, 1965.

———. "Slave Songs at the 'Sing for Freedom.'" *Broadside* 46 (May 30, 1964).

Dyer, Thomas. *Theodore Roosevelt and the Idea of Race.* Baton Rouge: Louisiana State University Press, 1980.

Edet, Edna Smith. *The Griot Sings: Songs from the Black World.* New York: Medgar Evers College Press, 1978.

Edwards, Walter, and Donald Winford, eds. *Verb Phrase Patterns in Black English and Creole.* Detroit, MI: Wayne State University Press, 1991.

Ellison, Ralph. *Shadow and Act.* New York: Vintage Books, 1972.

Epstein, Dena. "A White Origin for the Black Spiritual: An Invalid Theory for How It Grew." *American Music* 1, no. 2 (Summer 1983): 53–59.

———. "Black Spirituals: Their Emergence into Public Knowledge." *Black Music Research Journal* 10 (Spring 1990): 58–64.

———. *Sinful Tunes and Spirituals: Black Folk Music to the Civil War.* Urbana: University of Illinois Press, 1977.

Fallin, Wilson. *The African American Church in Birmingham, Alabama, 1815–1963: A Shelter in the Storm.* New York: Garland, 1997.

Fauset, Arthur. "Folklore from St. Helena, South Carolina." *The Journal of American Folklore* 38, no. 148 (April–June 1925): 217–38.

Feather, Leonard. *Inside Jazz.* New York: Da Capo Press, 1977.

Federal Writer's Project. *Virginia: A Guide to the Old Dominion.* New York: U.S. History Publishers, 1952.

Fenner, Thomas, *Religious Folksong of the Negro as Sung on the Plantations.* Hampton, VA: Hampton Institute, 1909.

Ferrell, Robert. *America's Deadliest Battle: Meuse-Argonne, 1918 (Modern War Studies).* Lawrence: University Press of Kansas, 2007.

Fisher, Miles Mark. *Negro Slave Songs in the United States.* New York: Carol Publishing, 1981.

Fisher, William Arms. *Seventy Negro Spirituals.* Boston: Oliver Ditson, 1926.

———. "Swing Low, Sweet Chariot: The Romance of a Famous Spiritual." *Etude* 50 (August 1932): 536.

Floyd, Samuel. "Black Music in the Circum-Caribbean." *American Music* 17, no. 1 (Spring 1999): 1–38.

———. "Ring Shout! Literary Studies, Historical Studies, and Black Music Inquiry." *Black Music Research Journal* (Spring 2002): 49–70.

———. *The Power of Black: Interpreting Its History from Africa to the United States.* New York: Oxford University Press, 1996.

———. "Troping the Blues: From Spirituals to the Concert Hall." *Black Music Research Journal* 13, no. 1 (Spring 1993): 31–51.

Foote, Henry Wilder. *The Penn School on St. Helena Island.* Hampton, VA: Hampton Institute Press, 1904.

Forten, Charlotte (Grimké). *The Journal of Charlotte L. Forten.* New York: Dryden, 1953.

———. "Life on the Sea Islands: Part 1." *Atlantic Monthly* 13 (May 1864): 587–96.

———. "Life on the Sea Islands: Part 2." *Atlantic Monthly* 13 (May 1864): 666–76.

Forten, Charlotte, and Brenda Stevenson. *The Journals of Charlotte Forten Grimké.* New York: Oxford University, 1988.

Fortune, Thomas. "Two Views of Negro Music," *The New York Age,* January 25, 1919.

Fowle, William Bentley. *The Common School Speller: In Which About 14,000 Words of the English Language Are Carefully Arranged According to Their Sound, Form, or Other Characteristics, so That the Difficulties of English Orthography Are Greatly Diminished, and the Memory of the Pupil Is Greatly Aided by Classification and Association.* Boston: Wm. B. Fowle and N. Capen, no. 184 Washington Street, 1842.

Frankenburger, David, and William F. Allen. *Essays and Monographs.* Boston: G. H. Ellis, 1890.

Frazier, E. Franklin. *The Negro Church in America.* New York: Schocken Books, 1974.

Frey, Sylvia R. *Water from the Rock: Black Resistance in a Revolutionary Age.* Princeton, NJ: Princeton University Press, 1993.

Gannett, William Channing. "The Freedmen at Port Royal." *North American Review* 101 (July 1865): 1–28.

Garst, John. "Mutual Reinforcement and the Origins of Spirituals." *American Music* 4 (Winter 1986): 390–406.

Gates, Henry L., Jr. *The Signifying Monkey: A Theory of African-American Literary Criticism.* New York: Oxford University Press, 1988.

Gates, Henry Louis, and Gene Andrew Jarrett. *The New Negro: Readings on Race, Representation, and African American Culture, 1892–1938.* Princeton, NJ: Princeton University Press, 2007.

Gaul, Harvey, *Nine Negro Spirituals.* New York: The H. W. Gray, 1918.

Gay, Kathlyn. *African-American Holidays, Festivals, and Celebrations: The History, Customs, and Symbols Associated with both Traditional and Contemporary Religious and*

Secular Events Observed by Americans of African Descent. Detroit, MI: Omnigraphics, 2007.

Gellert, Lawrence. *Me and My Captain.* New York: Hours Press, 1939.

Genovese, Eugene. *Roll, Jordan, Roll: The World the Slaves Made.* New York: Oxford University Press, 1974.

Georgia Writer's Project. *Drums and Shadows: Survival Studies among the Georgia Coastal Negroes.* Athens, GA: University of Georgia Press, 1940.

Geraty, Virginia Mixson, *Gulluh fuh oonuh = Gullah for you: A Guide to the Gullah Language.* Orangeburg, SC: Sandlapper, 1997.

Gilbert, Alma. *The Make Believe World of Maxwell Parrish and Sue Lewin.* San Francisco: Pomegranate Artbooks, 1990.

Glanton, Dahleen. "Gullah Culture in Danger of Fading Away." *Chicago Tribune,* June 8, 2001.

Glen, Isabella. *Life on St. Helena Island.* New York: Carlton, 1980.

Glen, John. *Highlander: No Ordinary School.* Knoxville: University of Tennessee Press, 1996.

Gloag, Kenneth. *Tippett, A Child of Our Time.* Cambridge: Cambridge University Press, 1999.

Goins, Leonard. "The Music of the Georgia and Carolina Sea Islands." *Allegro* 74, no. 5 (1974): 5.

Gomez, Michael. *Exchanging Our Country Marks: The Transformation of African Identities in the Colonial and Antebellum South.* Chapel Hill: University of North Carolina Press, 1998.

Gonzales, Ambrose Elliot. *The Black Border: Gullah Stories of the Carolina Coast.* Columbia, SC: The State Company, 1992.

———. *With Aesop along the Black Border.* Columbia, SC: The State Co., 1924.

Goodwine, Margaretta L., ed. *The Legacy of Ibo Landing: Gullah Roots of African American Culture.* Atlanta, GA: Clarity, 1998.

Goosman, Stuart. *Group Harmony: The Black Urban Roots of Rhythm & Blues.* Philadelphia: University of Pennsylvania Press, 2005.

Graham, Sandra. "The Fisk Jubilee Singers and the Concert Spiritual: The Beginning of an American Tradition." PhD diss., New York University, 2001.

Grainger, Percy. "Mrs. Burlin's Study of Negro Folk-Music." *New York Times,* April 14, 1918.

Grant, Frances R. "Negro Patriotism and Negro Music." *New Outlook* (February 26, 1919): 343–347.

Graydon, Nell S. *Tales of Edisto.* Orangeburg, SC: Sandlapper, 1986.

Graziano, John. "The Use of Dialect in African-American Spirituals: Popular Songs, and Folk Songs." *Black Music Research Journal* 24, no. 2 (Autumn 2004): 261–286.

Greene, Harlan. *Mr. Skylark: John Bennett and the Charleston Resistance.* Athens: University of Georgia Press, 2001.

Grew, Sydney. "Random Notes on the Spiritual." *Music & Letters* 16, no. 2 (April 1935): 96–109.

Grissom, Mary Allen. *The Negro Sings of a New Heaven.* Chapel Hill: University of North Carolina Press, 1930.

Griswold, Francis. *A Sea Island Lady.* New York: W. Morrow, 1939.

Guthrie, Patricia. "Catching Sense: The Meaning of Plantation Membership among Blacks on St. Helena Island, South Carolina." PhD diss., University of Rochester, 1977.

Guy, Nancy. *Peking Opera and Politics in Taiwan.* Urbana: University of Illinois Press, 2005. W. P. "Leading Negro Choir's European Visit." *Musical Times* 71, no. 1047 (May 1930): 416–17.

Haines, Michael. "Fertility and Mortality in the United States," In EH.Net Encyclopedia, edited by Robert Whaples, accessed March 19, 2008, http://eh.net/encyclopedia/article/haines.demography.

Hall, Edward. *Memoir of Mary L. Ware, Wife of Henry Ware.* Boston: American Unitarian Association, 1859.

Hallowell, Emily. *Calhoun Plantation Songs.* Boston: C. W. Thompson, 1907.

Hamilton, Virginia. *The People Could Fly: American Black Folktales.* New York: Alfred Knopf, 1985.

Hampton, Henry. *Voices of Freedom: An Oral History of the Civil Rights Movement from the 1950s Through the 1980s.* New York: Bantam, 2011.

Hampton Institute. *Hampton Normal and Agricultural Institute.* Hampton, VA: Normal School Steam Press, 1888.

Handy, William. *W. C. Handy's Collection of Negro Spirituals.* New York: Handy Brothers Music, 1938.

Harlan, Louis, and Raymond Smock. *The Booker T. Washington Papers, 2.* Urbana: University of Illinois Press, 1972.

Harris, Carl Gordon. "A Study of Characteristic Stylistic Trends Found in the Choral Works of a Selected Group of Afro-American Composers and Arrangers." DMA Thesis, University of Missouri-Kansas City, 1972.

Harris, Carmen. "Well I just generally bes the president of everything: Rural Black Women's Empowerment Through South Carolina Home Demonstration Activities." *Black Women Gender and Families* 3, no. 1 (Spring 2009): 101–2.

Harris, Joel Chandler. *Uncle Remus, His Songs and Sayings* (1895). New York: D. Appleton-Century, 1989.

Harris, Yvonne Bailey. *The History of the Penn School Under Its Founders at St. Helena Island, Frogmore, South Carolina, 1862–1908.* Ann Arbor, MI: University Microfilms International, 1981.

Harrison, Hubert H., and Jeffrey Babcock Perry. *A Hubert Harrison Reader.* Middletown, CT: Wesleyan University Press, 2001.

Harrison, Paul Carter, Victor Leo Walker II, and Gus Edwards. *Black Theatre: Ritual Performance in the African Diaspora.* Philadelphia, PA: Temple University Press, 2002.

Hart, Edward Brantley. *Gullah Spirituals in Prayer Meetings on Johns Island, South Carolina.* Published by Author, 1993.

Haskins, James. *Black Dance in America: A History Through Its People.* New York: Harper Collins, 1990.

Hast, Dorothy, James Cowdery, and Stanley Scott. *Exploring the World of Music: An Introduction to Music from a World Music Perspective.* Princeton, NJ: Recording for the Blind & Dyslexic, 2008.

Hawley, Thomas Earl, Jr. "The Slave Tradition of Singing among the Gullah of Johns Island South Carolina." PhD diss., University of Maryland, Baltimore County, 1993.

Hayes, Arthur. *Souvenir of the Class of 1902.* Hampton, VA: Hampton Institute, 1902.

Hayes, Michael G. "The Theology of the Black Pentecostal Praise Song." *Black Sacred Music* 4, no. 2 (Fall 1990): 30–34.

Hays, Lee, and Robert S. Koppelman, *"Sing Out, Warning! Sing Out, Love!": The Writings of Lee Hays.* Amherst, MA: Publisher Name?, 2010.

Hazzard-Donald, Katrina. *Mojo Workin': The Old African American Hoodoo System.* Urbana: University of Illinois Press, 2013.

Henderson, Stephen Evangelist. *Understanding the New Black Poetry; Black Speech and Black Music as Poetic References.* New York: W. Morrow, 1973.

Henry, Mellinger E. "Negro Songs from Georgia." *The Journal of American Folklore* 44, no. 174 (October–December 1931): 437–47.

Herbert, Joanna. *Negotiating Boundaries in the City: Migration, Ethnicity, and Gender in Britain.* Aldershot: Ashgate Publishing, 2008.

Herder, Nicole, and Ronald Herder. *Best-Loved Negro Spirituals: Complete Lyrics to 178 Songs of Faith.* Mineola, NY: Dover Publications, 2001.

Herskovits, Melville. "Some Recent Developments in the Study of West African Native Life." *The Journal of Negro History* 24, no. 1 (January 1939): 14–32.

Heyward, Dubose. "The Negro in the Low Country." In *The Carolina Low Country,* edited by Augustine Smythe et al., 185–86. New York: MacMillan, 1931.

Hicks, Elias. *Journal of the Life and Religious Labours of Elias Hicks.* 5th ed. New York: Isaac T. Hopper, 1832.

Higginson, Thomas Wentworth. *Army Life in a Black Regiment.* Boston: Beacon, 1962.

———. "Negro Spirituals." *Atlantic Monthly* 19, no. 116 (June 1867): 685–94.

Higginson, Thomas Wentworth, and Howard Meyer. *The Magnificent Activist: The Writings of Thomas Wentworth Higginson.* New York: Da Capo, 2000.

Hinton, Elizabeth, and Manning Marable. *The New Black History Revisiting the Second Reconstruction.* New York: Palgrave Macmillan, 2011.

Hod, Boz. *Terrorism in America: The Ritualistic Murder of Blacks.* Briarcliff Manor, NY: AOM Publishing Unit, 2004.

Holloway, Joseph E. *Africanisms in American Culture.* Bloomington: Indiana University Press. 1990.

Holmgren, Virginia C. *Hilton Head: A Sea Island Chronicle.* Easley, SC: Southern Historical Press, 1986.

Holzknecht, K. J. "Some Negro Song Variants from Louisville." *The Journal of American Folklore* 41, no. 162 (October–December 1928): 558–78.

Horn, Dorothy. "Quartal Harmony in the Pentatonic Folk Hymns of the Sacred Harp." *Journal of American Folklore* 71 (October–December 1958): 564–81.

House, Grace Bigelow. "How Freedom Came to Big Pa." *Southern Workman* 45 (April 1916): 217–26.

———. "Origin of the Hymn." *The Southern Workman* 47 (1918): 476.

———. "Roads of Learning on St. Helena." *Progressive Education* 4 (April 1937): 246–55.

———. "The Fiftieth Anniversary of the Penn School." *Southern Workman* 41 (1912).

———. "The Hymn in the Camps." *The Southern Workman* 47 (1918): 477.

———. "The Little Foe of All the World." *Southern Workman* 35 (November 1906): 598–614.

Howard, John Tasker, Jr. "Capturing The Spirit of the Real Negro Music." Book Review. *The Musician* 24 (1919): 13.

Howe, Arthur. "Hollis Burke Frissell." *Christian Statesman.* 40 (October 1931): 507–12.

Hudson, Larry E. *Working Toward Freedom: Slave Society and Domestic Economy in the American South.* Rochester, NY: University of Rochester Press, 1994.

Hudson, William Henry. *Sir Walter Scott (Scots Epoch Makers).* London: Sands and Company, 1901.

Huebner, Andrew. *The Warrior Image: Soldiers in American Culture from the Second World War to the Vietnam Era.* Chapel Hill: University of North Carolina, 2008.

Hutchison, James, and Harlan Green, eds. *Renaissance in Charleston: Art and Life in the Carolina Low Country, 1900–1940.* Athens: University of Georgia Press, 2003.

Hutchison, Janet. "Better Homes and Gullah." *Agricultural History* 67, no. 2 (Spring 1993): 102–18.

———. "The Cure for Domestic Neglect: Better Homes in America, 1922–1935." *Perspectives Vernacular Architecture* 2 (1986): 168–78.

Jackson, Bruce. *The Negro and His Folklore in Nineteenth-Century Periodicals.* Austin: University of Texas Press, 1967.

Jackson, George Pullen. *Spiritual Folk-Songs of Early America; Two Hundred and Fifty Tunes and Texts with an Introduction and Notes.* Locust Valley, NY: J. J. Augustin, 1953.

———. "Stephen Foster's Debt to American Folk-Song." *The Musical Quarterly* 22, no. 2 (April 1936): 154–69.

———. *White and Black Spirituals: Their Lifespan and Kinship.* Locust Valley, NY: J. J. Augustin, 1943.

———. *White and Negro Spirituals.* New York: Augustin, 1943.

———. *White Spirituals in the Southern Uplands.* Chapel Hill: University of North Carolina Press, 1933.

Jackson, Irene V. *Afro-American Religious Music: A Bibliography and a Catalog of Gospel Music.* Westport, CT: Greenwood, 1979.

Jackson, Irene V., ed. *More than Dancing: Essays on Afro-American Music and Musicians.* Westport, CT: Greenwood, 1985.

Jackson, L. P. "The Educational Efforts of the Freedmen's Bureau and the Freedmen's Aids Societies in South Carolina, 1862–1972." *The Journal of Negro History* 8, 1923, 1–40.

Jacoway, Elizabeth. *Yankee Missionaries in the South: The Penn School Experiment.* Baton Rouge: Louisiana State University Press, 1980.

James, Edward T., Janet Wilson James, and Paul S. Boyer. *Notable American Women 1607–1950: A Biographical Dictionary.* Cambridge, MA: Belknap Press of Harvard University Press, 1971–80.

James, Willis Laurence, and Jon Michael Spencer. *Stars in De Elements Study of Negro Folk Music.* Durham, NC: Duke University Press, 1995.

Johnson, Charles Spurgeon. "A Southern Negro's View of the South." *Journal of Negro Education* 26 (Winter 1957): 4–9.

Johnson, Guion Griffs. *A Social History of the Sea Islands with Special Reference to St. Helena Island, South Carolina.* New York: Negro Universities Press, 1969.

Johnson, Guy B. *Folk Culture on St. Helena Island, South Carolina.* Chapel Hill: University of North Carolina, 1930.

———. "Review: Untitled." *Social Forces* 14, no. 1 (October 1935): 157.

———. "The Negro Spiritual: A Problem in Anthropology." *American Anthropologist* 33, no. 2 (April–June 1931): 157–71.

Johnson, James Weldon, and J. Rosamond Johnson. *The Books of American Negro Spirituals.* New York: Viking, 1926.

Johnson, Robert Underwood, and Clarence Clough Buel. *Battles and Leaders of the Civil War. Being for the Most Part Contributions by Union and Confederate Officers. Based Upon "The Century War Series" Volume IV.* New York: Century, 1884.

Jones, A. M. *Studies in African Music.* London: Oxford University Press, 1959.

Jones, Arthur. *Wade in the Water: The Wisdom of the Spirituals.* New York: Orbis Books, 1993.

Jones, Bessie, John Davis, Willis Proctor, and Alan Lomax. *Georgia Sea Islands.* Cambridge, MA: Rounder, 1998.

Jones, Charles Colcock. *A Catechism for Colored Persons.* Savannah, GA: Thomas Purse, 1837.

———. *The Religious Instruction of the Negroes in the United States.* Savannah, GA: Thomas Purse, 1842.

Jones, Charles Colcock, Jr. *Gullah Folktales from the Georgia Coast.* Athens: University of Georgia Press, 2000.

Jones, Katharine M. *Port Royal Under Six-Flags.* Indianapolis, IN: Bobbs-Merrill, 1960.

Jones Jackson, Patricia, "Contemporary Gullah Speech: Some Persistent Linguistic Features." *Journal of Black Studies* 13, no. 3 (March 1983): 289–303.

———. "The Status of the Gullah: An Investigation of Convergent Processes." PhD diss., University of Michigan, 1978.

———. *When Roots Die: Endangered Traditions on the Sea Islands.* Athens: University of Georgia Press, 1989.

Jordan, Francis H. "Across the Bridge: Penn School and Penn Center." EdD diss., University of South Carolina, 1991.

Joseph, Peniel. *The Black Power Movement Rethinking the Civil Rights-Black Power Era.* Florence: Taylor and Francis, 2013.

Joyner, Charles. *Down by the Riverside: A South Carolina Slave Community.* Urbana: University of Illinois Press, 1984.

Kaplan, Carla. *Zora Neale Hurston: A Life in Letters.* New York: Anchor, 2003.

Katz, Bernard, *Social Implications of Early American Negro Music.* New York: Arno, 1969.

Kebede, Ashenafi. *Roots of Black Music: The Vocal, Instrumental, and Dance Heritage of Africa and Black America.* Englewood Cliffs, NJ: Prentice Hall, 1982.

Kemble, Fanny. *Journal of a Residence on a Georgian Plantation in 1838–1839.* New York: Harper & Bros, 1863.

Kent, Josiah. *Northborough History.* New York: Garden City, 1921.

Kester, Howard, and Mary Frederickson. Oral History Interview with Howard Kester,

August 25, 1974, Interview B-0007-2, Southern Oral History Program Collection (#4007). [Chapel Hill, NC]: University Library, UNC-Chapel Hill, 2007.

Kieffer, Aldine. *The Musical Million*. Rockingham County, Virginia, ca. 1873.

Kilson, Marion. "The Ga Naming Rite," *Anthropos* 64/64 (1968/1969): 904–20.

Kinlaw-Ross, Eleanor. *Dat Gullah and Other Geechie Traditions*. Atlanta, GA: Crick-Edge Productions, 1996.

Kirby, Percival. "A Study of Negro Harmony." *The Musical Quarterly* 16 (July 1930): 404–14.

Kiser, Clyde Vernon. *Sea Island to City: A Study of St. Helena Islanders in Harlem and other Urban Centers*. New York: Athenaeum, 1932.

Koenig, Karl. *Jazz in Print (1856–1929): An Anthology of Selected Early Readings in Jazz History*. Hillsdale, NY: Pendragon, 2002.

Kolinski, Mieczyslaw. "A Cross-Cultural Approach to Metro-Rhythmic Patterns." *Ethnomusicology* 17, no. 3 (September 1973): 494–506.

Krehbiel, Henry. *Afro-American Folk Songs: A Study in Racial and National Music*. New York: F. Ungar, 1962.

Krull, Kathleen. *Bridges to Change: How Kids Live on a South Carolina Sea Island*. New York: Lodestar, 1995.

Kuyper, George A. "The Powerful Influence of a Notable School." *Southern Workman* 60 (January 1931): 29–32.

Lake, Joy Jordan. *Whitewashing Uncle Tom's Cabin: Nineteenth-Century Women Novelists Respond to Stowe*. Nashville, TN: Vanderbilt University Press, 2005.

Lawrence, Levine. *Black Culture and Black Consciousness: Afro-American Folk Thought from Slavery to Freedom*. New York: Oxford University Press, 1977.

Lawrence-McIntyre, Charshee Charlotte. "The Double Meanings of the Spirituals." *Journal of Black Studies* 17, no. 4 (June 1987): 379–401.

Lawson, Warner. "Review." *The Journal of Negro History* 39, no. 2 (April 1954): 142–44.

Lawton, Samuel Miller. "The Religious Life of the South Carolina Coastal and Sea Island Negroes." PhD diss., George Peabody College for Teachers, 1939.

Levine, Lawrence. *Black Culture and Black Consciousness: Afro-American Folk Thought From Slavery to Freedom*. New York: Oxford University Press, 1977.

Lightfoot, William. "The Three Doc (k)s: White Blues in Appalachia." *Black Music Research Journal* 23, no. 1/2 (Spring–Autumn 2003): 167–93.

Lincoln, Eric, and Lawrence H. Mamiya. *The Black Church in the African American Experience*. Durham, NC: Duke University Press, 1990.

Lindsey, Donal. *Indians at Hampton, 1877–1923*. Urbana: University of Illinois Press, 1995.

Linneman, Russell. *Alain Locke: Reflections on a Modern Renaissance Man*. Baton Rouge: Louisiana State University Press, 1982.

Littlefield, Daniel C. *Rice and Slaves: Ethnicity and the Slave Trade in Colonial South Carolina*. Baton Rouge: Louisiana State University Press, 1981.

Locke, Alain. *The New Negro: An Interpretation*. New York: A. and C. Boni, 1925.

Logan, William A., and Allen M. Garrett. *Road to Heaven: Twenty-Eight Negro Spirituals*. Tuscaloosa, AL: University of Alabama Press, 1955.

Lomax, Alan, and John Lomax. *American Ballads and Folk Songs*. New York: MacMillan, 1958.

———. *Sounds of the Sounds: A Musical Journey from the Georgia Sea Islands to the Mississippi Delta.* Sound Recording. 4 sound discs: digital; 4 ¾ in. + 1 booklet. New York: Atlantic, 1993.

Lomax, John. "Sinful Songs of the Southern Negro." *The Musical Quarterly* 20, no. 2 (April 1934): 177–87.

Longstreet, Wilma. "Review." *Journal of Aesthetic Education* 8, no. 4 (October 1974): 115–17.

Lornell, Kip. *From Jubilee to Hip Hop: Readings in African American Music.* Upper Saddle River, NJ: Prentice Hall, 2010.

Lovell, John, Jr. *Black Song: The Forge and the Flame: The Story of How the Afro-American Spiritual Was Hammered Out.* New York: Macmillan, 1972.

———. "The Social Implications of the Negro Spiritual." *Journal of Negro Education* 8, no. 4 (October 1939): 634–43.

Ludlow, Helen W. *Tuskegee Normal and Industrial School, For Training Colored Teachers at Tuskegee, Alabama: Its Story and Its Songs.* Hampton, VA: Normal School Steam Press, 1884.

Lynskey, Dorian. *33 Revolutions Per Minute.* London: Faber, 2013.

Manning, Susan. *Modern Dance, Negro Dance: Race in Motion.* Minneapolis: University of Minnesota Press, 2004.

Marscher, Bill, and Fran Marscher. *The Great Sea Island Storm of 1893.* Macon, GA: Mercer University Press, 2004.

Marscher, Fran. *Remembering the Way It Was in Beaufort, Sheldon, and the Sea Islands.* Charleston, SC: History Press, 2006.

Marsh, J. B. T. *The Story of the Jubilee Singers: Including Their Songs.* London: Hodder and Stoughton, 1903.

Martin, Josephine W. *"Dear Sister": Letters Written on Hilton Head Island.* Beaufort, SC: Beaufort Book Company, 1977.

Maultsby, Portia K. "Africanisms in African American Music." In *Africanisms in American Culture,* edited by Joseph E. Holloway, 185–210. Bloomington: Indiana University Press, 1991.

———. "Black Spirituals: An Analysis of Textual Forms and Structures." *The Black Perspective in Music* 40, no. 1 (Spring 1976): 54–69.

McBrier, V. F. "The Life and Works of Robert Nathaniel Dett." PhD thesis, Catholic University of America, 1967.

McCutcheon, John. *Army Song Book.* Washington: United States Commission on Training Camp Activities, 1918.

McDaniels, Joseph Hetherington. *Letters and Memorials of Wendell Phillips Garrison: Literary Editor of "The Nation" 1865–1906.* New York: Riverside Press, 1909.

McGowan, Pierre. *The Gullah Mailman.* Raleigh, NC: Pentland, 2000.

McIlhenny, E. A. *Befo' de War Spirituals.* Boston: Christopher Publishing House, 1933.

McIntosh County Shouters. *Slave Shout Songs from the Coast of Georgia.* Washington, DC: Smithsonian Folkways Recordings, 2003.

McKelya, Micki. *Clinging to Mammy: The Faithful Slave in Twentieth-Century America.* Cambridge, MA: Harvard University Press, 2007.

McKenzie, Wallace. "E. A. McIlhenny's Black Spiritual Collection from Avery Island, Louisiana." *American Music* 8, no. 1 (Spring 1990): 95–110.

McKim, Lucy. "Songs of the Port Royal Contrabands." *Dwight's Journal of Music* 21 (November 8, 1862): 254–55.

McNeil, W. K. *Encyclopedia of American Gospel Music.* New York: Routledge, 2005.

McPherson, James. *The Abolitionist Legacy: From Reconstruction to the NAACP.* Princeton, NJ: Princeton University, 1975.

McTeer, James. *High Sheriff of the Low Country.* Beaufort, SC: Beaufort Book Co., 1970.

Mencken, H. L. "Songs of the American Negro." *World Review* 1 (February 8, 1926).

Merriam, Alan. "Flathead Indian Instruments and Their Music." *The Musical Quarterly* 37, no. 3 (July 1951): 368–75.

———. "The Bashi Mulizi and Its Music: An End-Blown Flute from the Belgian Congo." *The Journal of American Folklore* 70, no. 276 (April–June 1957): 143–56.

Michaelson, Patricia Howell. *Speaking Volumes: Women, Reading, and Speech in the Age of Austen.* Stanford, CA: Stanford University Press, 2004.

Miller, Edward. *Gullah Statesman: Robert Smalls from Slavery to Congress, 1839–1915.* Columbia, SC: University of South Carolina Press, 1995.

Miller, Francis Trevelyan, Robert Sampson Lanier, and Henry Wysham Lanier. *The Photographic History of the Civil War.* New York: The Review of Reviews Co., 1911.

Miller, Richard. "The Guitar in the Brazilian Choro: Analyses of Traditional, Solo, and Art Music." PhD diss., Catholic University of America, 2006.

Miner, Leigh Richmond, and Edith M. Dabbs. *Face of an Island: Leigh Richmond Miner's Photographs of Saint Helena Island.* New York: Grossman Publishers, 1971.

Mitchell, Faith. *Hoodoo Medicine: Sea Island Herbal Remedies.* Berkeley, CA: Reed, Cannon and Johnson, 1978.

Mitchell, Frank. *Navajo Blessingway Singer: The Autobiography of Frank Mitchell, 1881–1967.* Tucson: University of Arizona Press, 1980.

Monson, Ingrid T. *Freedom Sounds: Civil Rights Call Out to Jazz and Africa.* New York: Oxford University Press, 2007.

Montgomery, Michael. *The Crucible of Carolina: Essays in the Development of Gullah Language and Culture.* Athens, GA: University of Georgia Press, 2008.

Moon, Brian. "The Old Songs Hymnal: Harry Burleigh and His Spirituals During the Harlem Renaissance." PhD diss., University of Colorado, 2006.

Moore, Janie Gilliard. "Africanisms Among Blacks of the Sea Islands." *Journal of Black Studies* 10 (June 1980): 467–80.

Moore, Leroy. "The Spiritual: Soul of Black Religion." *Church History* 40, no. 1 (March 1971): 79–81.

Moore, Thomas. *The Poetical Works of Thomas Moore Including His Melodies, Ballads, etc . . . .* Philadelphia: Crissy and Markley, 1849.

Mufwene, Salikoko S., and Charles Gilman. "How African Is Gullah, and Why?" *American Speech* (Summer 1987): 120–39.

Murray, Ellen. *Aunt Jane's Prayer.* St. Helena Island, SC: Penn Normal, Industrial, and Agricultural School, 1905.

Myers, Helen. *Ethnomusicology: An Introduction.* New York: W. W. Norton, 1992.

National Baptist Publishing Board. *The New National Baptist Hymnal.* Nashville, TN: National Baptist Pub. Board, 1977.

National Parks Service. "Low Country Gullah Culture: Special Resource Study and Final Environmental Impact Statement, accessed February 8, 2010, www.nps.gov/sero /planning/gg_srs/ggrs_ section2.

Nettl, Bruno. *The Study of Ethnomusicology: Thirty-Three Discussions,* 3rd ed. Urbana: University of Illinois Press, 2015.

Nichols, Elaine, ed. *The Last Miles of the Way: African American Homegoing Traditions 1890-Present.* Columbia, SC: Dependable Printing Company, 1989.

Nichols, Patricia Causey. "Linguistic Change in Gullah: Sex, Age, Mobility." PhD diss., Stanford University, 1976.

Niles, John, and Margaret Thorniley Williamson. *Singing Soldiers.* New York: Scribner, 1927.

Nketia, J. H. Kwabena. *The Music of Africa.* New York: W. W. Norton, 1974.

Oakley, Giles. *The Devil's Music: A History of the Blues.* New York: Harcourt Brace Jovanovich, 1976.

O'Brien, Alicia DeRocke. *The Development of the Gullah Church.* Oxford, OH: Miami University, 2006.

Odum, Howard. "From Community Studies to Regionalism." *Social Forces* 23, no. 3 (March 1945): 249–50.

———. "Religious Folk-Songs of the Southern Negro." *American Journal of Religious Psychology and Education* 3 (July 1909): 265–365.

Odum, Howard W., and Guy B. Johnson. *The Negro and His Songs: A Study of Typical Negro Songs in the South.* Chapel Hill: University of North Carolina Press, 1925.

Odum, Howard W., and Guy B. Johnson. *The Negro and His Songs: A Study of Topical Negro Songs in the South.* New York: Negro Universities Press, 1925.

Oliver, Paul. *Songsters and Saints: Vocal Traditions on Race Records.* Cambridge: Cambridge University Press, 1984.

Oliver, Paul, Max Harrison, and William Bolcom. *The New Grove Gospel, Blues, and Jazz, with Spirituals and Ragtime.* New York: Norton, 1986.

Opala, Joseph. *The Gullah: Rice, Slavery, and the Sierra Leone–American Connection.* Freetown, Sierra Leone: USIS, 1987.

Otto, John Solomon, and Augustus Marion Burns III, "Black Folks and Poor Buckras: Archeological Evidence of Slave and Overseer Living Conditions on an Antebellum Plantation." *Journal of Black Studies* 14, no. 2 (December 1983): 185–200.

Owens, Thomas. "Forms." *The New Grove Dictionary of Jazz,* 2nd ed., edited by Barry Kernfeld, *Grove Music Online. Oxford Music Online,* accessed February 7, 2010, http://o -www.oxfordmusiconline.com.library.nsu.edu/subscriber/article/grove/music/J154400.

Page, Yolanda Williams. *Encyclopedia of African American Women Writers* (Westport, CT: Greenwood, 2007.

Paris, Arthur. *Black Pentecostalism: South Religion in an Urban World.* Amherst: University of Massachusetts Press, 1982.

Parrish, Lydia. *Slave Songs of the Georgia Sea Islands.* Athens: University of Georgia Press, 1942.

Parsons, Elsie Crews. *Folk-Lore of the Sea Islands, South Carolina.* New York: American Folk-Lore Society, 1969.

Patterson, Michelle Wick. "'Tawi Mana' (The Song Maid): Natalie Curtis Burlin and Her Search for an American Identity." PhD diss., Purdue University, August 2003.

Payne, Bishop Daniel Alexander. *Recollections of Seventy Years.* Nashville, TN: A. M. E. Sunday School Union, 1888.

Peabody, Francis Greenwood. *Education for Life: The Story of Hampton Institute.* Garden City, NY: Doubleday, Page, 1918.

Pearson, Elizabeth Ware, ed. *Letters from Port Royal, 1862–1868.* Boston: W. B. Clarke, 1906.

Pease, William D. "An African Background for American Negro Folktales?" *Journal of American Folklore* 84 (April–June 1971): 204–14.

Penn School (Saint Helena Island, SC). *Growing Up from a One Room Cabin: A Few Facts about Penn School.* [S.l]: s.n. 1933.

Penn School (Saint Helena Island, SC). *Penn School News.* Frogmore, St. Helena Island, SC: Penn School, 1942.

Penn School Graduates Club. *Official Program of the Observation of Founders Day in Connection with the . . . Anniversary of Penn Normal, Industrial and Agricultural School.* St. Helena Island, SC: s.n., 1970.

Perkins, A. E. "Negro Spirituals from the Far South." *The Journal of American Folklore* 35, no. 137 (July–September 1922): 223–49.

Peterson, Merrill. *John Brown: The Legend Revisited.* Charlottesville: University of Virginia Press, 2004.

Pierce, Edward L. "The Freedmen at Port Royal." *Atlantic Monthly* 12, no. 71 (September 1863): 293–315.

Pierce, Edward L. "The Freedmen at Port Royal." *The Atlantic Monthly* (September 1863): 307–8.

Pierce, Paul Skeels. *The Freedmen's Bureau: A Chapter in the History of Reconstruction.* Iowa City: The State University of Iowa, 1904.

Pike, Gustavus Dorman. *The Jubilee Singers and Their Campaign for Twenty Thousand Dollars.* Boston: Lee and Shephard, 1873.

Pinckney, Roger. *Blue Roots: African-American Folk Magic of the Gullah People.* St. Paul, MN: Llewellyn, 1998.

Pinn, Anthony. *The African American Religious Experience in America.* Westport, CT: Greenwood, 2006.

Pisani, Michael. "From Hiawatha to Wa-Wan: Musical Boston and the Uses of Native American Lore." *American Music* 19 (Spring 2001): 39–50.

Pitts, Walter. "Like a Tree Planted by the Water: The Musical Cycle in the African-American Baptist Ritual." *The Journal of American Folklore* 104, no. 413 (Summer 1991): 318–40.

Plair, Sally, and Annie Lyle Viser. *Something to Shout About: Reflections on the Gullah Spiritual.* Mt. Pleasant, SC: Molasses Lane, 1972.

Pollitzer, William S., and David Moltke-Hansen. *The Gullah People and Their African Heritage.* Athens: University of Georgia Press, 1999.

Poole, W. Scott. "Memory and the Abolitionist Heritage: Thomas Wentworth Higginson and the Uncertain Meaning of the Civil War." *Civil War History* 51, no. 2 (2005): 206.

Porcher, Richard. *The Story of Sea Island Cotton.* Charleston, SC: Wyrick, 2005.

Pound, Louise. "Nonsinging Games of American Children." *American Speech* 29, no. 1 (February 1954): 55–56.

Prahlad, Anand. *The Greenwood Encyclopedia of African American Folklore.* Westport, CT: Greenwood Press, 2006.

Price, Franklin. *Vital Records of Northborough, Massachusetts, to the End of the Year 1850.* Worcester, MA: Franklin Price, 1901.

Puckett, Newbell N. *Folk Beliefs of the Southern Negro.* Chapel Hill: University of North Carolina Press, 1926.

Pyatt, Thomas. *Gullah History Along the Carolina Low Country.* Published by the Author, 2006.

Qureshi, Regula. "Music Sound and Contextual Input: A Performance Model for Musical Analysis." *Ethnomusicology* 31 (1987), 56–86.

Rabaka, Reiland. *Civil Rights Music: The Soundtracks of the Civil Rights Movement.* Lanham, MD: Lexington Books, 2016.

Raboteau, Albert J. *Slave Religion: The Invisible Institution in the Antebellum South.* New York: Oxford University Press, 2004.

Radano, Ronald. "Denoting Difference: The Writing of the Spiritual." *Critical Inquiry* 22, no. 3 (Spring 1996): 506–44.

Rahn, Jay. "Turning the Analysis Around: Africa-Derived Rhythms and Europe-Derived Theory." *Black Music Research Journal* 16, no. 1 (Spring, 1966): 71–89.

Ramey, Lauri. *Slave Songs and the Birth of African American Poetry.* New York: Palgrave Macmillan, 2008.

Ramsey, Guthrie. *Race Music: Black Cultures from Bebop to Hip-Hop.* Berkeley, CA: University of California Press, 2003.

Rawick, George, ed. *The American Slave: A Composite Autobiography.* Westport, CT: Greenwood, 1972.

Raymond, Charles A. "The Religious Life of the Negro Slave, Part 1." *Harpers New Monthly Magazine* 27, no. 160 (September 1863): 479–85.

———. "The Religious Life of the Negro Slave, Part 2." *Harpers New Monthly Magazine* 27, no. 161 (October 1863): 676–82.

———. "The Religious Life of the Negro Slave, Part 3." *Harpers New Monthly Magazine* 27, no. 161 (November 1863): 816–25.

Reagon, Bernice Johnson. *If You Don't Go, Don't Hinder Me: The African American Sacred Song Tradition.* Lincoln: University of Nebraska Press, 2001.

———. "Movement Songs that Moved the Nation." *Perspectives: The Civil Rights Quarterly* 15, no. 3 (Summer 1983): 27–35.

———. "Music in the Civil Rights Movement." Interviewed by Maria Daniels, WGBH Boston, July 2006.

Rhyne, Nancy. *Chronicles of the South Carolina Sea Islands.* Winston-Salem, NC: John Blair, 1998.

Rice, Marianne. *Music Education through Gullah: The Legacy of a Forgotten Genre.* Bloomington, IN: Xlibris, 2009.

Richards, Paul. "A Pan-African Composer." *Black Music Research Journal* 21, no. 2 (Autumn 2001): 245–46.

Roach, Hildred. *Black American Music: Past and Present.* Boston: Crescendo Pub. Co., 1973.

Robb, John, Jack Loeffler, and Enrique R. Lamadrid. *Hispanic Folk Music of New Mexico and the Southwest A Self-Portrait of a People.* Albuquerque: University of New Mexico Press, 2014.

Robbins, Gerald. "Laura Towne: White Pioneer in Negro Education, 1862–1901." *Journal of Education* 143 (April 1961): 40–54.

———. "Rossa B. Cooley and the Penn School; Social Dynamo in a Negro Rural Subculture, 1901–1930." *The Journal of Negro Education* 33 (Winter 1964): 43–51.

Roberts, Helen. "Spirituals or Revival Hymns of the Jamaica Negro." *Ethnomusicology* 33, no. 3 (Autumn 1989): 419–74.

Robinson, Carline S., and William R. Dortch. *The Blacks in These Sea Islands: Then and Now.* New York: Vantage, 1985.

Rose, Peter. *Slavery and Its Aftermath.* New Brunswick, NJ: Aldine Transaction, 2007.

Rose, Willie Lee. *Rehearsal for Reconstruction.* Indianapolis: Bobbs-Merrill, 1964.

Rose, Willie Lee Nichols. *Rehearsal for Reconstruction: The Port Royal Experiment.* Oxford: Oxford University Press, 1964.

Rosenbaum, Art, and Johann S. Buis. *Shout Because You're Free: The African American Ring Shout Tradition in Coastal Georgia.* Athens: University of Georgia Press, 1998.

Rosengarten, Dale. *Grass Roots: African Origins of an American Art.* New York: Museum for African Art; Seattle:University of Washington Press, 2008.

———. *Row Upon Row: Sea Grass Baskets of the South Carolina Lowcountry.* Columbia: McKissick Museum, University of South Carolina, 1986.

Rosenthal, Rob, and Richard Flacks. *Playing for Change: Music and Musicians in the Service of Social Movements.* Boulder, CO: Paradigm Publishers, 2011.

Rowe, George C. "The Negroes of the Sea Islands." *Southern Workman* 29 (December 1900): 709–15.

Rowland, Lawrence Sanders, Alexander Moore, and George C. Rogers. *The History of Beaufort, South Carolina, 1514–1861.* Columbia: University of South Carolina Press, 1996.

Russell, William. *My Diary, North and South, by William Howard Russell.* London: Bradbury and Evans, 1863.

Ryder, Georgia. "Harlem Renaissance Ideals in the Music of Robert Nathaniel Dett." In *Black Music in the Harlem Renaissance, A Collection of Essays,* edited by Samuel A. Floyd Jr., 55–70. New York: Greenwood, 1990.

Sanders, Lynn Moss. *Howard W. Odum's Folklore Odyssey: Transformation to Tolerance Through African American Folk Studies.* Athens: University of Georgia Press, 2004.

Sandilands, Alexander. *A Hundred and Twenty Negro Spirituals.* Morija, Lesotho: Morija Sesuto Book Depot, 1981.

Sankey, Ira. *Sacred Songs and Solos, Sung by I. D. Sankey, etc. . . . .* London: Morgan and Scott, 1873.

Saunders, William C. "Sea Islands: Then and Now." *Journal of Black Studies* 10, no. 4 (1980): 481–92.

Scarborough, Dorothy. *On the Trail of Negro Folk-Songs*. Cambridge: Cambridge University Press, 1925.

Schenbeck, Lawrence. "Representing America, Instructing Europe: The Hampton Choir Tours Europe." *Black Music Research Journal* 25, no. 1/2 (Spring–Fall 2005): 3–42.

Schuller, Gunther. *Early Jazz: Its Roots and Musical Development*. New York: Oxford University Press, 1968.

Scott, Emmett. *Scott's Official History of the American Negro in the World War: A Complete and Authentic Narration, from Official Sources, of the Participation of American Soldiers of the Negro Race in the World War for Democracy: A Full Account of the War Work Organizations of Colored Men and Women and Other Civilian Activities, Including the Red Cross, the Y.M.C.A., the Y.W.C.A. and the War Camp Community Service, with Official Summary of Treaty of Peace and League of Nations Covenant*. Chicago: Victory Pub., 1919.

Seabrook, Whaley, Marcellus. *The Old Types Pass: Gullah Sketches of the Carolina Sea Islands*. Boston: The Christopher Publishing House, 1925.

Sears, Ann. "A Certain Strangeness: Harry T. Burleigh's Art Songs and Spirituals." *Black Music Research Journal* 24, no. 2 (Autumn 2004): 227–49.

Seashore, Carl. *Psychology of Music*. New York: Dover, 1967.

Seeger, Peter, Bob Reiser, Guy Carawan, and Candie Carawan. *Everybody Says Freedom*. New York: Norton & Company, 2009.

Sernett, Milton C. *Afro-American Religious History: A Documentary Witness*. Durham, NC: Duke University Press, 1985.

Sharp, Cecil. *English Folk-Song: Some Conclusions*. London: Simpkin, 1907.

Shipley, Lori Rae. "A History of the Music Department at Hampton Institute/University, 1868–1972." PhD diss., Boston University College of Fine Arts, 2009.

Siceloff, Elizabeth, Courtney Siceloff, and Dallas A. Blanchard. Oral History Interview with Elizabeth and Courtney Siceloff, July 8, 1985 Interview F-0039, Southern Oral History Program Collection (#4007). [Chapel Hill, NC]: University Library, UNC-Chapel Hill, 2006. Accessed November 9, 2009, http://docsouth.unc.edu/sohp/F-0039/menu.html.

Silverman, Jerry. *Songs of Protest and Civil Rights*. New York: Chelsea House, 1992.

Simawe, Saadi A. *Black Orpheus: Music in African American Fiction from the Harlem Renaissance to Toni Morrison*. New York: Garland, 2000.

Simms, Lois A. *Profiles of African American Females in the Low Country of South Carolina*. Charleston, SC: College of Charleston, 1992.

Simpson, Robert. "The Shout and Shouting in the Slave Religion of the United States." *Southern Quarterly* 23, no. 3 (Spring 1985): 34–48.

Sims, Christine. "Assessing the Language Proficiency of Tribal Heritage Language Learners: Issues and Concerns for American Indian Pueblo Languages." *Current Issues in Language Planning* (August 2008): 327–43.

Sklaroff, Lauren. "Variety for the Servicemen: The Jubilee Show and the Paradox of Racializing Radio during World War II." *American Quarterly* 56, no. 4 (December 2004): 945–973.

Smalls, Cynthia Gregory. "Elements that Impact the Retentions of the Gullah Culture on the Sea Islands." PhD diss., Walden University, 2004.

Smith, Efrem. *The Hip-Hop Church: Connecting with the Movement Shaping our Culture.* Downers Grove, IL: InterVarsity, 2005.

Smith, Jessie, ed. *Notable Black Women.* Detroit, MI: Gale Research, 1996.

Smith, John P. "Cultural Preservation of the Sea Island Gullah: A Black Social Movement in the Post–Civil Rights Era." *Rural Sociology* 56 (1991): 284–98.

Smith, Julia Floyd. *Slavery and Rice Culture in Low Country Georgia 1750–1860.* Knoxville: University of Tennessee Press, 1985.

Smith, Thérèse. *Let the Church Sing: Music and Worship in a Black Mississippi Community.* Rochester, NY: University of Rochester Press, 2004.

Smith, Vernon. "The Hampton Institute Choir." PhD diss., Florida State University, 1985.

Snyder, Jean. "A Great and Noble School of Music: Dvořák, Harry T. Burleigh, and the African American Spiritual." In *Dvorak in America: 1892–1895,* edited by John C. Tibbetts, 123–48. Portland, OR: Amadeus, 1993.

Society for the Preservation of Spirituals. *Gullah Lyrics to Carolina Low Country Spirituals.* Charleston, SC: Society for the Preservation of Spirituals, 2007.

Sotiropoulos, Karen. *Staging Race: Black Performers in the Turn of the Century America.* Cambridge, MA: Harvard University Press, 2006.

South Carolina Department of Archives and History. African American Historic Places in South Carolina (Columbia, SC: June 2009), accessed May 1, 2010, http://www.state.sc.us/scdah/afamer/aframsitespdf.

Southern, Eileen. *The Music of Black Americans.* New York: W. W. Norton, 1971.

Southern, Eileen, and Josephine Wright. *African-American Traditions in Song, Sermon, Tale, and Dance, 1600's–1920: An Annotated Bibliography of Literature, Collections, and Artworks.* New York: Greenwood, 1990.

Spaulding, Henry George. "Under the Palmetto." *Continental Monthly* 4 (August 1863): 195.

Spencer, Jon Michael. "R. Nathaniel Dett's Views on the Preservation of Black Music." *Black Perspective in Music* 10 (Fall 1982): 132–48.

———. *Protest and Praise: Sacred Music of Black Religion.* Minneapolis, MN: Augsburg Fortress, 1990.

———. *The New Negroes and Their Music: The Success of the Harlem Renaissance.* Knoxville: University of Tennessee Press, 1997.

Spener, David. *We Shall Not Be Moved/No Nos Moverán: Biography of a Song of Struggle.* Philadelphia, PA: Temple University, 2016.

Spivey, Donald. *Schooling for the New Slavery: Black Industrial Education, 1868–1915.* Westport, CT: Greenwood, 1978.

Stanley, May. "R. N. Dett, Of Hampton Institute: Helping to Lay Foundation for Negro Music of Future." *The Black Perspective in Music* 1, no. 1 (Spring 1973): 64–69.

Starks, George L., Jr. "Singing 'bout a Good Time: Sea Island Religious Music." *Journal of Black Studies* 10, no. 4 (1980): 437–44.

Stayton, Corey. "Kongo Cosmogram: A Theory in African American Literature." Master's thesis, Clark Atlanta University, 1997.

Stewart, Sadie E. "Seven Folktales from the Sea Islands, SC." *Journal of American Folklore* 32, no. 125 (July 1919): 394–96.

Stoddard, Albert Henry. *Gullah Tales and Anecdotes of South Carolina Sea Islands.* Savannah, GA: Privately printed, 1940.

Stoney, Samuel, ed. The Autobiography of William John Grayson." *South Carolina Historical and Genealogical Magazine* 49, no. 1 (January 1948): 24.

Stoney, Samuel G., and Gertrude M. Shelby. *Black Genesis: A Chronicle.* New York: Macmillan, 1930.

Stuckey, Sterling. *Slave Culture: Nationalist Theory and the Foundations of Black America.* New York: Oxford University Press, 1987.

Tallmadge, William. "Folk Organum: A Study of Origins." *American Music* 2, no. 3 (Autumn 1984): 47–65.

———. "Dr. Watts and Mahalia Jackson: The Development, Decline, and Survival of a Folk Style in America." *Ethnomusicology* 5, no. 2 (May 1961): 95–99.

Taylor, Clarence. *Black Churches of Brooklyn.* New York: Columbia University, 1994.

Thompson, De Bora A. *Negro Spirituals and the Formation of the Negro Church: Survival Techniques, Protests, and Accommodations.* Master's thesis, Rutgers University, 2004.

Thompson, Robert. *The Four Moments of the Sun.* Washington, DC: National Gallery of Art, 1981.

Thurman, Howard. *Deep River, Reflections on the Religious Insight of Certain Negro Spirituals.* New York: Harper & Brothers, 1945.

———. *The Negro Spiritual Speaks of Life and Death.* New York: Harper, 1947.

Tindall, George B. *South Carolina Negroes 1877–1900.* Columbia, SC: University of South Carolina Press, 1952.

Tirro, Frank. "Review." *19th-Century Music* 1, no. 3 (March 1978): 266–67.

To Live as Free Men. Directed by John Silver. Saint Helena Island, SC: Castle Films, 1942.

Towne, Laura. "Pioneer Work on the Sea Islands." *Southern Workman* 30 (July 1901): 397–401.

Tufts, John, and Hosea Holt. *The Normal Music Course: A Series of Exercises, Studies, and Songs.* Boston: W. Ware, 1885.

Turner, Kristen. "Guy and Candie Carawan: Mediating the Music of the Civil Rights Movement." PhD diss., University of North Carolina at Chapel Hill, 2011.

Turner, Lorenzo D. *Africanisms in the Gullah Dialect: By Lorenzo D. Turner.* Ann Arbor: University of Michigan, 1974.

———. "Notes on the Sounds and Vocabulary of Gullah." *American Dialect Society* 3 (1945): 1–28.

Turner, Richard Brent. *Jazz Religion, the Second Line, and Black New Orleans.* Bloomington: Indiana University Press, 2009.

Twining, Mary A. *Bibliography of the Sea Islands.* Atlanta, GA: Atlanta University, 1974.

———. "An Examination of African Cultural Retentions in the Folk Culture of South Carolina and the Georgia Sea Islands." PhD diss., Indiana University, 1977.

Twining, Mary Arnold, and Keith Baird. "Introduction to Sea Island Folklife." *Journal of Black Studies* 10, no. 4 (1980): 387–416.

United States of America. *Army Song Book*. Washington, DC, 1941.

United States Department of the Treasury. *The Negroes at Port Royal.: Report of E. L. Pierce, Government Agent to the Hon. Salmon P. Chase, Secretary of the Treasury*. Boston: R. F. Wallcut, 1862.

Unknown author. "Folk Song in the Camps." *New York Times*, September 19, 1918.

Vance, Rubert B., and Katharine Jocher. "Howard W. Odum." *Social Forces* 33, no. 3 (March 1955): 205–6.

Vaughn, Steve. "Making Jesus Black: The Historiographical Debate on the Roots of African-American Christianity." *The Journal of Negro History* 82, no. 1 (Winter 1997): 25–41.

Visser-Maessen, Laura. *Robert Parris Moses: A Life in Civil Rights and Leadership at The Grassroots*. Chapel Hill: University of North Carolina Press, 2017.

von Hornbostel, E. M. "Review of American Negro Songs." *International Review of Missions* 15 (October 1926): 748–53.

Wallaschek, Richard. *Primitive Music: An Inquiry into the Origin and Development of Music, Songs, Instruments, Dances, and Pantomimes of Savage Races*. London: Longmans, Green, and Co., 1893.

Walker, Lois, and Susan Silverman [comp]. *A Documented History of Gullah Jack Pritchard and the Denmark Vesey Slave Insurrection of 1822*. Lewiston: E. Mellen, 2000.

Walker, Margaret. "Review." *The Journal of Southern History* 20, no. 2 (May 1954): 265–66.

Walker, Wyatt Tee. *"Somebody's Calling My Name": Black Sacred Music and Social Change*. Valley Forge, PA: Judson, 1979.

Ward, John. "The Morris Tune." *Journal of the American Musicological Society* 39, no. 2 (Summer 1986): 294–331.

Ware, Louise. *George Foster Peabody: Banker, Philanthropist, Publicist*. Athens: University of Georgia, 1951.

Washington, Booker T. "Plantation Melodies, Their Value." *Musical Courier* 71 (December 23, 1915): 47.

Waterman, Christopher, and Adebis Adeleke. *Jùjú: A Social History and Ethnography of an African Popular Music*. Chicago: University of Chicago Press, 1990.

Waterman, Richard. "African Influence on the Music of the Americas." In *Mother Wit from the Laughing Barrel*, edited by Alan Dundes, 81–94. Upper Saddle River, NJ: Prentice-Hall, 1973.

———. "Review." *The Journal of American Folklore* 68, no. 269 (July–September 1955): 370–71.

Watkins, June T. "Strategies of Social Control in an Isolated Community: The Case of the Gullah of South Carolina's St. Helena Island." PhD diss., Indiana University of Pennsylvania, 1993.

Watley, William. "The Tradition of Worship." In *Readings in African American Church Music and Worship*, edited by James Abbington, 284. Chicago, IL: GIA, 2001.

Weatherford, W. D. *The Negro from Africa to America*. New York: Negro University Press, 1969.

———. "First Steps in Solving the Race Problem." *Southern Workman* 39 (November 1910): 589–92.

———. "Negro Training in the South." *Southern Workman* 41 (October 1912): 550–58.

Whaley, Marcellus S. *The Old Types Pass; Gullah Sketches of the Carolina Sea Islands.* Boston: Christopher, 1925.

White, Clarence Cameron. *Forty Negro Spirituals.* Philadelphia, PA: T. Presser, 1927.

White, James Cameron. "The Story of the Spiritual 'Nobody Knows the Trouble I've Seen.'" *Musical Observer* 23 (1924): 29.

White, Newman Ivey. *American Negro Folk-Songs.* Hatboro, PA: Folklore Associates, 1928.

White, Shane, and Graham White. *The Sounds of Slavery: Discovering African American History Through Songs, Sermon, and Speech.* Boston: Beacon Press, 2005.

———. *Somewhat More Independent: The End of Slavery in New York City, 1770–1810.* Athens: University of Georgia Press, 1991.

Whittier, John Greenleaf. *The Letters of John Greenleaf.* New York: Harvard University Press, 1977.

Williams, Robert. "Preservation of the Oral Tradition of Singing Hymns in Negro Religious Music." PhD diss., Florida State University, 1973.

Williams, W. T. B. "The Yankee School Ma'am in Negro Education." *Southern Workman* 44, 1915, 73–80.

Willson, Marcius. *The Second Reader of the School and Family Series.* New York: Harper & Bros, 1860.

Wilson, G. R. "The Religion of the American Negro Slave: His Attitude Toward Life and Death." *The Journal of Negro History* 8 (1923): 41–71.

Wilson, Olly. "The Significance of the Relationship Between Afro-American Music and West African Music." *The Black Perspective in Music* 2, no. 1 (Spring 1974): 3–22.

Wilson-Dickson, Andrew. *The Story of Christian Music: From Gregorian Chant to Black Gospel: An Authoritative Illustrated Guide to all the Major Traditions of Music for Worship.* Minneapolis, MN: Fortress, 1996.

Wintz, Cary D., ed. *The Politics and Aesthetics of "New Negro" Literature.* New York: Garland, 1996.

Wolfe, Michael. *The Abundant Life Prevails: Religious Traditions of Saint Helena Island.* Waco, TX: Baylor University Press, 2000.

Wolfram, Walt, and Nona H. Clarke, eds. *Black-White Speech Relationships.* Washington, DC: Center for Applied Linguistics, 1971.

Wood, John. *The Natural History of Man; Being an Account of the Manners and Customs of the Uncivilized Races of Men.* London: G. Routledge and Sons, 1868.

Wood, Peter H. *Black Majority: Negroes in Colonial South Carolina from 1670 Through the Stono Rebellion.* New York: W. W. Norton and Company, 1996.

Woodson, Carter G. *The Education of the Negro Prior to 1861: A History of the Education of Colored People of the United States from the Beginning of Slavery to the Civil War.* New York: Arno, 1919.

Woofter, Thomas Jackson. *Black Yeomanry, Life on St. Helena Island.* New York: H. Holt and Company, 1930.

Work, John. *American Negro Songs: 230 Folk Songs and Spirituals, Religious and Secular.* New York: Dover Publications, 1998.

Wright, Roberta Hughes, and Wilbur Hughes. *Lay Down Body: Living History in African American Cemeteries.* Detroit, MI: Visible Ink Press, 1996.

Wright, Roberta H. *A Tribute to Charlotte Forten 1837–1914.* Detroit, MI: Charro, 1992.

Young, Alan. *Woke Me Up This Morning: Black Gospel Singers and the Gospel Life.* Jackson: University of Mississippi Press, 1997.

Young, Jason Randolph. *Rituals of Resistance African Atlantic Religion in Kongo and the Lowcountry South in the Era of Slavery.* Baton Rouge: Louisiana State University, 2007.

INDEX